THE CHURCH'S MAGNA CHARTA

for

MIGRANTS

Exsul Familia

The
CHURCH'S
MAGNA CHARTA
for
MIGRANTS

Edited by the Rev. Giulivo Tessarolo, P.S.S.C., S.T.D.
With Commentaries

Introduction
by
The Most Rev. Edward E. Swanstrom, D.D.
Executive Director of Catholic Relief Services—NCWC
Representative of the United States Hierarchy
on the Supreme Council for Migration
of the
Sacred Consistorial Congregation

ST. CHARLES SEMINARY
Staten Island, N. Y.

IMPRIMI POTEST:

Very Reverend Louis Riello, P.S.S.C.

Superior Provincial

NIHIL OBSTAT:

Vincent Paolucci, P.S.S.C.

Censor Deputatus

IMPRIMATUR:

✠Patrick A. O'Boyle

Archbishop of Washington

The nihil obstat and imprimatur are official declarations that a book or pamphlet is free of doctrinal or moral error. No implication is contained therein that those who have granted the nihil obstat and the imprimatur agree with the content, opinions or statements expressed.

Library of Congress Catalogue Card Number: 62-15993

APOSTOLIC CONSTITUTION
of August 1, 1952

On the Spiritual Care to Migrants
PIUS BISHOP
SERVANT OF THE SERVANTS OF GOD
IN EVERLASTING REMEMBRANCE

(Exsul Familia in *AAS* Vol. XXXXIV
Sept. 30, 1952. No. 13, pp. 649-704)

CONTENTS

PART II

TWO COMMENTARIES
BY JOSEPH CARDINAL FERRETTO

I

Historical—Juridical Commentary of "Exsul Familia":
Spiritual Assistance to Migrants.

II

Commentary on Norms and Faculties for Priests engaged in
the Spiritual Care of Sea Travellers, Seamen and
Migrants

A

PART III

TWO OUTSTANDING HISTORICAL
COMMENTARIES ON "EXSUL FAMILIA"

EDITOR'S REMARKS

THE United States of America has been a haven to immigrants regardless of their reasons for migration. Father T. McAvoy, C.S.C., in *Roman Catholicism and The American Way of Life,* University of Notre Dame Press, 1960, p. 123, has stated: "Only the redmen are really natives as far back as we have records. This may seem a contentious statement, and perhaps it is, but this fact is important in placing in perspective some of the worst evils of the agitation against immigrants that has appeared at times in the history of the United States."

The United States is a country of immigrants and the Catholic Church in America is a Church of immigrants. The restrictive immigration laws of the United States, called unjust even by some of its recent Presidents, are grounded on historico-psychological reasons, deeper and more complicated than one, at first, would be inclined to believe.

By and large, the Catholic viewpoint has supported the liberal outlook on the immigration policy of the United States as typified by the brave and successful fight of one of the Catholic institutions with which I am familiar, to wit, the American Committee on Italian Migration, which was organized as, and still is, a member agency of the National Catholic Resettlement Council—NCWC.

Without attempting to slant history in any way, it may be stated that the national parish was at the core of the very organizational phase of the Catholic Church in America.

"During the early period of its development, this country was considered as a missionary country, and actually depended for it jurisdiction upon Europe.... The priests who came to this country usually came with a particular group of settlers to minister to their needs...." Joseph E. Ciesuik, *National Parishes in The United States,* the Catholic University of America Press, Washington, D. C., 1944, p. 28, "These were the general conditions under which the language parishes arose and thrived. They received their initial *sanction* from the Very Rev. John Carroll, as Prefect Apostolic. After his consecration as the first bishop of the United States, in one of his pastoral letters, he expressed the thought uppermost in his mind, exhorting the faithful, whose number had increased rapidly through immigration, ... reminded them that ... their duty was to erect a church suitable to their needs...." (*Ibid.,* p. 31) This thought "uppermost" in the mind of the first Catholic bishop of America seems re-echoed in the Apostolic Constitition, *Exsul Familia,* published here for the first time in English in its entirety, together with the main juridico-historico-theological commentaries. In fact, this seems the turning point of the pontifical document. In the third *paragraph* before the conclusion of the first part thereof, the Supreme Pontiff affirmed: "For we were eagerly awaiting an opportunity to draw up suitable regulations for the bishops, to provide them with proper authority to offer aliens, whether immigrants or travellers, the religious assistance, appropriate to their needs and not inferior to that available to other Catholics in the dioceses."

I am well aware that the national parishes have stirred much controversy in the past and are objects of controversy even today. It is also a known fact that "when immigration became a matter of national concern, there was no general agreement among Catholics to its desirability ... continued agitation for restrictive legislation took the form of a literacy test which became required in 1917. Catholic opinion was not solidly opposed to the establishment of such a requirement for admission to the United States.... The inability of the Church to provide for the hordes arriving, as well as philanthropic reasons, were cited by those Catholics who favored some type of restrictive legislation." (Thomas T. McAvoy, *ibid.*, p. 224)

All this, however, neither diminishes the value of the authoritative provisions of the Holy Father in the *Exsul Familia*, nor offsets the great record on behalf of immigrants established by the United States as a country, and by the Catholic Church in that country.

I feel confident, therefore, that this English translation of the Apostolic Constitution, *Exsul Familia*, with its most significant commentaries will be welcomed. The *Exsul Familia* has been called the "Magna Charta" of the Church on Emigration, a landmark in the field of the assistance to be offered to immigrants. It should be of service to university and college libraries, to professors and students of Canon Law, to Chancery offices and the priests, as well as seminarians. There are hardly any places, today, where aliens are not present.

In undertaking this work, I took cognizance of a signfi- cant social fact of our time; that, due to enormous financial implications, the phenomenon of emigration will find some relief only in the English-speaking countries. The vast influx of immigrants into Canada and Australia confirms that fact.

It is my hope that the revolutionary tactics of the *Exsul Familia,* in the apostolate on behalf of aliens, will be made available throughout the English-speaking world. Under this apostolic point of view, it may not be out of place to recall here the meaning of a pontifical document designated as "Apostolic Constitition."

Dr. Theodor Grentrup, in the introduction to *Die Apostolische Konstitution—Exsul Familia—Zur Auswanderer Und Fluchtlingsfrage,* Verlag Christ Unterwegs, Munchen, 1955-56, defines that term, thus: "The papal documents on the spiritual care of migrants bears as its official title— Apostolic Constitution. Even though the word—Constitution —has a rather broad meaning, it is true, however, that when used by the Holy See, it carries an exact significance; namely, it indicates a document which is a solemn enactment carrying juridical binding force, an ordinance coming directly from the Holy Father. Hence, it is an ordinance of the church deriving from the highest source, in the clearest form. Consequently, only the most important laws are issued through a Constitution. Some newspapers have translated the word—Constitution—in our instance with "disposition." This is plainly wrong ... Constitution differs from encyclical. Even though an encyclical can be binding, it aims directly at explaining truths and dogmas, not at formally issuing new laws. A Constitution, however, contains clearly formulated laws. On the other hand, the legislative nature of a Constitution does not include the fact that the documents may also carry considerations of another nature. It is, indeed, one of the characteristics of a Constitution to have an historical or theoretical part introducing the laws issued, thereby enlightening the very nature of those laws. So it is that our Constitution has a long introduction with practical considerations and a documentation of facts. This introduction stands before the juridical section as a wide plateau before a mountain peak."

I wish to express my appreciation to all those who have assisted me herein, without whose cooperation this book could not have been written. A special word of thanks to Mr. John Doebele who prepared a popular translation of the *Exsul Familia* including some of the notes inserted in the text itself, based primarily on the French translation. I used it introducing changes I thought were necessary and adding notes that were not translated. The Latin text I interpreted with the help of the Italian, French and Portugese versions listed in the bibliography.

This has been a work of long duration, most of it being written while teaching, full time, Moral Theology and Canon Law at St. Charles Seminary in Staten Island, New York. As I neared completion, I was assigned to parish work. I offer this explanation as an apology for any inaccuracies which may be present.

In reading all the commentaries on the *Exsul Familia* which I assembled, I realized that their publication would have made a rather repetitious and cumbersome volume. Hence, the commentaries for publication were chosen on the basis of authority and originality. I wish to thank all the authors of such commentaries and the publishers for having given me permission to translate and publish them.

Special thanks go the the Most Rev. Edward E. Swanstrom, D.D., for a most splendid and authoritative introduction.

Above all, I thank my superiors for extending me the privilege to do this work and for making possible its publication.

Rev. Giulivo Tessarolo, P.S.S.C., S.T.D.

Washington, D.C.

Easter, 1962

FOREWORD

IT IS most fitting and noteworthy that the year in which we are celebrating the Tenth Anniversary of its promulgation should witness this publication of the English translation and commentary of the Apostolic Constitution *Exsul Familia* by Father Tessarolo, a priest of the Pious Society of St. Charles and now pastor of Holy Rosary Parish in Washington, D.C. It is equally fitting that such a translation should come from the pen of a son of the saintly Bishop Scalabrini, since it is in this year also that the priests of his congregation are celebrating the Seventy-fifth Anniversary of their dedication to the cause of Italian emigrants.

It was on August 1, 1952 that Pope Pius XII of revered and happy memory promulgated the Apostolic Constitution *Exsul Familia* which has come to be considered as the "Magna Charta" of spiritual assistance to migrants and refugees. To celebrate the Tenth Anniversary of this important papal document, the Sacred Consistorial Congregation, to whom the concerns of the Church for the migrant are entrusted, is promoting a worldwide pilgrimage to Rome of migrants and refugees as a sign of gratitude to the saintly author of *Exsul Familia* and of filial affection for His Holiness, Pope John XXIII, who in his recent Encyclical *Mater et Magistra* and repeated messages, has reaffirmed the doctrine of the Church in regard to modern migratory movements.

This Tenth Anniversary celebration of the historic document will undoubtedly elicit a new interest in and study of its principles.

From its earliest days, the Catholic Church in the English-speaking world, in harmony with the teachings of the founder of the Church Himself, Jesus Christ, has had a special concern for the migrant. In recent years particularly, it has been countries such as the United States, Canada and Australia that have been in a position to provide a home and haven for most of the thousands of refugees who have been forced to flee from their native lands because of tyranny and oppression of one kind or another. The Catholic Church, in each of these countries, has played a very significant part in these migratory movements of our own age.

The principles enunciated in the *Exsul Familia* are not only well-known to the leaders of the Church in these countries, but they are being translated into effective activity for the material and spiritual welfare of the immigrant of every nationality. However, this newest translation and commentary of this important document into English, will help to bring it to the attention of even greater numbers of people who may not be thoroughly familiar with its contents.

As one who has had the privilege of being associated with many groups in the field of immigration and emigration, as Chairman of the National Catholic Resettlement Council and the representative of the hierarchy of the United States on the Supreme Council for Emigration of the Sacred Consistorial Congregation, I see in Father Tessarolo's translation of this magnificent and historic document, a timely corollary to the Tenth Anniversary celebration of its promulgation.

✠ Edward E. Swanstrom

PART I

THE APOSTOLIC CONSTITUTION
"EXSUL FAMILIA"

INTRODUCTION

THE émigré Holy Family of Nazareth, fleeing into Egypt, is the archetype of every refugee family. Jesus, Mary and Joseph, living in exile in Egypt to escape the fury of an evil king, are, for all times and all places, the models and protectors of every migrant, alien and refugee of whatever kind who, whether compelled by fear of persecution or by want, is forced to leave his native land, his beloved parents and relatives, his close friends, and to seek a foreign soil.

For the almighty and most merciful God decreed that His only Son, "being made like unto men and appearing in the form of a man," [1] should, together with His Immaculate Virgin Mother and His holy guardian Joseph, be in this type too of hardship and grief, the firstborn among many brethren,[2] and precede them in it.

In order that this example and these consoling thoughts would not grow dim but rather offer refugees and migrants a comfort in their trials, and foster Christian hope, the Church had to look after them with special care and unremitting aid. She sought to preserve intact in them the Faith of their fathers and a way of life that conformed to the moral law. She also had to contend strenuously with numerous difficulties, previously unknown and unforseeable, which were encountered abroad. Above all, it was necessary to combat the evil work of those perverse men who, alas, associated with migrants under the pretext of bringing material aid, but with the intent of damaging their souls.

How serious and grave would be the reasons for anxiety and anguish had the Church's spiritual care been lacking or found wanting in the past or the present! The disasters would have been more lamentable than those of the tragic days of St. Augustine! Then, the Bishop of Hippo insistently urged his priests not to leave their flocks without pastors during the oppressive catastrophes. He reminded them what benefits their presence would bring and what havoc would inevitably follow if their flocks were abandoned.

> When the priests are absent, what ruin for those who must leave this world either unbaptized or still chained by sin! What sadness for their friends, who will not have them as companions in the repose of eternal life! What grief for all, and what blasphemy by some, due to the absence of the priest and of his ministry.
>
> One can readily understand what the dread of passing evils can do, and what great eternal evil follows! On the other hand, when the priests are at their posts they help everyone with all the strength the Lord has given them. Some are baptized, others make their peace with God. None is deprived of receiving the Body of Christ in Communion; all are consoled, edified and urged to pray to God, Who can ward off all dangers.[3]

The Church's Motherly Solicitude for Migrants

Holy Mother Church, impelled by her ardent love of souls has striven to fulfill the duties inherent in her mandate of salvation for all mankind, a mandate entrusted to her by Christ. She has been especially careful to provide all possible spiritual care for pilgrims, aliens, exiles and migrants of every kind. This work has been carried out chiefly by priests who, in administering the Sacraments and preaching the Word of God, have labored zealously to strengthen the Faith of the Christians in the bond of charity.

Let us briefly review what the Church has done in this matter in the distant past and then discuss more fully the implementation of this work in our own times.

First, let us recall what the great St. Ambrose did and said when that illustrious Bishop of Milan succeeded in ransoming the wretched captives who had been taken after the defeat of the Emperor Valentine near Adrianopolis. He sacrificed the sacred vessels in order to protect the destitute ones from physical suffering and to relieve them of their pressing spiritual dangers which were even a greater hazard. "For who," said Ambrose,

> is so callous, unfeeling, hard-hearted and cruel that he does not want men saved from death and women from barbarous attacks worse than death?

> For who is not willing to rescue girls and boys or little children from the service of pagan idols, into which they have been forced under pain of death? We have not undertaken this work without reason; and we have done it openly to proclaim that it is far better to preserve souls for the Lord than to preserve gold.[1]

Equally noble were the vigorous ardent labors of bishops and priests who sought to bring to newcomers the blessings of the true Faith and to introduce them into the social customs of these new countries. They also facilitated the assimilation of the uncultured invaders whom they introduced both to the Christian religion and to a new culture.

We indeed are happy to recall those religious orders founded specifically to ransom prisoners. Their members, burning with Christian love, endured great hardships on behalf of their enchained brothers for the purpose of liberating, or at least, of consoling many of them.

With the discovery of the New World, Christ's priests were the tireless companions of the men who founded colonies in those far distant lands. It was these priests who made sure that these colonists would not desert Christian ways nor become proud because of the riches acquired in the new lands. These priests also wished to move forward suitably and readily as missionaries to teach the Gospel to the natives, who previously were entirely ignorant of the Divine Light. And they zealously proclaimed that the natives were to be treated as brothers by the colonists.

We must also mention those apostles of the Church who labored for the relief and conversion of those Negroes who were barbarously deported from their own land and sold as slaves in American and European ports.[2]

We wish also to say a few words concerning the unceasing care exercised in behalf of pilgrims by a number of devout associations. Providentially set up during the Middle Ages, these groups flourished throughout the Christian world, and especially here in Rome. Under their influence, innumerable hospices and hospitals for strangers, churches and national societies were established. Many traces of them are found even today.

Especially worthy of note were the Pilgrims' Halls: Saxon, Frankish, Frisian, which by the 8th century had been established around the Vatican beside the tomb of St. Peter, Prince of the Apostles. These Halls housed visitors from countries north of the Alps who had journeyed to Rome to venerate the memory of the Apostles.

These Halls were provided with their own churches and cemeteries, and staffed by priests and clerics of their respective nationalities, who provided for the material and spiritual welfare of their people, especially the sick and the poor. In the following centuries other monasteries were built, with their associated hospices for pilgrims. Included among them were Ethiopian or Abyssinian, Hungarian and Armenian Halls. All this happily echoed words of the Apostle Paul: ". . . sharing the needs of the saints, practising hospitality." [3]

This experience proves that the sacred ministry can be carried on more effectively among strangers and pilgrims if it is exercised by priests of their own nationality or at least who speak their language. This is especially true in the case of the uneducated or those who are poorly instructed in the Catechism. The Fourth Lateran Council solemnly affirmed that this rightly was so, declaring in 1215: "We find in most countries, cities and dioceses in which people of diverse languages who, though bound by one Faith, have varied rites and customs. Therefore we strictly enjoin that the Bishops of these cities or dioceses provide the proper men, who will celebrate the Liturgical Functions according to their rites and languages. They will administer the Sacraments of the Church and instruct their people both by word and by deed." [4] The Church has followed this instruction scrupulously, even down to our own days.

Indeed, as we know, special parishes have been established for the various languages and nationality groups. At times, even dioceses have been established for the different rites. It is this aspect to which we now turn our attention.

Such parishes, most frequently requested by the emigrants themseleves, were a source of great benefit both to dioceses and to souls. Everyone recognizes this and respects it with due esteem. Therefore, the Code of Canon Law duly provides for them (Can. 216, 4). And as the Holy See gradually gave its approval, numerous national parishes were established, especially in America. Very recently, to cite but one example, parishes were set up, by decree of the Consistorial Congregation, for the Chinese living in the Philippine Islands.[5]

Indeed, there never has been a period during which the Church has not been active in behalf of migrants, exiles and refugees. But to be brief, we will recount only her work of recent years.

It is well to begin this survey by mentioning the fifty volumes preserved in the Vatican Archives: *Holy See's Care in behalf of the French.*[6] Truly they constitute a magnificent proof of the never-ending devotion of the Roman Pontiffs to the hapless persons banished from their country by revolution or war.

These volumes reveal the fatherly care taken of the French by our predecessors Pius VI and Pius VII. Driven from their native land, many of these émigrés were received with open arms in the Papal State, and particularly in Rome, while others took refuge in other countries.

We are happy to mention Blessed Vincent Pallotti, the eminent founder of the Catholic Apostolic Society. We ourselves have called him the "pride and glory of the Roman Clergy" and at the beginning of the recent Jubilee year, we gladly announced that he was among the resplendent company of the Beatified. Urged on by love of souls and eager to strengthen the Catholic Faith of Italian immigrants in England, Blessed Vincent sent several of his Congregation to London to provide for the spiritual care of their people. Our predecessor Pius IX granted Blessed Vincent's request for permission to collect funds for the construction of a new church building in London which was to be dedicated to the glory of God in honor of St. Peter, Prince of the Apostles, and it was intended chiefly for Italian immigrants.[7]

Toward the end of the 19th century, when the social means of prosperity became available to the poor in a manner previously unknown, great waves of people left Europe and moved especially from Italy to America. As usual the Catholic Church devoted special effort and care to the spiritual welfare of these emigrants. Inspired by devotion towards her exiled sons, she has through the centuries been ever quick not only to approve new methods of Apostolate, more suitable to the progress of peoples and the changed circumstances of the times, but she has also zealously integrated them into this new social system, for she is ever careful to warn of the dangers that threaten society, morality, and religion.

The record of our predecessor Leo XIII provides clear evidence of the Holy See's diligent solicitude, a solicitude which became more ardent as public officials and private

institutions seemed the more dilatory in meeting the new
needs. Leo XIII not only upheld vigorously the dignity and
rights of the working man but also defended strenuously
those emigrants who sought to earn their living abroad. On
July 9, 1878, when he had been Pope for only a year, he
graciously approved the Society of St. Raphael, established
by the Bishops of Germany to aid emigrants from that
nation.[8] Through the years, the Society worked advanta-
geously in behalf of emigrants in the ports of departure and
arrival, and aided other nationalities, such as Belgian,
Austrian and Italian, as their own.

Later, in an Apostolic Letter of 1887, he approved as most
beneficial and timely the project of the Servant of God,
John Baptist Scalabrini, then Bishop of Piacenza. The plan
was "to found an institute of priests ready and willing to
leave their native land for remote places, particularly, for
America, where they could carry on the priestly ministry
among the numerous Italian Catholics, who were forced by
economic distress to emigrate and to take up residence in
foreign lands." [9]

Then, aided by energetic priests and far-sighted prelates,
this apostolic man, whom we ourselves in 1946 proclaimed
most valuable to the Church and State,[10] founded a Society
of priests. In the apt words of Leo XIII, in the letter which
we shall mention later, Leo said: "In that Society, priests
burning with love of Christ gather together from all parts of
Italy to devote themselves to studies and to practices of
these duties and ways of life that would make them effective
and successful ambassadors of Christ to the Italians scattered
abroad." [11]

Thus was founded a new religious community, the
Missionaries of St. Charles for Italian Emigrants. The

Servant of God John Baptist Scalabrini is honored as its Founder.

We are happy likewise to mention another letter that the same great Leo, our predecessor, sent the following year to the Archbishops and Bishops of America.[12] Fortunately that letter inspired many new projects and developed an eager rivalry in giving aid to the emigrants. Numerous priests, as well as many members of religious communities journeyed to every part of America in order to help their scattered brethren. At that same time, societies and institutions were established to aid the masses of emigrants from Italy, Germany, Ireland, Austria, Hungary, France, Switzerland, Belgium, Holland, Spain and Portugal, and very prominent national parishes were established.

In his wisdom and charity, Leo XIII did not neglect mere temporary migrations or those migrations within Europe. More than one letter from the Secretary of State to the Italian Bishops testifies clearly to this concern of the great Pontiff.[13]

Again inspired by the earnest call of Leo XIII and impelled by the love of souls, Jeremias Bonomelli, Bishop of of Cremona, founded an Agency for the Assistance of Italians who had migrated to other parts of Europe. From this Agency arose many institutions and flourishing centers of civic education and welfare. In 1900, devout priests and eminent laymen attracted to the work founded successful "missions" in Switzerland, Austria, Germany and France. So that such a beneficial work might not cease, with the death of Bonomelli our predecessor Benedict XV entrusted Ferdinand Rodolfi, Bishop of Vicenza, with the care of Italians who had emigrated to various countries of Europe.[14]

It is well also mention here, those numerous institutions

for the education of boys and girls, the hospitals and other welfare agencies most beneficially established for the faithful of various language groups and national origins. These institutions daily became more and more prosperous. It is in this type of work that St. Frances Xavier Cabrini stands out most brilliantly. Advised and encouraged by that Servant of God, John Baptist Scalabrini, this saintly woman was also supported by the authority of Leo XIII of happy memory. The Holy Father persuaded her to look westward rather than towards the East.[15] Having decided to go to North America, she persevered in her missionary undertakings with such love that she herself reaped the richest harvests. Moreover, because of her extraordinary devotion and outstanding work for Italian emigrants, she was rightly called the "Mother of Italian Emigrants." [16]

It is to our predecessor St. Pius X that we must attribute the systematic organization of Catholic labors in behalf of emigrants in Europe, in the East and in America. While he was still a pastor in Salzano, he went to the assistance of those of his beloved people who were emigrating, seeking to assure them a safe voyage and a secure living in the new country. Later, as Pope he looked with a special care after the uprooted and dispersed sheep of his universal flock and made special provision in their behalf.

St. Pius X was aflame with love for the faithful who had emigrated to distant lands, such as North and South America. The zeal of the Bishops and priests in welcoming them was a great joy to him, as is clearly evident from a letter he sent the Archbishop of New York, on February 26, 1904. In this letter he praised and approved the concern the Archbishop had shown for Italian immigrants to guard them from many dangers and help them to persevere in the practice of the

Faith of their Fathers. He also praised the Archbishop's efforts in founding a seminary for the proper training of priests from the Italian community.[17]

St. Pius' interest is also attested by remarks he made in an address to pilgrims from the Argentine Republic [18] and in a letter to the Bishops of Brazil.[19] And similarly in letters to the Superior General of the Missionaries of St. Charles [20] and to the Director of the Antonian Society. Likewise to the President of the Catholic Society for Immigrants, which had been recently founded in Canada.[21]

As a matter of fact the Missionary Society of St. Anthony of Padua was established in 1905 with the approval of St. Pius X specifically to provide proper spiritual care for the emigrants both during the voyage and in the ports of disembarkation and after their settlement in their adopted countries.[22]

As to Italy itself, most important were the regulations issued by the Secretary of State of the Bishops of that land.[23]

Both the Bishops of the emigrants and those of the émigrés constantly kept the Consistorial Congregation informed of their conditions.[24] The same Consistorial Congregation carried out promptly the Pontiff's order by properly reorganizing existing agencies for migrants and by setting up new agencies where necessary, as well as recommending to Bishops the establishment of committees and sponsorships on behalf of emigrants.[25]

In his great solicitude, St. Pius X did not confine himself to one method of spiritual aid. Because of the hardships and the circumstances of the places in which they found themselves, some people, after emigrating from Europe to distant lands, were contracting marriage without the canonical formalities and even resorted to attempted marriage. Since such formalities were designed to prevent certain highly undesirable evils, the Pontiff was anxious that they be fully observed. When he learned of their neglect, he directed the Congregation of Sacraments to issue instructions concerning proof of freedom to marry and, likewise, the notification of the contracted marriage. These instructions were issued again,[27] by the same Congregation a few years later and afterwards even these were supplemented by prudent rules for the benefit of migrants contracting marriage by proxy.[28]

While the great St. Pius X was governing the Universal Church, special rules were promulgated for the priests and laypeople of the Ruthenian Rite living in the United States, even a Ruthenian Bishop was assigned to them[29] and still another Ruthenian Bishop was entrusted with the spiritual care of Catholics of the Rite who were resident in Canada.[30]

Under the same pontificate, a society for the extension of the Catholic Church was founded in Toronto, Canada. This worthy society was abundantly successful, for it protected from the inroads of heretics the Ruthenian Catholics living in Northwest Canada.[31] The rules governing the relations between the Canadian Hierarchy and the Ruthenian Bishop, and between the priests and laity of both rites, were clearly established.

In Rome, the Church of Our Savior and its adjoining rectory on the *Via delle Copppelle* were given to the Rumanian Bishop from the ecclesiastical province of Fagaras and Alba Julia.[33]

The most important, however, of all the measures in behalf of the emigrants was the establishment, in the Consistorial Congregation, of the Special Office for the Spiritual

Care of Migrants. "Its purpose," in the words of St. Pius X, was:

> To seek out and provide everything to improve the condition of the migrants of the Roman Rite in all that pertains to the welfare of souls. With regard to migrants of Eastern Rites, however, the rights of the Congregation for the Propagation of the Faith are to be preserved. This Congregation may, within its competence, make appropriate provision for them. The Special Office, however, has exclusive charge of migrants who are priests.[34]

Neither could provision and guidance for migrant priests be neglected. Indeed the Holy See had long before cared for them through the Congregation of the Council,[35] and through the Congregation for the Progapation of the Faith for clerics of Oriental Rites,[36] as well as through the Consistorial Congregation.[37] Since, in fact, some of the priests who emigrated overseas were victimized by material comforts and overlooked the welfare of souls, timely rules were published by the same Consistorial Congregation. The rules applied also to priests "discharging their mission among farmers and other workers." [38] By these rules potential abuses would be rooted out and penalties fixed for violations.

In another decision of the Consistorial Congregation, these rules were made to conform with the Code of Canon Law, [39] published a short time before, and they are still beneficially in force. As time passed, other regulations were added by the Congregation for the Oriental Church [40] and by the Congregation for the Propagation of the Faith,[41] each for priests under its own jurisdiction.

The same Pontiff must also be credited with the beginning of the Roman College established for the benefit of Italians who had emigrated to other lands.[42] Young priests from the secular clergy were to be given a special course of studies and be trained for the sacred ministry among emigrants. In order that the number of students might correspond to the need, he urged the Italian Bishops, and particularly those who had an ample supply of priests, "to send to the college any of their priests who seemed qualified." [43]

Finally in the last days of his pontificate, when this saintly Pontiff was heartbroken at the prospect of a catastrophic war and was about to receive his eternal reward, it was he who personally, as a most loving father, drew up the by-laws of the College subsequently turning them over to the Consistorial Congregation for publication.

Earnestly following the distinguished path of his predecessor, and accepting the care of migrants as an inheritance bequeathed to him, the Pontiff Benedict XV had scarcely ascended the Chair of St. Peter when he secured the residence for the above mentioned College at St. Apollinaris.[44] The Holy See, at this time, was providing a great deal of financial war relief for the areas ravaged by war easing inflicted on the victims. Hence the Vatican could no longer support the College single-handedly. It was then that the Consistorial Congregation did not hesitate to ask the Bishops of Italy and America for funds to maintain it.[45]

In order to assist Catholic endeavors in behalf of the spiritual care of Italian migrants, this same Congregation requested the Bishops of Italy to establish an annual day for taking up a collection for this work.[46] Later, it directed that every pastor should each year offer one Mass for the intention of the Holy Father, instead of *pro populo,* and should contribute the offering from such Mass to the apostolate in behalf of emigrants.[47]

Full well do all know, especially migrants and missionaries, that this money was exclusively spent to support relief agencies which were established in foreign lands to provide timely and secure aid to migrants, "whose Catholic Faith and Catholic practices were often threatened with almost incredible dangers." [48] In fact, these agencies are either under the direction of the Consistorial Congregation or of missionaries of religious communities of men or women.

The same Pontiff proposed to the Bishops of Calabria that ecclesiastical sponsorships be established for the benefit of Italian migrants.[49]

Foreign workers were then pouring into Brazil from Europe; some in the hope of becoming prosperous, others driven by want. Benedict XV, therefore, earnestly requested the Archbishop of Sao Paulo and the other Bishops of Brazil to undertake their care, "with the cooperation of their good Brazilian priests," so that the new workers would not, once they had left their native countries, give up the Christian customs of their ancestors.[50]

Benedict XV also recommended the same practices to the Bishop of Trenton, while praising his great diligence in this work. For, when an Italian community developed in that diocese, a church and an adjacent building were immediately erected for them. In fact, the Pontiff expressed his ardent wish that Italian immigrants would be the object of the same solicitude and assistance everywhere in the United States.[51]

At this same time, Benedict XV also interested himself in those Italians who were leaving their homes and migrating temporarily into other parts of Italy, as the women who work in the rice fields do even today.[52]

Later, he very wisely decided to appoint a prelate, who,

empowered with the necessary faculties and free from diocesan duties, could devote himself entirely to the spiritual welfare of Italian migrants. It was, therefore, in 1920 that Benedict XV established the office of prelate for the Italian migrants [53] with the exclusive duty of choosing missionaries destined for such work. The function of the office was also to assist and supervise them and to direct the College for priests who were to be assigned to provide religious and moral guidance to Italian emigrants abroad. So as to speed the development of this College, he set up the following year new by-laws to govern it in a manner more adapted to the needs of the times and circumstances.[54]

Deeply moved by the tragic distress of numberless men taken prisoners in the prolonged disastrous war, Benedict XV directed that the bishop of the dioceses in which prisoners were held should without delay appoint one or, if necessary, several priests, sufficiently familiar with the language of the prisoners, to provide for their care. "The priests chosen for this work should do everything possible for the welfare of the prisoners, whether it be for their souls, or for their physical health. They should console them, help and assist them in their manifold needs, which at times prove so pressing." [55]

As the war continued, he appointed a special Ordinary to care for the spiritual needs of refugees who had entered Italy.[56] And he did not ignore the very grave dangers of corruption to which German citizens, including many Catholics, were then exposed, compelled as they were in the misfortunes of war, to seek other lands to obtain the essentials of life. The Consistorial Congregation therefore urged the Bishops, not only of Germany but also Central Europe, to consider the problem of migrants carefully; to discuss it in their meetings and episcopal conferences and then to provide necessary means for the immediate and proper alleviation of such great need.

At the same time, he pointed out the advantage of expanding the activities of the Society of St. Raphael. It had, before the war, offered innumerable benefits to all travelers providing every kind of aid suggested by prudence and charity.[57]

Later in 1921, the Archbishop of Cologne was appointed patron of the St. Raphael Society, founded in 1904, so that this Society might provide for the religious care of German -speaking Catholics then living in Italy.[58] And this same Society in the following years also undertook the spiritual care of Germans throughout Western Europe.[59] With the appointment of the Bishop of Osnabruck as its second patron, it cared for Germans in Eastern Europe and even outside Europe.[60]

When civil war flared up in Mexico, a number of Mexican Bishops, priests, religious and many laymen were unjustly expelled from their native country and sought refuge in the United States. Benedict XV warmly commended them to the charity of American Catholics, writing first to the Bishop of San Antonio [61] and then to the Archbishop of Baltimore, through whose generosity poor boys destined for the priesthood were received into the seminary. Such interest was, as the Pontiff said, "a great satisfaction to us."[62]

We recall also what the same Pontiff very wisely did in behalf of the faithful of the Oriental Rites. The spiritual assistance provided to the Catholics of the Greek-Ruthenian Rite, who had emigrated to South America, was widely extended.[63] A Seminary for the Italo-Greek boys was founded at the Monastery of Grottaferrata near Rome.[64] The diocese of Lungro in Italy was established for Catholics of the Greek Rite who had once lived in Epirus and Albania, but had fled the Turkish Rule and reached Italy, settling in Calabria and Sicily.[65]

Nor do we consider it out of place to mention the decree of the Congregation of Rites, designating Our Lady of Loreto the heavenly patroness of those who travel by air. "May they who confide in her protection arrive safely at their destination." [66]

We ourselves desired that the faithful should have an opportunity of going to Confession while travelling by air. We, therefore, later decreed that the permission granted to priests by Canon 883 of the Code of Canon Law, giving faculties for hearing confessions while travelling by sea, should apply also and be extended to priests travelling by air.[67]

Our beloved predecessor, Pius XI, allowed no obstacle to hinder this very important and successful development in behalf of migrants. Innumerable migrants and refugees in America and Europe experienced abundant proof of the universal fatherhood of Pius XI. Of the many provisions which he made, we wish merely to recall some of the more important ones beginning with those on behalf of Oriental peoples.

In the first year of his pontificate, Armenia was devastated and many loyal faithful were either slain or otherwise sent wandering far from their native country. He generously supported his unfortunate sons thus deprived of all their possessions. In particular he welcomed with fatherly hospitality sick and orphaned children into a section of his palace of Castel Gandolfo and carefully maintained them at his own expense.[68]

In 1925, matters pertaining to Russians exiled from their country were entrusted to the Russian Commission, [69] and then, a special office was set up in the Congregation for the Oriental Church to care for the Catholics of the Slavic Rite[70] all over the world.

Consequently, an episcopal See was established in Harbin, China, and a priest of the Byzantine-Slavic Rite was placed in charge of it, and as the Russian Bishop of Harbin, he was spiritual ruler of all the clergy and lay people living in China.[71]

Preceding Pontiffs had provided special churches in Rome for Armenians, Syrians, Maronites, Greeks, Ruthenians and Rumanians. Following their example, Pius XI assigned the Church of St. Anthony, the Hermit, on the Esquiline to Catholics of the Slavic Rite who were resident in or passing through Rome, so that they might worship according to the customs of their fathers.[72]

A Russian Seminary, erected by his command, was therefore set up in a brand new building within the premises.[73] Refugees from Eastern Europe of any religion or nationality were aided more than once by Pius XI by his encouragement, example and spontaneous offers of financial aid as well as by arousing in their behalf the generosity of the Bishops and peoples of Poland.

He sought to promote the spiritual welfare of the Byzantine Rite community which persecutions had earlier driven to Italy, where subsequently he separated the Byzantine parishes from the dioceses of Palermo and Monreale, forming the new Greek diocese or Eparchy of Piana.[75] Likewise, he set up timely rules for the spiritual administration of the Greek-Ruthenian dioceses in the United States[76] and Canada.[77]

As a token of his special good-will toward the Poles, he raised to the rank and dignity of Minor Basilica the Church of St. Josaphat, Bishop and Martyr, in Milwaukee, a Church which cares for Polish-speaking Catholics.[78] Then, in 1931, he appointed the Archbishop of Gniezno to be protector of all Polish emigrants.[79]

Following the example of the Pious Society of the Missionaries of St. Charles for Italian migrants, a new religious institute was founded in the city of Godesberg in 1924 for the assistance of German Catholics emigrating to foreign lands. Pius XI rightly praised this worthy and promising undertaking and when the institute attained its desired development, he gave it the noble name: Society of the Holy Angels.

When bishops, priests, members of religious communities and lay people had to flee Spain because of the most detestable antireligious persecution raging there, he received them humanely and consoled them most affectionately.[80]

In order that Mexicans who emigrated to foreign countries might not become the prey of the enemies of Christ nor lose the Christian ways of their fathers, he urged the Mexican Bishops to confer with their brother bishops in the United States, and he appealed for the cooperation of Catholic Action groups.[81]

This is the place to duly note the love that this same Pontiff demonstrated for Negroes scattered throughout the world. It is clearly evident from a letter to the Superior General of the Society of the Divine Word, April 5, 1923, in which he sent his best wishes for the seminary shortly to be augurated for Nego students. He described as most beneficial their plan to receive into the Society of the Divine Word those Negroes who seemed called to the religious life.

Then, when these students had attained the priesthood, they might exercise the sacred ministry more effectively among their own people.[82]

With regard to the Italians, the chaplains aboard ships, who until then belonged to the Missionary Society of St. Anthony of Padua, were in January 26, 1923 placed by Pius XI under the direct guidance of the head of the College of priests which had been established for Italian people migrating abroad and, subsequenly, he had the Consistorial Congregation provide practical rules for the training of these priests.[83]

Similarly, all priests already engaged in the work of assisting Italian migrants were placed under a single director, chosen and appointed by the Consistorial Congregation. He commanded that the Italian immigrants should be provided with proper identification cards from the ecclesiastical authority before departure so that they could be more readily recognized in their new home lands.[85]

He gave the direction of the Pious Society of the Missionaries of St. Charles to the Consistorial Congregation, a provision which brought many advantages to the Society. For through the efforts of our most beloved Raphael Cardinal Rossi, who was Secretary of the Consistorial Congregation and quite properly considered to be the second founder by the Missionaries of St. Charles, the Constitutions of the Society were brought into harmony with the Code of Canon Law and then approved. This society was restored to its original religious vows. Many new houses were established especially for training priests; likewise, several autonomous religious provinces and missions were erected. Consequently, the membership grew and its field of activity developed so rapidly in America, in Europe and more recently in Australia, that there appeared well founded hope for a more certain and permanent assistance to Italian migrants.

Finally, on April 17, 1922, that noble Pontiff bestowed his own benevolence on and enhanced the work of the Apostleship of the Sea with official Papal approval. Such work was first established in Glasgow, Scotland, in 1920 for the spiritual welware of sailors. After numerous congresses and through the approval of Bishops, the Apostolate had so developed and so widely spread that we ourselves were happy, on May 30, 1942, to place it under the beneficial direction of the Consistorial Congregation.

To usher this subject into our own pontificate, we need only describe what the Church has accomplished during these last few years. As it is well known, soon after we were raised to the See of Rome there daily appeared more bold and violent symptoms of unrestrained desire for extending national boundaries, for an idolized supremacy of race and the unbridled tendency to occupy foreign lands, and for reliance on might rather than on right with the consequent cruel and shameless deportation of entire nations and the forced migration of peoples. These new crimes were, indeed, far worse than the ancient ones.

Soon there developed a whirlwind of most sorrowful events leading to barbarous war. Our own efforts on behalf of charity and peace began immediately.

We tried everything possible, striving, urging, entreating, pleading, and appealing directly to the heads of governments to prevent the disastrous war.[89] Even when this tragic war broke out and spread horror throughout the world, we still sought by word and deed to mitigate and restrain it as much as we could. In these sorrowful circumstances, the Church, as a universal mother, failed neither in her duty nor in what was expected of her. She, the "Head of the universal society of love," [90] became, as was her custom, a comfort for the afflicted, a refuge for the persecuted, a homeland for the exiled.

No matter how enormous the difficulties that faced us and how impossible the times, we left nothing untried to bring some aid to our suffering sons, without discrimination as to their status or nationality. We also exerted great efforts for the displaced Jews who were victims of the cruelest persecutions. [91]

We approved, initiated, and furthered many works of charity for the relief of countless untold wartime disasters and hardships from which practically no one escaped. But in all these works of charity, we were especially solicitous for prisoners of war, refugees, exiles and our other sons who, for whatever reason, had to wander far from their homelands. And along with these, our chief concerns were children and orphans. Yet this being well known to all, since the record is amply documented, there is no need to recount it further. We can however touch on a few specific items.

During the First World War, we assisted our predecessor, Benedict XV, in his extensive charity. Again the Second World War had scarcely broken out when, following his example, we established a special office under our Secretary of State to bring assistance to the poor and needy everywhere. [92] Still another office, for inquiring about and exchanging information on prisoners was maintained through the war. [93]

We also appointed a number of other commissions, among them the commission for the victims of war, for civilian refugees and for those detained in custody. [94] This one was later replaced by the Pontifical Commission for Relief[95] for all those who were in need. Equally worthy of mention are the missions arranged by our Secretariate of State and sent more than once into Germany and Austria, chiefly to provide for the welfare of refugees and displaced persons.[96]

Then when peace was finally restored, at least in part, the necessity of providing for millions of refugees became daily more urgent. Many of them were prevented from returning to their homes; while at the same time, a large number of other people in many over-populated countries were oppressed by want and had to seek refuge in other lands. Hence, we decided to establish an Office of Migration in the very Secretariae of State itself. It was comprised of two sections: one for voluntary migration, the other for enforced deportation.[97] We also delegated an ecclesiastic to the Migration Office established in Geneva so that he might attend international meetings and congresses held in that city.

Very recently, we approved the International Catholic Migration Commission, whose function is to unite and organize existing Catholic associations and committees, and to promote, reinforce and coordinate their projects and activities in behalf of migrants and refugees.[98]

Nor should we forget to mention how our nuncios and delegates and other ecclesiastics specifically sent to organize [99] committees or commissions for needy refugees and for migrants, successfully founded them in every country, indeed in almost every diocese.[100] This of course, was brought about with the aid of the local bishop and of priests, and of the members of Catholic Action and other apostolic associations as well as other worthy laymen.[101]

The diligence and skill of these committees and commissions worthy of our praise achieved many benefits which we ourselves witnessed and which we hope will safeguard migrants and refugees.

The war that broke out in Palestine in 1948 brought new reasons for sadness and mourning. Innumerable refugees underwent horrible suffering, being forced to abandon their possessions and to wander throughout Libya, Syria, Jordan, Egypt and the district of Gaza. United in a common disaster, both the rich and the poor, the Christians and the non-Christians, offered a sad and morurnful spectacle.

Immediately, following the custom of the Catholic Church to provide assistance for the wretched and the abandoned, we sent as much aid as possible. As was customary in Apostolic times, we specifically established the Pontifical Mission for Palestine,[102] which still relieves the want of Arab refugees through money collected [103] from Catholics everywhere, but particularly through the aid of the special agency established by American bishops, called the Catholic Near East Welfare Association.[104]

We have tried earnestly to produce in the minds of all people a sympathetic approach towards exiles and refugees who are our needier brothers. In fact, we have often spoken of their wretched lives, upheld their rights, and more than once appealed in their behalf to the generosity of all men and especially of Catholics. This we have done in radio addresses,[105] in talks and discourses given as occasion arose,[106] and in letters to archbishops and bishops.[107]

We wrote, for example, to our Venerable Brothers, Archbishops, Bishops and Ordinaries of places in Germany:

In the present circumstances, what seems most likely to stimulate and heighten your own charity and that of the German clergy is the necessity of assisting refugees by every resource and means of your ministry. We refer both to refugees from your land who live abroad in scattered regions and to alien refugees in Germany who, often deprived of their friends, their goods and their homes, are forced to lead a squalid and forlorn existence, usually in barracks outside the towns. May all good Germans, and especially the priests and members of Catholic Action, turn their eyes and hearts toward these suffering neighbors and provide them with everything required by religion and charity.[108]

Similarly, in our Encyclical *Redemptoris Nostri* on the Holy Places in Palestine, we lamented sadly:

Very many fugitives of all ages and every state of life, driven abroad by the disastrous war, cry pitifully to us. They live in exile, under guard, and exposed to disease and all manner of dangers.

We are not unaware of the great contributions of public bodies and private citizens to the relief of this stricken multitude; and we, in a continuation of those efforts of charity with which we began our Pontificate, have truly done all in our power to relieve the greatest needs of these millions.

But the condition of these exiles is indeed so critical, so unstable that it cannot last much longer. Therefore, since it is our duty to urge all generous and well-minded souls to relieve as much as possible the wretchedness and want of these exiles, we most earnestly implore those in authority to do justice to all who have been driven far away from homes by the tempest of war and who long above all to live in quiet once more.[109]

We have indeed made our gratitude known to our very dear brothers in the episcopate, as well as to priests and to citizens of every rank, to the public authorities as well to benevolent agencies that have aided refugees and emigrants in many different ways through their activities and advice.[110]

Of these, we here recall with pleasure our letter of December 24, 1948, to the Chairman of the National Catholic Welfare Conference established by the bishops of the United States to promote the Catholic welfare;[111] similarly, our personal letter of April 1951, which we sent to the Bishops of Australia, congratulating them on the 50th Anniversary of the Commonwealth.[112]

Moreover, we have repeatedly addressed the Rulers of States, the heads of agencies, and all upright and cooperative men, urging upon them the need to consider and resolve the very serious problems of refugees and migrants,[113] and, at the same time, to think of the heavy burdens which all peoples bear because of the war and the specific means that should be applied to alleviate the grave evils. We asked them also to consider how beneficial for humanity it would be if cooperative and joint efforts would relieve, promptly and effectively, the urgent needs of the sufferings, by harmonizing the requirements of justice with needs of charity. Relief alone can remedy, to a certain extent, many unjust social conditions. But we know that this is not sufficient. In the first place, there must be justice, which should prevail and be put into practice.[114]

Likewise, from the first days of our Apostolic Office, we have directed our earnest attention to all our migrant sons, and we have been most anxious about their welfare, both temporal and eternal.[115]

For this reason, on June 1, 1951 in a radio address on the fiftieth anniversary of the Encyclical *Rerum Novarum*, we

did speak of the right of people to migrate, which right is
founded in the very nature of land.

Let us recall here a section of that address:

> Our planet, with all its extent of oceans and seas and lakes,
> with mountains and plains covered with eternal snows and ice,
> with great deserts and tractless lands, is not, at the same time,
> without habitable regions and living spaces now abandoned to
> wild natural vegetation and well suited to be cultivated by
> man to satisfy his needs and civil activities: and more than
> once, it is inevitable that some families migrating from one
> spot to another should go elsewhere in search of a new home-
> land.
>
> Then,—according to the teaching of "Rerum Novarum,"—the
> right of the family to a living space is recognized. When this
> happens, migration attains its natural scope as experience often
> shows. We mean, the more favorable distribution of men on
> the earth's surface suitable to colonies of agricultural workers;
> that surface which God created and prepared for the use
> of all.
>
> If the two parties, those who agree to leave their native land
> and those who agree to admit the newcomers, remain anxious
> to eliminate as far as possible all obstacles to the birth and
> growth of real confidence between the country of emigration
> and that of immigration, all those affected by such transference
> of people and places will profit by the transaction.
>
> The families will receive a plot of ground which will be
> native for them in the true sense of the word; the thickly
> inhabited countries will be relieved and their people will
> acquire new friends in foreign countries; and the States which
> receive the emigrants will acquire industrious citizens. In this
> receive the migrants will acquire industrious citizens. In this
> way, the nations which give and those which receive will both
> contribute to the increased welfare of man and the progress of
> human culture.[116]

We again recalled these general principles of natural law

the following year on Christmas Eve before the Sacred College of Cardinals.[117]

We wrote specifically on this subject in a letter of December 24, 1948 to the American Bishops:

> You know indeed how preoccupied we have been and with what anxiety we have followed those who have been forced by revolutions in their own countries, or by unemployment or hunger to leave their homes and live in foreign lands.
>
> The natural law itself, no less than devotion to humanity, urges that ways of migration be opened to these people. For the Creator of the universe made all good things primarily for the good of all. Since land everywhere offers the possibility of supporting a large number of people, the sovereignty of the State, although it must be respected, cannot be exaggerated to the point that access to this land is, for inadquate or unjustified reasons, denied to needy and decent people from other nations, provided of course, that the public wealth, considered very carefully, does not forbid this.
>
> Informed of our intentions, you recently strove for legislation to allow many refugees to enter your land. Through your persistence, a provident law was enacted, a law that we hope will be followed by others of broader scope. In addition, you have, with the aid of chosen men, cared for the emigrants as they left their homes and as they arrived in your land, thus admirably putting into practice the precept of priestly charity: "The priest is to injure no one; he will desire rather to aid all." (St. Ambrose, "De Officiis ministrorum," lib. 3, c. IX)[118]

But no one who has heard our words, whether in our Christmas Address of 1945, [119] or in our allocution of February 20, 1946 to the newly created cardinals, and in our address on the 25th of February to the Diplomatic Corps accredited to the Holy See, certainly, no one can be unaware of the grave concern gripping the heart of the worried father of all the faithful.

In these addresses and in our radio talks, we have condemned severely the ideas of the totalitarian and the imperialistic state, as well as that of exaggerated nationalism. On one hand, in fact they arbitrarily restrict the natural rights of people to migrate or to colonize while on the other hand, they compel entire populations to migrate into other lands, deporting inhabitants against their wills, disgracefully tearing individuals from their families, their homes and their countries.

In that address to the Diplomatic Corps, in the presence of a solemn gathering, we again affirmed our desire, often previously expressed, for a just and lasting peace. We pointed out another way of attaining this peace, a way that promotes friendly relations between nations; that is, to allow exiles and refugess to return finally to their homes and to allow those in need, whose own lands lack the necessities of life, to emigrate to other countries.[121]

In our allocution to the cardinals on the feast of our patron, St. Eugene, on July 1, 1946,[122] we again called upon the nations with more extensive territory and less numerous populations to open their borders to people from overcrowded countries. Of the latter, as is well known, Japan today happens to be the most overpopulated one.

We expressed the same view in our Christmas Address of 1948. It is better, we said, to facilitate the migration of families into those countries able to provide them with the essentials of life, than to send foodstuffs at great expense to refugee camps.[123]

Therefore, when Senators from the United States, who were members of a Committee on Immigration, visited Rome a few years ago, we again urged them to try to administer as liberally as possible the overly restrictive provisions of their immigration laws.[124]

Nor did we neglect to state and urge this same principle in an audience to which we were pleased to admit also eminent American Congressmen in charge of European refugee affairs [125] and who were likewise members of a Committee on Public Expenditures.[126] We reaffirmed that stand very recently, on June 4th of this year, in our paternal address to our dear people of Brazil.[127]

In an address of July 2, 1951, to the members of an International Catholic Congress for the Improvement of Rural Living Conditions, held in Rome, we said that there would be very great benefits from international regulations in favor of emigration and immigration.[128]

Later, we described the gravity of this matter to many distinguished members of an International Catholic Migration Congress, held in Naples, whom we gladly received in audience.[129]

We therefore offer endless thanks to God, the Bountiful Giver of every good gift, Who has most generously assisted His Holy Church. In fact it has been because of His aid and with the effective co-operation and initiative of all commissions and agencies, that it has been possible to carry out among other endeavors, the following relief and welfare projects:

Settlements for boys and girls, some open during the summer months and some permanently, which settlements also accepted children of immigrants from many different nations, welcoming them with great care; institutes to care for orphans and children crippled in the war; kitchens and tables with food for the needy; shelters for receiving newly-released prisoners and refugees on their return to their homeland, and for assisting migrants and their families; Christmas presents given on our instructions to children and prisoners.

Provision was made for youths from every nation so that, although they were far from their native lands, they could resume in foreign schools the studies they had earlier been forced to drop. Likewise, there were undertaken many trips through various European nations to bring aid, food, clothing, medicine for the poor and victims of the war; recreation centers for soldiers far from home.

While the disastrous war waged, there converged on Rome almost hourly a vast mass of people, children, women, the sick and the aged, to seek from the common father of all, a place of safety and refuge. They came from the towns and villages laid waste by the invading enemies, particularly from devastated areas of Italy. This caused us to enlarge, yet further, the scope of our charity, for the cries of so many exiles and refugees touched our heart, and, moved by that same pity, we felt the need to repeat those words of Our Lord: "I have compassion on the multitude." [130]

For this reason, we threw open the doors of all our buildings at the Vatican as well as at the Lateran, and especially those at Castel Gandolfo; and at the Roman Basilicas, as well as these religious communities, seminaries and ecclesiastical colleges of Rome. So while almost the whole world was aflame with bitter hatred and the blood of brothers flowed freely, the Sacred City of Rome and the buildings mentioned became centers and homes of charity.

It was also our privilege to bring comfort to millions of soldiers and prisoners by means of religious and charitable undertakings and to encourage, as well, their chaplains with extraordinary spiritual aids; it was, likewise, our privilege to bring those who had been exiled back to their own lands and to obtain freedom for civilians condemned unjustly to prison or exile; again to release from prison and rescue from almost certain death those people deported to remote regions, and to return them to their anxious families.

It was our privilege to assure the means of travel to refugees and migrants about to migrate to hospitable foreign lands; to receive cordially those banished clerics and priests who endured so much for the Apostolic Faith and Catholic Unity, and to assign them a new field of apostolic labor among migrants and refugees from their own nations; to relieve, in every way, great numbers of migrants, and especially laborers dwelling outside their homelands because of their work; to nourish and protect the delicate lives of children and to attend to the healing of the sick; to provide for the burial of those fallen in battle, to guard their revered remains and to return them to their homelands.

We wish also to express our thanks to all those who, even though they were besieged by many private and public troubles, responded generously to our appeals.

Even now, it is with an aching heart that we recall the great masses of refugees who poured into Rome while the war raged. And we recall our unfortunate sons, exiles or internees who, as pilgrims to Rome, later set out from many regions of Europe to win expiatory indulgences of the Jubilee. We were very happy to receive them and addressed them as a father. We dispelled their tears and comforted their embittered spirits with Christian hope.[131]

With grieving heart we recall, again and again, our very dear sons, the bishops, priests, and nuns dragged unjustly from their homes and all those others who, condemned to prison or forced labor, have been kept in absolutely inhuman living conditions.

All these hapless wanderers have been an unceasing source of anguish to us.[132]

In order that these uprooted peoples might be renewed through heavenly gifts and comforts, we have prayed ardently and continuously in their behalf to the Eternal Father and to Our Most Loving Redeemer, Source of every consolation.[133] We still beseech God constantly that "the refugees, the prisoners and the deported who have been carried far from their native lands may return to their own beloved countries as soon as possible."[134]

We believe we fulfilled an urgent duty of our office when we appointed certain prelates, distinguished by their zeal, to advance the spiritual welfare of people of their nationality living in settlements far from their native land. By reason of their authority, they were to direct and support everything that was to be undertaken in behalf of the settlers by priests of their native language. We were happy to see how these prelates, whom we invested with a special mandate as Visitors and provided with appropriate powers, have faithfully fulfilled our hopes.

Meanwhile, it was with profound satisfaction that we learned of the work of the Dutch Catholic Agency for the Care of Migrants. This institution, established by the Bishops of Holland, has worked very successfully on behalf of Catholics preparing to emigrate or those who had already emigrated from that country.[135] We were equally happy to find that a growing number of priests went abroad, especially to Belgium, France, Germany, Switzerland, Holland, Great Britain and also distant regions of America; not only to assist emigrants of their nationality, but also to toil in behalf of the poor in places where there is a scarcity of priests as in certain Latin American dioceses.

We must honor by special mention the Bishops of Italy who, at the prompting of the Consistorial Congregation,[136] permitted a number of priests to leave their country. Also worthy of honor are the Spanish Bishops, for the Hispano-American Institute for priestly co-operation[137] is due to their efforts.

Lest anyone think that the religious communities made only a small contribution to this work, it is enough simply to recall that Order priests voluntarily became companions of the secular priests and of the bishops in their sufferings and labors. They have gone, more than in the past, into remote regions and, working with their usual ardor, have earned high praise.

Along with the older Orders and the regular clerics, and the newer congregations and communities, a new Society, approved by the Holy See,[138] has also distinguished itself in this branch of the apostolate. This is the Society of Christ, founded in the archdiocese of Gniezno in 1932, for the spiritual care of Poles living abroad.

In our constant solicitude for Eastern refugees, we have among other things erected the Maronite Patriarchal Vicariate in the Diocese of Cairo for Maronite Catholics, who often migrate from Lebanon into Egypt or else live there permanently.[139]

In Canada, we divided the Ruthenian province into three provinces or exarchates; the central, eastern and western.[140] Later, a part of the central province was divided off and established as the new province of Saskatchewan.[141] Very recently, we likewise erected a diocese in Brazil for Catholics of Oriental Rite living in that country.[142]

We also established the Lithuanian College of St. Casimir in Rome for refugee bishops and priests from Lithuania.[143]

We were very happy to appoint St. Francis of Paula heavenly patron of associations dedicated to the service of seamen, of navigation companies and of all sailors of Italy.[144] We were likewise glad to canonize St. Frances Xavier Cabrini[145] and proclaim her as the heavenly patroness of all migrants.[146]

These timely projects have seemed altogether worth noting here. Initiated by this Apostolic See, they were undertaken by the bishops with the eager co-operation of priests, members of religious communities and laymen. The names of these collaborators, although, for the most part, not recorded in history books, are nevertheless written in heaven. Again, these works have appeared worth recounting here, if only briefly, so that the universal and benevolent activity of the Church on behalf of migrants and exiles of every kind—to whom she has extended every possible aid: religious, moral and social,—might thus become better appreciated.

Besides, it seemed that these things badly needed to be publicized, especially in our times, when the provident enterprises of Mother Church are so unjustly assailed by her enimies and scorned and overlooked, even in the very field of charity where she was first to break ground and often the only to continue its cultivation.

Frequent letters, which we have recently received, report, as can be read every day in newspapers and magazines, that the number of immigrants in Europe and America, and lately in Australia and the Philippine Islands, has continued to increase.

True, many organizations—including a number of official

agencies, both national and international—have vied and still vie with one another in assisting migrants, relieving moral as well as material want. Nevertheless, because of our supreme and universal ministry, we must continue to look with the greatest love after our sons who are caught in the the trials and misfortunes of exile, and to strive with all our resources to help them. While we do not neglect whatever material assistance is permitted, we seek primarily to aid them with spiritual consolation.

Moved by their desire for the good of souls, many of our venerable brothers, the bishops and archbishops, including a number of cardinals have urged us to publish new regulations to better organize, for diocesan administration, the spiritual care of immigrants. Their requests were directed to us through our venerable brother, Cardinal A. G. Piazza, Bishop of Sabina and Poggio Mirteto, and Secretary of the Consistorial Congregation.

These requests were in full accord with our own intentions. In fact, we were eagerly awaiting an opportunity to draw up suitable regulations for the bishops, to provide them with proper authority to offer aliens, whether immigrants or travellers, the religious assistance appropiate to their needs, and not inferior to that available to other Catholics in the dioceses. These regulations were not to conflict with the provisions of the Code of Canon Law, but rather to conform faithfully both to its spirit and practice.

We thought it would be very useful for the salvation of souls and for the improvement of the Church's discipline to present a brief historical summary of at least the most important activities of our Holy Mother the Catholic Church on behalf of migrants. We have also outlined, starting with the end of the 19th century and coming down to our own days, some of the regulations, still in force, governing pastoral work among migrants.

But most of all, we thought it important to arrange in a systematic collection the relevant laws as adapted to present times and circumstances, while the old rules are either annulled in part or modified or expanded. We hope, in this way, to make better provision for the spiritual care of all emigrants and aliens. We wish this care to be entrusted permanetly to the Consistorial Congregations because of its authority over Catholics of the Latin rite.

Having accomplished the first part of this plan, we now proceed to the second part.

TITLE II

Norms for The
Spiritual Care of Migrants

CHAPTER I

THE COMPETENCY OF THE
CONSISTORIAL CONGREGATION REGARDING
MIGRANTS

WE now review, approve and confirm the enactments of our predecessors of happy memory, and especially those of St. Pius X; at the same time however, we modify them somewhat, as seems necessary. We hereby wish and decree that the following rules be observed in the future.

1. a) The Consistorial Congregation alone has the authority to seek and to provide everything pertaining to the spiritual welfare of migrants of the Latin rite, wheresoever they may have migrated. However, if their migration is to countries under the jurisdiction of the Congregation for the Oriental Church, or the Congregation for the Propagation of the Faith, then these Congregations must be consulted depending upon the region.

b) It is likewise within the competence of the Consistorial Congregation to seek and to provide, in like manner, for emigrants of the Oriental rite, whenever emigrants of one or another Oriental rite leave for areas which are not under the jurisdiction of the Congregation for the Oriental Church, and where no priests of such rite are available, but in all cases previous consultation must be taken up with the Congregation for the Oriental Church.

2. a) Whenever priests of the Latin rite migrate it is always the Consistorial Congregation alone which has jurisdiction over them.

b) If the priests of the Latin rite subject to the Congregation for the Oriental Church or the Congregation for the Propagation of the Faith desire to migrate into an area not under jurisdiction of the same Congregation, they also will be subject to the regulations concerning such migration, made or to be made by the Consistorial Congregation, without prejudice of the rights of the Congregation for the Oriental Church or for the Propagation of the Faith.

c) These same regulations are binding on priests of the Oriental rite migrating into areas not under the jurisdiction of the Congregation for the Oriental Church, likewise without prejudice to the laws and rights of this same Congregation for the Oriental Church.

3. a) 1. The Consistorial Congregation alone can authorize priests to migrate from Europe or Mediterranean regions to other lands overseas. This applies regardless of any length of time they wish to be gone, whether it be brief or long, indefinite or permanent. Such authorization may be merely for departure or for a brief residence in the new country, or for a more prolonged residence there.

2. Nuncios, Internuncios and Apostolic Delegates may grant this permission to priests of that nation where they regularly fulfil their assignments, provided that this faculty has been granted and reserved to them.

b) 1. The priests referred to in a) 1. must obtain

permission and comply with all other regulations before being incardinated into the new diocese overseas.

2. This permission is also necessary for religious priests unless it is a matter of their going, on orders of their superiors, to another house of their order. Similarly, religious excloistered need it, during the time of their exclaustration; also, religious who have been "secularized," whether they have been accepted outright by a friendly bishop or simply on a trial basis.

c) This permission, without prejudice to the other requirements of the decree *Magni Semper Negotii*,[1] is not to be granted unless it is certain that there are:

1. The testimonials of good conduct of the petitioner;

2. a proper and reasonable motive for migration;

3. consent both of the bishop of the place he is leaving, or of his superior in the case of a religious, and of the bishop to whose diocese he is going;

4. an indult from the Congregation of the Council, if it is a case of a pastor to be absent more than two months from his parish.

d) Priests, whether secular or religious, who have obtained permission to migrate to an overseas country, must obtain new permission if they wish to go to still another country, even in that same continent.

e) Priests who, disregarding these rules, heedlessly and boldly migrate, shall incur the penalties of the decree *Magni Semper Negotii*.[2]

4. An apostolic indult to establish special nationality parishes for the benefit of immigrants can, according to Canon 216, 4 of the Code of Canon Law, be granted only by the Consistorial Congregation.

5. a) It is likewise the Consistorial Congregation which has the right:

1. After first reviewing the applicant's previous life, morals and fitness, and making sure of the Ordinary's consent, then to grant permission to priests, whether they be secular or religious who now desire to dedicate themselves to the religious care of migrants of their own nationality or language, or to the care of people who may be travelling by sea or who, for many reasons, may be aboard ships or who are attached to ships, in whatever capacity. Likewise, the said Congregation has the right to appoint, by special rescript, priests as missionaries to migrants or as chaplains aboard ships; similarly, to assign their destinations, to transfer them, to accept their resignations, and in a proper case, to dismiss them.

2. To choose and appoint in any nation Moderators or Directors of Missionaries for migrants of the same nationality or language.

3. To direct and supervise all these priests, whether through the local Ordinaries or the Delegate for Migration Affairs, or other ecclesiastics delegated for this task.

b) 1. If the rescript mentioned in a) 1. is granted, notice must be sent to both the Ordinaries, the Ordinary from whom and the Ordinary to whom the priest is going.

2. The Consistorial Congregation must not delay in notifying bishops of the appointments of moderators or directors for their nations or territories.

6. a) We approve with our authority the special committees or episcopal commissions set up in many European and American countries for the spiritual aid of migrants, and wish that these timely committees be set up also in other

areas. We have, therefore, decided that the priests appointed by Bishops to serve as Secretaries of these committees may be named Directors of Migration Affairs, each for his own country, by the Consistorial Congregation.

b) Where this type of committee has not yet been established, the Consistorial Congregation may choose a director from among the priests presented by the Bishops of the country.

7. a) In order to facilitate the work of assisting emigrants, we hereby establish and institute, in the offices of our Consistorial Congregation, a Supreme Council on Migration.

b) The president of this Council will be the Assessor of the same Congregation. Its secretary will be the Delegate for Migration Affairs.

c) The following may be members of this Council:

1. Those priests who in their own country or region either serve as secretaries of the episcopal commissions for the spiritual care of immigrants or are otherwise engaged, at the direction of their bishops, in this type of spiritual care.

2. Those priests, whether secular or regular, resident in Rome who seem outstanding because of their knowledge of this field and their zeal for souls.

8. a) We also establish within the Consistorial Congregation another agency, the General International Secretariate, to direct the work of the Apostolate of the Sea. The chief work of this Apostolate is to promote the spiritual and moral welfare of maritime people, that is, of both those who board ships as officers and those who go as crew members, together with those who are employed in ports to prepare sailings.

b) The Assessor of the Consistorial Congregation shall direct this Secretariate as its president. The Delegate for Migration Affairs shall be its secretary.

c) The following may be chosen as members of the Secretariate:

1. Those ecclesiastics who in each country have been appointed as Directors of such work by the bishops.

2. Other priests who, having worked notably in the development of this work, are recommended by proper testimonials.

CHAPTER II

THE DELEGATE FOR MIGRATION AFFAIRS

9. We establish in the Consistorial Congregation the Office of Delegate for Migration Affairs.

10. a) The function of this Delegate is to foster and promote by every apt means the welfare, especially spiritual, of Catholic migrants of whatever language, race, nationality or, with necessary exceptions, rite. In doing this, the Delegate is to confer, when necessary, with our Secretary of State or with government officials or agencies.

b) To this end, the Delegate is, in the name and by authority of the Consistorial Congregation, to assist and support by his activities and counsel all Catholic organizations, institutions and agencies, whether national or international, including—without prejudice to the rights of bishops—diocesan and parochial groups that aim at the same goal.

11. a) The Delegate has charge of missionaries to migrants and chaplains on ships, whether secular or regular, and their directors.

b) He shall, by order of the Consistorial Congregation, direct and supervise these men, and not neglect to report on them.

12. It will also be the duty of the Delegate to recruit and present to the Consistorial Congregation priests who wish to devote themselves to the spiritual care of those who are migrating or have migrated and of those who ply the seas or are for whatever reason on board ships or service them.

13. a) Priests approved for the work and appointed missionaries to migrants or ship chaplains by rescript of the Consistorial Congregation will be assigned to a mission or to a special ship by the Delegate.

b) The Delegate shall be careful to provide these men with aid they need, whether he does so personally and immediately, or indirectly through other ecclesiastics, preferably through their Directors.

14. The Delegate shall notify the local Ordinaries and the Directors of the imminent arrival of immigrants.

15. The Delegate shall strive to promote and guide everything that might contribute to the success of an annual Migrant Day.

16. At the end of each year, the Delegate shall prepare and send to the Consistorial Congregation a report on the material and spiritual state of the missions and on the observance of ecclesiastical discipline by the missionaries to migrants and by ship chaplains.

cern the spiritual welfare of immigrants of their nationality or language.

b) To direct, without prejudice to the rights of the Ordinaries, the missionaries or chaplains.

21. a) The Director should therefore investigate:

1. Whether the missionaries or chaplains lead a a life in conformity with the standards of the sacred canons and are careful to fulfil their duties.

2. Whether these men properly carry out the decrees of the Consistorial Congregation and of their local Ordinary.

3. Whether they preserve carefully the decorum and dignity of churches or chapels or oratories and of sacred furnishings, especially in regards to the custody of the Most Blessed Sacrament and the celebration of Mass.

4. Whether the sacred rites are celebrated according to requirements of liturgical laws and decrees of the Congregation of Rites. Similarly, whether the church revenues are carefully administered, and the obligations connected with them, particularly those of Mass, are properly met. Also whether the parochial records, mentioned below in No. 25 c) and No. 35 b), are correctly written and preserved.

b) To assure himself of all this, the Director must visit the missions or ships frequently.

c) It is also up to the Director, as soon as he learns that a missionary or chaplain is seriously ill, to provide assistance, so that neither spiritual nor material aid will be lacking, nor, in case of death, a decent funeral. He must also take care that during the priest's sickness or on his death the records, documents, sacred furnishings and other mission property are not lost or carried off.

22. The Director may, where possible and for good reasons approved by the Consistorial Congregation, bring all the missionaries or chaplains together, especially in order to make a retreat or to attend conferences on the best methods for carrying on their ministry.

23. At least once a year, the Director shall send an accurate report to the Consistorial Congregation on the missionaries and chaplains, and on the state of the missions. He is to recount not only the good accomplished during the year, but also the evils that have crept in, what measures have been taken to obviate them and what seems necessary to promote the growth of the missions.

24. Missionaries to migrants engaged in the spiritual care of Catholics of their own nationality or language come under the jurisdiction of the local Ordinary, according to the norms of Chapter IV below.

25. a) It is the duty of the chaplains aboard ships to attend, throughout the voyage, to the spiritual care of all those who, for whatever reason happen to be aboard. The only exception would be in the case of marriage.

b) The chaplains will be given, without prejudice to the provision of Canon 883 of the Code of Canon Law, special rules and faculties by the Consistorial Congregation.

c) They must keep a record of baptisms, confirmations and deaths. At the end of each trip they are to send their Director a copy of this record, together with a report of their work done on that trip.

26. If there is a chapel legitimately erected on the ship, the chaplains shall, with due allowances, be deemed equivalent to rectors of churches.

27. a) Chaplains may celebrate the Divine Services, even solemnly, in the chapel aboard ship as long as they

observe the canonical and liturgical laws and are careful to
hold the services at a convenient time for all on board.

    b) The chaplains are to:

    1. Announce feast days to those on board.

    2. Give catechetical instructions, especially to the
young people, and an explanation of the Gospel.

    28. Chaplains on ships are to watch:

    a) That in the chapel, the Divine Services are cele-
brated properly according to the prescription of the sacred
canons and that priests celebrating Mass be assisted by
another priest if there is one, vested in a surplice, in order to
avoid the danger of spilling the Sacred Species from the
chalice.

    b) That the sacred furnishings are kept up and the
decorum of the chapel looked after;that nothing be done
there incompatible, in any way, with the holiness of the place
or the reverence due the House of God, and that neither the
chapel nor the altar nor the sacred vestments be used at the
service of non-Catholic sects.

    29. a) No one may celebrate Mass, administer the sacra-
ments, preach, or perform other divine functions in the ship's
chapel, without the permission, at least presumed, of the
chaplain.

    b) This permission must be granted or refused
according to the ordinary rules of the canon law.

    30. The right to erect and bless a chapel on ship belongs
to the Ordinary of the place in which the home port of the
ship is located.

    31. Missionaries and chaplains may, with the consent
of the Director, and the Superior in case of a religious, be
absent from their mission or ship for any one month within
the same year, provided the needs of emigrants or sea-

men be met by a priest who has the proper rescript from the Consistorial Congregation. Directors, who must obtain the authorization of the Consistorial Congregation, and if they are religious, of their Superior, are granted this same privilege, provided they can find a priest approved by the Consistorial Congregation to substitute for them.

CHAPTER IV

THE SPIRITUAL CARE
LOCAL ORDINARIES ARE TO PROVIDE ALIENS

32. Local Ordinaries are to provide for the spiritual care of aliens of every sort, whether they have a quasi-domicile or they have no domicile at all. Whenever, in this ministry it seems for one reason or another inexpedient to apply to the Consistorial Congregation for permission to establish parishes for various language or nationality groups, local Ordinaries are in the future to observe carefully the following rules:

33. Every local Ordinary is to make an earnest effort to entrust the spiritual care of aliens or immigrants to priests, whether secular or regular, of the same language or nationality, i.e., to missionaries to migrants who have, as stated above, a special license from the Consistorial Congregation.

34. In like manner, after consultation with the Consistorial Congregation, and having observed all other requirements of law, every local Ordinary shall try to grant these missionaries to migrants the authority to undertake the

spiritual care of immigrant Catholics of their own language or nationality with no canonical quasi-domicile or without any canonical domicile.

35. a) A missionary to migrants, supplied with such authority in exercising the care of souls, is to be considered equal to a pastor. He therefore possesses, making due allowances, the same faculties for the spiritual care as a pastor and is bound by the same obligations and held to the requirements of the common law.

b) They must therefore in the first place, keep the parish records mentioned in Canon 470 of the Code of Canon Law. An accurate copy must be sent at the end of each year to the pastor of the place and to his Director.

36. a) Parochial authority of this type is personal, to be exercised over aliens or immigrants.

b) This same authority is cumulative on equal terms with that of the pastor of the place, even if it is exercised in a church or chapel or public or semi-public oratory, entrusted to the missionary to migrants.

37. a) Wherever possible, every missionary to migrants is to be assigned a church, chapel or public or semi-public oratory for carrying on the sacred ministry.

b) Otherwise, the Ordinary of the place shall set up regulations to enable the missionary to migrants freely and completely to fulfill his duties in another church, not excluding the parish church.

38. Missionaries to migrants are, while in this work, completely subject to the jurisdiction of the local Ordinary, both with respect to the exercise of the sacred ministry and with respect to discipline, excluding every privilege of exemption.

39. For receiving the Sacraments, including marriage, every alien, whether with canonical quasi-domicile or without any canonical domicile is free to approach a missionary to migrants or the pastor of the place.

40. For the purpose under discussions, under the designation of immigrants with no canonical quasi-domicile (*advenae*) or without any canonical domicile (*peregrini*) are included:

      1. All aliens—not excluding those who migrate from colonies—who for whatever length of time or whatever reason, including studies, are in a foreign land.

      2. Their direct descendants of the first degree of the direct line even though they have acquired the rights of citizenship.

CHAPTER V

THE SPIRITUAL CARE TO BE PROVIDED MIGRANTS BY ITALIAN BISHOPS

41. Since migration has been more common among Italians than other peoples, the Holy See has been especially active in caring for Italian migrants.[4] We, by this Apostolic Letter, confirm those special regulations drawn up by our predecessors with regard to Italians emigrating to foreign countries, and warmly commend those norms to the zeal, well known to us, of Italian Ordinaries. We take this opportunity to urge these local Ordinaries earnestly to fulfill our wishes.

42. Let them keep in mind, as a rule in undertaking and accomplishing this work, those words with which St. Pius X praised the committees and agencies: "There are in Italy, at the service of migrants, numerous committees, as they are called, and agencies, as well as other institutions of the kind, established by the bishops, by members of the clergy, and by laymen themselves, men remarkably generous with their goods and much attached to Christian wisdom."[5]

43. Let them see that, at their initiative and under their direction, and with the co-operation of members of Catholic Action and of other Catholic groups devoted to the religious, moral and social aid of workers, there are set up committees and sub-committees for migrants, especially in those dioceses from which more migrants are departing.

44. Similarly, let them watch diligently that the committees thus established perform properly the duties assigned them and strive to attain their goal, the salvation of souls.

45. a) The local Ordinaries must not neglect to recommend that the pastors, engaged in this phase of their ministry, with their usual diligence, should warn their people against the spiritual dangers which ordinarily confront them as soon as they leave their homes, their families, and their country.

b) Therefore, pastors shall give suitable catechetical instructions to those of their parishioners who are preparing to migrate.

46. The Ordinaries must not hesitate to urge pastors to keep in contact with their people even after they migrate.

47. The following precepts of the Consistorial Congregation are to be observed scrupulously: "The Ordinaries of

Italy, especially through pastors and through the agencies devoted to the assistance of migrants, shall see that departing migrants and travellers are given ecclesiastical identfication cards."[6]

48. They must do their best, using the methods that seem most useful, to ensure the success both of the Day for Italian Migrants, to be held annually, and of the collection for the spiritual assistance of migrants. This collection should be forwarded to the Consistorial Congregation.[7]

49. a) We congratulate those Ordinaries of dioceses outside Italy, whether in Europe or overseas, who try, through national or diocesan agencies and commissions to provide every alien with spiritual and moral help, receiving them, though they are strangers, as members of their own flock. We request that in parishes where all or most of the members are of Italian descent, there be celebrated an annual Day for Italian Migrants, as provide in No.48 for the Ordinaries of Italy, and to see that the collection taken be sent to the Consistorial Congregation in support of the work for Italian migrants.[8]

b) Similarly, this should also be done with necessary modifications, for migrants of other nationalities and languages, so that a Day for Migrants may be celebrated throughout the whole Catholic world at one and the same time, on the first Sunday in Advent.

50. The Ordinaries of Italy may wish, finally, to urge their pastors to offer one Mass a year for the Holy Father's intention, rather than *pro populo*. They can call on them to adopt faithfully and voluntarily such a change since it is done for the benefit of Italian migrants.

CHAPTER VI

THE PONTIFICAL COLLEGE OF PRIESTS
AT THE SERVICE OF ITALIAN MIGRANTS

51. We recognize and approve the Pontifical College of priests, established to provide missionaries for Italians migrating abroad.[9]

52. a) We wish this College to remain dependent on the Consistorial Congregation, without, however, interfering with the jurisdiction of the Cardinal Vicar of Rome.

b) It is up to the Consistorial Congregation itself:

1. To direct the College and watch over it, both with respect to the maintenance of discipline and to its finances and to the administration of its material resources.

2. To make rules for it.

3. To appoint the Rector and other officials.

53. The special function of this College is to prepare young Italian priests of the secular clergy so that they may provide Italian migrants in foreign lands.[10] Since this function is the same as that of the Pious Society of the Missionaries of St. Charles, we permit the Rector and the other governing officials and professors to be chosen from priests of the same Pious Society, to which we freely entrust this College. The requirements of the preceding number are still to be observed.

54. We also direct that, in the future, no priest be entrusted with the spiritual care of migrants until he has been properly prepared for an adequate period of time in the College mentioned above, and is thus recognized as suitable for such duties by his qualities of mind and heart,

his doctrine, his knowledge of languages, his sound health and other requirements.

55. Especially in those dioceses from which the majority of migrants are leaving, let the bishops be mindful that they should do what is most useful to the cause of religion and most pleasing to us, namely, that they voluntarily send to the Pontifical College those young priests who are outstanding for virtue and zeal for souls and who wish to devote themselves entirely to the welfare of migrants.

56. Finally, in other regions and countries outside Italy to which migration is now taking place there may be a lack of adequate spiritual assistance for the Catholic migrants already there. In such areas the Ordinaries can, without doubt, provide this assistance if they follow carefully the methods used for Italian migrants, as fully publicized in the Acts of the Roman Pontiffs, and hereby approved by us, with necessary modifications for the place and circumstances.

Therefore, having seriously considered the importance of this whole matter, and being impelled by the examples of Our Predecessors, and having given careful attention to the views of Adeodato G. Cardinal Piazza, Bishop of Sabina and Poggio Mirteto and Secretary of the Consistorial Congregation, we, hereby, do establish and prescribe all which is contained therein.

We now decree that what we hereby establish shall not be subject to attack for any reason whatsoever, even though it be enacted without the consent of those who have or claim to have the right to express their opinion on this matter, or even if they were not consulted or their opinion was not accepted. Furthermore, we declare that what we, hereby, have stated shall possess and retain its force, its validity, and its effectiveness until such time as it shall have obtained its full results. Finally, we publicly state that all those who are expected or will be expected to benefit by it should do so by careful observance.

We reject as null and void every contrary measure, regardless of who impudently proposes to do so, whether knowingly or through ignorance, and irrespective of what his authority may be.

This Constitution shall remain valid, notwithstanding anything to the contrary, including any other Apostolic Constitutions or dispositions of the Roman Pontiffs, our predecessors, as mentioned above or other Acts, however worthy of special mention or calling for canonical derogation.

No one, therefore, shall modify this text which expresses what we, hereby, establish, ordain, reject, direct, unite, admonish, forbid, command, and desire, nor shall anyone rashly oppose it. But if someone presume to do so, he should know that he will incur the wrath of the omnipotent God, and of His apostles Peter and Paul.

Given at Castel Gandolfo, near Rome, on August 1, the feast of St. Peter in Chains, in 1952, the 14th year of our Pontificate.

Pius P. P. XII

APOSTOLIC CONSTITUTION *EXSUL FAMILIA*
REFERENCES

INTRODUCTION

1. *Phil.* 2:7.
2. Cf. *Rom.* 8:29.
3. St. Augustine, *Epistula*, CCXXVIII, 8; Migne, *Patrologia Latina*, XXXIII, 1016 ff.

TITLE I

1. St. Ambrose, *De officiss ministrorum*, II, 28, 136-137: *PL*, XVI, 148.
2. Cf. Pope Benedict XV, Letter to Paulinus Peter Cardinal Andrieu, Archbishop of Bordeaux, on the occasion of a collection for Negro Missions on Epiphany Sunday, *Quoniam Africanorum Galliae*, February 11, 1916, *Acta Apostoticae Sedis*, VIII, 57 ff: "Because of Our Apostolic office, We are greatly concerned about the wretched and abject condition of Negroes. Therefore We write to you, Beloved Brother, in order that We may offer them some relief. We need scarcely mention here the abolition of the sinister commerce of slaves. It is well established that the Church has from its very beginning zealously worked to abolish it.

She affirmed the identical personal dignity innate in every human being and his full equality of rights; she encouraged men to set free their slaves for the sake of a heavenly gain; she established religious communities with the specific purpose of redeeming slaves.

However, We are deeply grieved that such a blameful blot and stain of dishonor still remains in the bosom of human society, even though most of it has been removed. Accordingly, it is entirely proper for us to zealously follow the custom of the Holy See in this work also worthy of honor"; *Ibid.*, p. 57, Congregation of the Propagation of the Faith, Letter to all the Bishops of the world concerning a collection for the Negroes in Africa. *Summus Pontifex Leo XIII*, September 21, 1919, *AAS*, XII, 74 f.: "The Supreme Pontiff of glorious memory, having had pity on the distress of the Negroes who were abducted into slavery and were suffering great damage in mind and body, through an Encyclical (*Catholicae Ecclesiae*) to all the Bishops of the Catholic world, November 20, 1890 (*Leonis XIII Pontificis Maximi Acta*, Rome, Vatican Press, 1891, X, pp. 312 ff.), recommended to their charity the work undertaken by him for safeguarding the liberty of the Negroes in Africa, and for freeing them from their racial superstition." Leo XIII dealt with this dehumanizing toleration of slavery and more especially with the traffic in human beings in a Letter to the Venerable Brother Bishops of Brazil (*In plurimis*, May 5, 1888, *op. cit.*, VIII, pp. 169 ff.).
3. *Rom.* 12:13. Cf. in addition those passages from the New Testament in

which hospitality is commended: *Matt.* 25: 35, 38, 40; *Luke* 14: 13-14; I *Tim.* 3:2; *Titus,* 1:8; I *Pet.* 4:9; III *John,* 5, 8; *Heb.* 13:2; *Jas.* 1:27; or examples of hospitality referred to: *Luke* 10:38 and 19:6; *Acts,* 16:15 and 28:2,7.

4. IV Lateran Council, c. IX, Mansi, *Sacrorum Conciliorum Nova* et Amplis- *sima Collectio* (Venice, 1778) XXII, 998.

5. Sacred Consistorial Congregation, Rescript n. 510/52 in which, on June 10, 1952, an apostolic indult was granted to Archbishop Caebuano to erect in his arch-episcopal city a national parish for the fifteen thousand Chinese immigrants.

6. Vatican Archives, *Em. Riv. Franc.* These fifty manuscript volumes in folio, 29 x 20. 5m., make up what are commonly called the *Fund for Emigres of the French Revolution.* They were assembled from the records of the institution known as "Opera Pia dell' Ospitalita' Francese" set up in Rome by Pius VI. Opened towards the end of 1792, it was maintained until the end of 1805. It gave assistance to Bishops, clerics, nuns, and very many lay people who quickly fled from France and journeyed in groups to Rome and to the Papal States under the destructive fury of the revolutionaries and their persecution of the Catholic Church. (Cf. Augustin Theiner, *Documents inedit relatifs aux Affaires Religieuses de la France 1790 à 1800, extraits des Archives Secrètes du Vactican, vols. I and II* (Paris, Chez Firmin Didot Frères, Fils et C ie., 1858); Abbé E. Audard, *"L'Histoire religieuse de la Révolution Francaise aux Archives Vaticanes,"* Extrait de la Revue d'Histoire de l'Eglise de France (Sept.–Nov., 1913). Pietro Savio, *"Clero Francese ospite nei Conventi di Cappucini dello stato Pontificio,"* L'Italia Francescana VIII (1933). Surrel de Saint-Julien, *Annales de Saint-Louis des Francais,* I (1896), 327-41.

This series of volumes is rich with documentation, which for the most part is still unpublished. Among them are autograph letters from the Bishops of the Papal States to the Secretary of State, and to the Prelate especially designated to supervise the clerical emigrants from France. There are the replies prepared by the director of the Agency and transmitted to the Department of Public Affairs of the Church. There are a number of reports by Cardinals and Legates on the condition of the exiles. There are reports of several bishops and superiors of regulars on the French exiles living in their dioceses or religious houses, and letters in which refugees were asking for help or returning thanks. There are accounts of expenditures, grants and of all sorts of assistance provided; passports issued the refugees by the governors of provinces, as well as reference letters furnished clerics by prelates, etc.

There are printed copies of eleven encyclical letters sent by the Secretary of State to the bishops of the Papal States during the years 1792 to 1797. These letters urge properly supervised hospitality for the immigrants (cf. *De Charitate,* Vol. L, ff 1, 13, 164 ff; Vol. XXIV, ff., 105, 125, 130, 136, 143, etc.; Savio *op. cit.,* p. 29, n. 42).

Among other things an encyclical of May, 1797 expresses "the just and sovereign indignation against anyone who dares to be lacking in respect for their sacred character, their services to religion, and for that hospitality, because of which, His Holiness has not ceased to hope for the Divine Mercy in its fullness for all his beloved subjects and for the State: 'For God is not unjust that he should forget your work and the love that you have shown in His name, you who have ministered and still minister to the saints.' (Heb. 6:10.)" *De Charitate,*

Vol. XXIV, ff., 143; Cf. Audard, *op. cit.* p. 24: *Catologue des fonds de l'Oeuvre "De Charitate Sedis Sanctae erga Gallos"* (1792-1803).

The title of the collection is taken from volume 50, the report written by Laurence Caleppi and presented to the Pope on August 1, 1793: *"De Charitate Sedis Apostolicae erga Gallos* ... wishing on the first of August respectfully to offer His Holiness a complete picture of the system of hospitality accorded to clerical French immigrants in his domain, I have assembled an account of the principal lines along which the system mentioned has been carried out together with a list of immigrants. I presented it to His Holiness with the title indicated above and with the accompanying letter with which I render His Holiness a report of my assignment" (*De Charitate* Vol. XXIV, f. 8).

Pope Pius VI directed that the most important of these documents be collected as permanent and solid evidence of the inexhaustible disaster to the Church in France, of the grievous suffering of her clergy and of the extraordinary fortitude of her emigrants. Pius VII ordered these records to be stored carefully in the Vatican Archives (Theiner, *op. cit.*, II. pref. xxi). For this puropose Mark Anthony Cattaneo wrote on June 17, 1805 to Cajetan Marini, head of the Vatican Library: "Cattaneo submits to the most kind and esteemed Reverend Marini the voluminous records of matters concerning the French emigrants who were received and supported for thirteen and more years in this State of His Holiness. In the opinion of His Eminence, the Cardinal Secretary of State, it would be well to deposit these records in the Vatican Archives as a perpetual and glorious reminder of the beneficence and charity of the Holy See. They may offer too, a new proof of that charity for the present time" (Theiner, *op. cit.*, II, pref. xxiv n.1).

The Pope entrusted the relief work to a special commission presided over by himself and directed by a Cardinal in charge of the public affairs of the Church. The chief tasks of the Commission were: to provide the French emigrants with necessities of body and soul; to distribute the newcomers among the various provinces of the Papal States, and to direct them to religious houses and devout places; to keep in contact for a long time with the Ordinaries of the places, with the Superiors of the Regulars and the heads of those pious institutions housing the exiles, as well as with the exiles themselves; to guard against evil customs creeping in; to accept requests and fulfill them as far as possible.

A special prelate was appointed to supervise the refugees from France. It was his duty to prepare questions for decision by the Commission and to see that they were carried out promptly. The first of these Prelates was Laurence Caleppi, (who was made a Cardinal of the Holy Roman Church in 1816), the next was John Francis Falzacappa, who became a Cardinal of the Holy Roman Church in 1823), then Emanuel de Gregorio, (Secretary of the Sacred Congregation of the Council and created a Cardinal in 1816), and lastly Mark Anthony Cattaneo. The Prelate Laurence Caleppi drew up a very practical plan for hospitality (Piani dell' Ospitalita'). The Pope approved it and directed that it be carried out by the Secretary of State and by the Congregation newly appointed for State business in the Kingdom of Sardinia, occupied by French troops. (*De Charitate*, XXIV and L; Theiner, *op. cit.*, II, pref. xxi-xxviii; Pietro Savio, *op. cit.*, 22 ff.)

Orders were accordingly sent to the Papal Legates in Turin and Florence that the exiles arriving from France were to be divided up by an established norm. Offices were established for receiving them in the five largest cities of the Papal States: Rome, Bologna, Ferrara, Perugia and Viterbo. The Bishops and governors of these cities were given the letters and orders of the Secretary of State concerning the French immigrants and forwarded them to the Bishops of their districts, being careful to carry out the wishes of the Holy See.

An enormous sum of money was spent by the Holy See to provide for the support of the French exiles. Caleppi testified in 1793, "If, in fact, you estimate the cost of a year's maintenance for one person at only 12 scudi, you will have for two thousand people the imposing sum of 100,000 scudi. This made many immigrants say later that Pius VI had repaid to them alone the Holy See's debt to Charlemagne" (*De Charitate*, Vol XXIV, 10). We know that nearly 20,000 French exiles were thus given hospitality in the Papal States for 13 years (Theiner, *op. cit.*, II, pref. xxxii).

A few years before, Pope Clement XIII had withdrawn a large sum of money from the special treasury in the Castle of St. Angelo. (Allocution, Secret Consistory, April 9, 1764: *Bullarium Clementis XIII, I*, 871, ff., *Bullarii Romani continuatio*, pars II, vol. III (Pratti, Aldine Press, 1843). He used it to lower the price of grain and to relieve members of the Society of Jesus, who, banned from many European countries, had taken refuge in the Papal States. Pope Pius VI did not hesitate to do the same thing, for he took five hundred thousand scudi from the same treasury, not only to satisfy the urgent needs of the Papal States but also to provide a maximum aid to his exiled sons (Allocution, Secret Consistory, December 3, 1792: Pius VI, *Epistolae ad Principes*, an. XVIII, f. 203; Theiner, op. cit., I, no. 54, 161 ff.). This generous action was beautifully honored by a medal dedicated, July 4, 1795, bearing the inscription: *"Pius VI Pont. M. An. XXI—Clero Gallicano Pulso Hospit. et Alim. Praestita."*

Pius VI wrote many letters in behalf of the French exiles. He addressed Bishops in Europe, Papal Legates in various foreign lands and Catholic and non-Catholic kings and rulers. We will mention a few of the letters. To Our Venerable Brothers, the Archibishop of Paris and the Bishops of St. Bernard de Cominges, Nimes, St. Malo, Troyes and Langres, *Nova illa fuga*, November 21, 1792 (*Epist. ad Princ.*, an. XVI, f. 112; Theiner, I op. cit., n. 25, 160); to Our Venerable Brother, John Francis Bishop of Lyons, *Inter augustias*, November 2, 1793 (Epist. ad Princ., an. XIX, f. 67; Theiner, op. cit., I, n. 61, 194 ff.); to Our dear sons, governors and councillors of the Freiburg district, defenders of ecclesiastical liberties, *Valde gaudemus*, April 20, 1793 (Pius VI, *Epist. ad Princ.*, an. XIX, f. 9; Theiner, op. cit., I, n. 56, 169 ff.); to Our beloved sons Bajulivo and the Masters of the Seven Districts of Valais, *Quae plurima*, August 31, 1793 (*Epist. ad Princ.*, an. XIX, f. 59; Theiner, op. cit., I, n. 60, 193); to the most serene, powerful and illustrious George, King of Great Britain, *Non possumus*, September 7, 1793 (*Epist. ad Princ.*, an. XIX, f. 71; Theiner, op. cit., I, n. 51, 159 ff.); to the most illustrious Royal Prince Augustus, son of the King of Great Britain, *Haud ingratum fore*, September 2, 1793 (Pii VI P.M. *Epist. ad Princ.*, an. XIX, f. 6; Theiner, op. cit., n. 62, p. 197); and the same, *Quo Temporis momento*, September 7, 1793 (Pii VI P.M. *Epist. ad Princ.*, an. XIX, f. 72; Theiner, op. cit., I, n. 63, p. 198).

It is sufficient to reproduce here a few lines from a letter to the Archbishops, Bishops and beloved Sons, Abbots, Abbesses, Chapters and Clergy, both secular and religious, of Germany, *Ignotae nemini sunt*, November 21, 1792 (*Nuntiatura*

Galliae, f. 320; Theiner, *op. cit.,* I, n. 53, 162 ff.): "Everyone knows of, and must cry when he thinks over the events that forced Archbishops, Bishops, pastors, clergy, nuns and a great many regulars to leave France. They had given many distinguished proofs of their religion but now they have had to relinquish their sees, their houses and goods, and seek other regions, Catholic or non-Catholic, wherever they could take refuge more readily, seeking from strangers that support they could not obtain from their own countrymen.

"The dispersion of this noble clergy into scattered areas did not fail to move every heart indeed. We, certainly, ought to honor with the greatest praise those Catholic rulers, pastors and peoples who, taught by the Gospel and aflame with the true spirit of charity, have generously received these confessors of the Faith and taken upon themselves the burden of their support.

"Moreover, we must also honor those non-Catholic rulers and peoples, particularly the illustrious King and the distinguished people of Great Britain who, moved by the spirit of human compassion toward their neighbor, of which St. Ambrose spoke (*De officiis, II,* 31), furnished the exiles as though their own with abundant aid. Thus they rivalled in honor the ancient Romans who believed it altogether appropriate that the homes of the most distinguished men be opened for the most distinguished hospitality. It was an honor also for the State that men from other lands were not excluded from this kind of liberality in our city (Cicero, *De officis,* II, 18).

"We hold, through no merit of Our own, the position of Universal Shepherd and Father of all the faithful. We have therefore felt Ourselves bound more than anyone else to extend prompt aid to those poor exiles who have thrown themselves upon Us.

"We are sure or rather absolutely certain that nowhere and at no time can relief be provided with more justice or more liberality than for those who have suffered the loss of their possessions for the sake of Christ and who, outrageously and violently uprooted from their homelands, wander through other regions. Forced to live among alien peoples, they are brought to a life almost like that of hermits. Hence from the very beginning of this cruel abuse, We have opened Our heart affectionately to these French, whether clerical or lay, embracing them in all kindness and friendship.

"These wretched exiles had indeed hoped that their lives, if less comfortable, might at least be secure and quiet in those lands into which they first fled. But the unexpected advance of French troops, particularly into Savoy and into the city and country of Nice, forced them to undertake a new and sadder flight. We, of course, moved by the same charity, and guided by the same desire, ordered and directed, despite Our straitened circumstances, that the new refugees be admitted and cared for not only in Rome but also in the provinces of Our State.

"Therefore We tried in an encyclical letter of last October 10 to stimulate Our Brothers, the Archbishops and Bishops of the Papal States, hoping that each of them, together with his clergy and the devout of his diocese, would comply with Our fatherly wish and cooperate in the work of mercy. As a result, not only Our Venerable Brothers and the secular and regular clergy, but also many laymen of every class tried marvelously to imitate Our example, so much so that an increased number of new emigrants were received by Us after the occupation of Savoy and Nice until now there are 2,000.

17. a) We, therefore, abolish and hereby declare suppressed the Office of Prelate for Italian Emigrants.[3]

b) We likewise declare completely at an end the functions of the Visitors or Delegates of whatever language or nationality, previously established for the religious welfare of immigrants and refugees living in Europe and America.

CHAPTER III

DIRECTORS, MISSIONARIES TO MIGRANTS, AND SHIP CHAPLAINS

18. a) The missionaries to emigrants and chaplains aboard ships and their directors will carry on their work under the direction of the Consistorial Congregation and its Delegate for Migration Affairs.

b) Neither the office of missionary to migrants nor of ship chaplains, nor that of director effect excardination from a diocese. Nor do they offer exemption either from one's own Ordinary or religious Superior, or from the Ordinary of the place in which the work of the missionary or chaplain is done.

19. Directors of missionaries to migrants and ship chaplains have, by virtue of their office, no jurisdiction, either territorial or personal, except that described below.

20. The rights and duties of a Director are chiefly:

a) To make arrangements with the bishops of the nation or territory in which the missionaries maintain a settled residence, with respect to all those factors that con-

"We know that many other French ecclesiastics entered Germany through the kindness of Our dear son in Christ, Francis, Emperor of the Romans. It would scarcely be necessary to urge Germany to provide assistance and relief to the exiles. We are also aware, Venerable Brothers and dear Sons, that your devotion and charity far surpass the ancient glory of your ancestors, whose reputation for civility and kindness to strangers still survives. 'They freely offered hospitality to all travellers and vied with each other in generosity towards them' (Diodor., lib. V, post Tacit. *de morib. Germanor,* et *Mela,* lib. III)."

Pope Pius VII, who inherited the name of his predecessor and rivalled him in virtue, had scarcely begun his pontificate when he resumed with the same ardor the works of charity in behalf of the exiles. This is evident from a letter the famous Consalvi, then Director of the Church's Office of Public Affairs, wrote from Venice, April 5, 1800 to John Francis Falzacappa (*De Charitate,* XXII, f. 667; Theiner, *op. cit.,* II, n. 474, p. 631). Indeed, Pius VII had already, while still Bishop of Imola, striven to answer the urging of his predecessor to receive and care for the French émigrés. (*De Caritate,* XI, ff. 360-85; XXI, f. 210; Theiner *op. cit.,* II, n. 455-57, pp. 608 ff.)

This work of charity towards his exiled sons was meticulously continued by the Pontiff until 1801, when an agreement was happily signed between the Holy See and the French Government, permitting all the exiles to return gradually to their own country (Theiner *op. cit.,* II, pr. xxiv). This work of hospitality was in the words of Caleppi, to be "ever memorable in the annals of the Church" (*De Charitate,* XXIV, f. 10; L, initio).

7. Apostolic Letter declaring Blessed the Venerable Servant of God Vincent Pallotti, Roman priest, Founder of the Society of the Catholic Apostolate, *Ineffa-bilis et amantissima Dei benignitas* (January 22, 1950), *AAS,* XXXXII, 176 ff.; Lenten Allocution to the assembled pastors of Rome (March 2, 1950), *Siate benvenuti, AAS,* XXXXII, 302 ff. Cf. the collected writings of Blessed Vincent Pallotti sent to Pope Pius and the rescripts of the Congregation of the Propagation of the Faith: "18-6-1848. Pius IX (O: Prop. Fide; C. a C.R.) Holy Father, it is known to Your Holiness that some priests of the Congregation of the Catholic Apostolate are now working to procure the means whence to build in London a church for the special use of Italians, and that such church will be dedicated to the Prince of the Apostles, St. Peter. In order to secure that such church may be constructed and used in the Roman manner, and that it be continued for the purpose for which it was founded, the priest, Vincent Pallotti of that Congregation and Society, humbly begs Your Holiness graciously to grant that the ownership, direction and administration of the capital of this church shall belong to his Congregation while this exists or has sufficient subjects for the work, and when this shall cease to exist, or lack subjects for it, the right may be reserved to the Holy See to substitute for that Congregation another Congregation or Society of Italian priests."

From the Audience of His Holiness, June 18, 1848. "Our most holy Lord, by Divine Providence Pope, Pius IX, carefully considered what I, undersigned Pro-Secretary of the Sacred Congregation for the Propagation of the Faith related to him, having heard on the matter and obtained the consent of the Pro-vicar of London, graciously granted the request. Given at Rome from the above mentioned Sacred Congregation on the day and year for which see above. Free of charge without any fee for any reason whatsoever, Alexander Bernabò, Pro-Sec." Cf. also the reference letter sent by the Sacred Congregation for the Propagation of the Faith through James Cardinal Philip Fransoni, Prefect of the same Congregation to Raphael Melia of the Society of the Catholic Apostolate, Roman priest and Apostolic missionary, "who now for three years have labored much in the City of London for Italians" (December 7, 1847), (*Arch.*, *Vicariate of Rome, Opera della Propagazione della Fede, XII,* 1341).

8. *Opus S. Raphaels-Verein zum Schutze Katolischer Auswanderer,* canonically erected in Mainz, September 13, 1871.

9. Pope Leo XIII, Apostolic Letter under the seal of the Fisherman, *Libenter agnovimus,* November 25, 1887.

10. Decretal Letters for Frances Xavier Cabrini, Foundress of the Institute of the Missionaries of the Sacred Heart of Jesus, decreeing the honors of saints, *Spiritus Domini* (July 7, 1946), *AAS,* XXXIX, 44.

11. Pope Leo XIII, Letter *Quam aerumnosa* (December 10, 1888), *Leonis XIII Pontificis Maximi Acta* (Rome: Vatican Press, 1889), VIII, 383.

12. *Ibid.,* pp. 380-84.

13. Secretariate of State, Circular n. 57171, to the Archbishops of Italy, *E' noto come l'emigrazione temporanea* (June 19, 1900), *Leonis XIII Pontificis Maxima Acta,* XX, 168-72; Circular to the Archbishops of Milan, Turin and Vercelli (May 18, 1899).

14. Sacred Consistorial Congregation, Notification concerning the Missionaries of the "Society for the Assistance of Italian Workers migrating to the Foreign Countries of Europe," *Litteris Sacrae Congregationis* (January 31, 1915), *AAS,* VII, 95-96. "The Bishop of Vicenza was appointed honorary President and Adviser of the Society for the Assistance of the Italian Workers migrating to Foreign Countries of Europe, by order of our Most Holy Lord Benedict XV, through a letter of the Sacred Consistorial Congregation, January 18, 1915. He was also entrusted, at the will of the Holy See, with the office held up to that time in the same Society by a Milan Ecclesastical Board, called in Italian 'Consulta'." p. 95. This institution in Italian is called, *Opera di Assistenza agli Italiani in Europa.*

15. Decretal letters: The Honors of the Saints are decreed to Blessed Frances Xavier Cabrini, Foundress of the Institute of the Missionaries of the Sacred Heart of Jesus, *Spiritus Domini* (July 7, 1946), *AAS,* XXXIX, 44.

16. Pope Pius XI, Apostolic Letter in which the Venerable Servant of God, Frances Xavier Cabrini, Foundress of the Institute of the Missionaries of the Sacred Heart of Jesus is acclaimed Blessed, *Benignus Dei* (November 13, 1938), *AAS,* XXXI, 10-15.

17. Pope Pius X, Letter to Our Venerable Brother, John Murphy Farley, Archbishop of New York, *Haud ita pridem* (February 26, 1904), *Pii X Pontificis Maximi Acta* (Rome: Vatican Press, 1905), I, 180-1.

18. "We commend especially to your care the poor Italian emigrants who are far from their native land. They need your assistance to insure that their conduct will never dishonor the name of their country." (Pius X, *Sermo XV, Vi ringrazio* (November 18, 1908), *Pii X Pontificis Maximi Acta* (Rome: Vatican Press, 1914), IV, 305.

19. Letter *Quod hierarchia* (June 6, 1911), *AAS,* III, 262 f. "Considerable effort and zeal must also be expended on the welfare of emigrants . . . and so We

wish that an effort be made to have priests who know their language stationed at the ports of departure and at the usual ports of entry, in order to guide the emigrants properly."

20. *Secretariate of State,* Letter to the Reverend Father Vicentini, Superior General of the Institute of the Missionaries of St. Charles, whose zeal on behalf of Italian emigrants is highly commended, *Ho ricevuto* (January 15, 1912), *AAS,* IV, p. 333; Pius X, Letter to the Reverend Dominick Vincentini, priest, moderator of the Institute of St. Charles for the Italian emigrants, on the solemn occasion of the celebration in memory of John Baptist Scalabrini, founder of the same Institute, *Vehementer nobis* (September 4, 1912), *AAS,* IV, 581-2.

21. "We have heard that this same society, greatly increased in numbers, has made a practice of relieving the wants of their people and of erecting or maintaining many churches and chapels in honor of their saintly patron, both among Italians and other peoples. The group has also printed on their own presses books and leaflets defending Faith and morals and distributed them widely, spending in all this up to the present a huge amount of money.

"We have learned also that it is in large part due to you that in recent times great numbers of Italians living in America have kept faithfully to their religion. Indeed the more they were deprived of the safeguards of the spiritual life because of the vastness of the regions, the more zealously you have labored to increase their devotion and to aid them by your advice and by the wide circulation of your Bulletin Antoniano": Pius X, Letter to Our Beloved Son, President of the Pious Society of St. Anthony to which praises are offered, *Quo Societas* (March 25, 1914) *AAS,* VI, 259. Secretariate of State, Letter to H.D. Casgrain, Rector of the Catholic Society for Immigrants lately founded in Canada, *Il a été particulièrement* (February 12, 1914), *AAS,* VI, 132.

22. *Società dei Missionari d'Emigrazione di S. Antonio da Padova,* instituted July 1905 by the Reverend John James Coccolo and highly commended in the "Letter of His Eminence Cardinal Merry del Val, Secretary of State, to their Excellencies the Archbishops and Bishops of Italy," *Una iniziativa sommamente giovevole,* January 25, 1908.

23. Secretary of State, Letter to the Italian Ordinaries concerning Italian workers migrating from Italy to foreign lands, *Uno degli argomenti* (September 8, 1911) *AAS,* III, 513-18.

24. Sacred Consistorial Congregation, *De emigrantium cura:* questions proposed to the Ordinaries of places of immigration, prot. n. 502/12; questions proposed to the Ordinaries of places of immigration, prot. 894/13.

25. Pope Pius X, *Motu proprio* concerning Italian emigrants to foreign lands, *Iam pridem* (March 19, 1914), *AAS,* VI, 174-5.

26. Sacred Congregation of the Sacraments, Instruction of Ordinaries concerning the proof of liberty to marry and denunciation a previous marriage, *Perlatum haud semel* (March 6, 1911), *AAS,* III, 102-3.

27. Instructions to the Most Reverend Ordinaries concerning proof of freedom to marry and notification of contracted marriage, *Iterum conquesti sunt* (July 4, 1921),*AAS,* XIII, 348-9.

28. Sacred Congregation of the Sacraments, Circular Letter to their Excellencies the Archbishops, Bishops and Ordinaries of Italy relative to the celebration of marriage by proxy (May 1, 1932). n. 11255/32.

29. St. Pius X, Bull or Apostolic Letter, *Ea semper fuit* (June 14, 1907), *Pii X Pontificis Maximi Acta* (Rome: Vatican Press, 1914), V, 57-58. Sacred Congregation for the Propagation of the Faith, for affairs of the Oriental Rites, Decree concerning the spiritual administration of the Greek-Ruthenians in the United States, *Cum episcopo* (August 17, 1914), *AAS*, VI, 458-63.

30. St. Pius X Apostolic Letter, *Officium supremi* (July 15, 1912), *AAS*, IV, 555-56.

31. St. Pius X, Apostolic Letter to the Most Reverend Fergus Patrick McEvay, Archbishop of Toronto: the Association founded for the spread of the Catholic Church in Toronto, Dominion of Canada, is praised and enriched with indulgences. *Allata nuper* (June 9, 1910), *AAS*, II, 536-40.

32. Sacred Congregation for the Propagation of the Faith for affairs of the Oriental Rites, Decree *Fidelibus ruthenis* (August 18, 1913), *AAS*, V, 393-99.

33. St. Pius X, Apostolic Letter to Our Venerable Brother Victor Mihalyi de Apsia, Archbishop of Fagaras and Alba Julia, and to the suffragan Bishops of the province of the Greek-Rumanian Rite, concerning the Church of the Holy Savior on the *Via Delle Coppelle*, to be entrusted to the Rumanian episcopate, *Universi Episcopatus* (March 31, 1914), *AAS*, VI, 222-3.

34. St. Pius X, *Motu proprio* concerning the emigration of Catholics to foreign lands, *Cum omnes catholicos* (August 15, 1912), *AAS*, IV, 526 f.

35. Sacred Congregation of the Council, Letter of February 3, 1886 and March 27, 1889; Letter to the bishop and ordinaries of Italy and America, *Non sine magno*, July 27, 1890; Decree concerning Clerics leaving for America and Philippine Island, *Clericos peregrinos*, November 14, 1903; *Pii X, Pontificis Maximi Acta* (Rome, Vatican Press, 1905) I, p. 63: "Lest those norms laid down salutarily in the Lord be forgotten with the passing of years especially since at the present time it happens that quite a few priests go from Italy, particularly to America, without any permission of this Sacred Congregation of the Council, our most Holy Lord, Pope Pius, ordered to be again published the decree titled: *De Clericis in Americam et ad Insulas Philippinas profecturis,* issued by the same Sacred Congregation of the Council, November 14, 1903. Given at Rome by the Sacred Congregation of the Council, September 7, 1909," *AAS*, I, 692-95. Sacred Consistorial Congregation, concerning the admission of Polish clergy among the diocesan clergy of the United States of North American, *anno proxime elapso*, (Reply, December 9, 1909.) *AAS*, II, 102-8.

36. Sacred Congregation for the Propagation of the Faith, Letter of August 12, 1894; Sacred Congregation for the Propagation of the Faith for Affairs of Oriental Rite, Circular Letters to the Ordinaries of places of the Latin Rite on not permitting the Orientals the sollicitation of alms without permission of the same Sacred Congregation, *Sacrae huic*, (January 1, 1912). *AAS*, IV 532-3.

37. Sacred Consistorial Congregation, Decree concerning clergy about to go to America, to all Ordinaries of Dalmatia, Croatia, Slovenia, Bosnia and Herzegovina, *Neminem latet,* October 4, 1911, n. 567/11.

38. Sacred Consistorial Congregation, Decree concerning priests immigrating to some specified countries, *Ethnographica studia,* (March 25, 1914), *AAS,* into some specified countries, *Ethnographica studia,* (March 25, 1914), *AAS,* VI, 182-6; Declaration concerning the Decree of the Sacred Consistorial Con-

gregation in regard to priests immigrating to some specified countries, March 25, 1914, *AAS*, VI, 671.

39. Sacred Consistorial Congregation, Decree concerning priests immigrating to some specified countries, *Magni semper negotii*, (December 30, 1918), *AAS*, XI, 39-43.

40. Sacred Congregation for the Oriental Church, Decree concerning Oriental clergy, whether secular or religious, who from territories or Oriental dioceses immigrate to the countries of North, Central or South America, or to Australia, that they may care for the faithful in their own rites, *Qua sollerti alacritate*, (December 23, 1929), *AAS*, XXII, 99-105; Decree concerning the Oriental clergy, whether secular or religious, who go from territories or Oriental dioceses into North, Central or South America not to offer spiritual care to the faithful in their own rites, but for some other reason whether economic, moral or in order to remain there for a short time, *Non raro accidit*, (January 7, 1930), *AAS*, XXII, 106-8; Decree concerning Oriental clergy collecting or solliciting alms, money or Mass stipends outside the countries of Oriental regions or dioceses, *Saepenumero apostolica sedes*, (January 7, 1930). *AAS*, XXII, 108-10; Instruction concerning Oriental clergy living in foreign nations outside of their own patriarchate or their own country, *Quo facilior vetustorum*, (September 26, 1932), *AAS*, XXIV, 344-46; Instruction concerning the rules to be observed in regard to clergy of the Oriental Rite, journeying outside the territory of their own Patriarchate, *Sacrae Congregationi*, (July 20, 1937). *AAS*, XXIX 342-43; Decree on the annual report to be sent to the Sacred Congregation by priests of the Oriental Rite having the care of souls outside the territory of their own Patriarchate and under the jurisdiction of an Ordinary of a different Rite, *Cordi semper fuit*, (November 16, 1938), *AAS*, XXXI, 169-70.

41. Sacred Congregation of the Propagation of the Faith, Decree on clergy emigrating from European dioceses to Australia or New Zealand, *Ad tuendam disciplinam*, (October 21, 1948), *AAS*, XLI, 34-5.

42. St. Pius X, *Motu proprio* on emigrants from Italy to other countries, *Iam pridem*, (March 19, 1914), *AAS*, VI, 173-6.

43. *Ibid.* p. 175.

44. Benedict XV, Chirograph, *il Sommo Pontifice Pio X*, (October 16, 1915.)

45. Sacred Consistorial Congregation, Circular Letter to the Most Rev. Ordinaries of America on the care of Italian immigrants, *Cum in varias Americae*, (February 22, 1915), *AAS*, VII, 145-6; Circular, (December 24, 1915); Circular to the Most Rev. Ordinaries of Italy, (May 25, 1918).

46. Sacred Consistorial Congregation, Circular Letter to the Most Rev. Ordinaries of Italy concerning the spirtual care of emigrants, *Il dolore e le preoccupazioni*, (December 6, 1914), *AAS*, VI, 699-701.

47. Sacred Consistorial Congregation, Circular Letter to the Most Rev. Ordinaries of Italy, *Ad subveniendum patronatibus*, (January 2, 1918), n. 682/17.

48. St. Pius X, *Motu proprio*, concerning Italians emigrating to other countries, *Iam pridem*, (March 19, 1914), *AAS*, VI, 173-76.

49. Sacred Consistorial Congregation, Circular Letter to the Most Rev. Archbishops and Bishops of Calabria on founding ecclesiastical sponsorships on behalf of the emigrants, *Assai gradite*, (November 24, 1916), *AAS*, VIII, 437-38.

50. Benedict XV, Letter to the Most Rev. Leopold Duarte Silva, Archbishop

of São Paulo, extolling with well-deserved praise the work of his charity and episcopal office, *Tristia, laeta,* (May 24, 1919), *AAS,* XI, 272-73.

51. Benedict XV, Letter to the Most Rev. Thomas Joseph, Bishop of Trenton, whose paternal care for Italian immigrants he highly praised, *Inter praeclaras laudes,* (December 10, 1920), *AAS,* XIII, 89-90.

52. Sacred Consistorial Congregation, To the Ordinaries of Lombardy, Piedmont, Emilia and Liguria, for religious and economic assistance to the workers in the rice fields, *Mifaccio un dovere,* (July 20, 1918), n. 557/18.

53. Sacred Consistorial Congregation, Notification on the institution of a Prelate for Italian emigration, *Esistono in Italia,* (October 23, 1920), *AAS,* 534 f.

54. Sacred Consistorial Congregation, Note concerning the Pontifical College of Priests for Italian emigration to other countries, *Sacerdotum collegium,* (May 25, 1921). *AAS,* XIII, 309-11.

55. Sacred Congregation for Extraordinary Ecclesiastical Affairs, On the care of prisoners to be furnished by priests. From the Audience of His Holiness, (December 21, 1914): "Our Most Holy Lord Benedict XV, by Divine Providence Pope, greatly mourned the sufferings with which innumerable men made prisoners in this most shocking war are afflicted in misery, and the anxieties their families on this account are weighed down under, while they are deprived of information of their own. He thought how it would be possible for him to bring solace and aid . . . Eugene Pacelli, Secretary," *AAS,* VI, 710-11; cf. also the Letter of the Cardinal Secretary of State, *loc. cit.,* 711-12.

56. Sacred Consistorial Congregation, Decree for one common Ordinary on behalf of all refugees in Italy, *Considerando che i sacerdoti,* (September 3, 1918), *AAS,* X, 415 f.

57. Sacred Consistorial Congregation, Circular Letter to the Most Rev. Bishops of Germany and of Central Europe, *Coniiciunt statistae,* (April 12, 1920).

58. Sacred Congregation for Extraordinary Ecclesiastical Affairs, Dispatch n. B. 18808, (March 24, 1921) and n. 321/52, (January 24, 1952).

59. Sacred Congregation for Extraordinary Ecclesiastical Affairs, Dispatch n. 2743/26, (November 21, 1926).

60. Sacred Congregation for Extraordinary Ecclesiastical Affairs, Dispatch n. 3455/30, (December 2, 1930).

61. Benedict XV, Letter to the Most Rev. John G. Shaw, Bishop of San Antonio for the great charity with which he, his priests and religious congregations received some Mexican bishops and priests expelled from their country, *In summa animi,* (November 25, 1914), *AAS,* VI, 667-8.

62. Benedict XV, Letter to James Cardinal Gibbons, Archbishop of Baltimore, praising the extraordinary charity of the United States towards the unfortunate inhabitants of the Mexican nation, vexed by war, *Certiores quotidie,* (March 17, 1915), *AAS,* VII, 168-69.

63. Sacred Congregation for the Propagation of the Faith for the Affairs of the Oriental Rite, *Cum sat numerosiores,* (March 27, 1916), *AAS,* VIII, 105-7.

64. Sacred Congregation for the Oriental Church, Decree *Perspiciens Sacra Congregatio,* (July 10, 1918), *AAS,* X, 419.

65. Benedict XV, Apostolic Constitution, *Catholici fideles graeci,* (February 13, 1919), *AAS,* XI, 222-26.

66. Sacred Congregation of the Rites, Decree (March 24, 1920), *AAS*, XII, 175.

67. *Motu proprio, Animarum studio,* (December 16, 1947), *AAS*, XXXX, 17.

68. "We consider as a gift from Heaven this present by which it seems that the Lord and Saviour has wished to follow up the announcement of that other present, that We recently promised Your Eminences and the whole Church, and which We can now happily give you. A whole troop of children has come to gather round Us. They are more than 400 orphans from the distant East, representatives of a people that has endured suffering to the point of bleeding and dying. They have been sent to Us by the Divine Infant. We are happy to receive them and to press them to Our Heart and even more happy to be able to do so, for We are deeply consoled by that contest of charity in which the whole world has come to the aid of the Vicar of Christ." Pius XI, Discourse to the Sacred College in reply to Christmas greetings. *Il vostro aspetto, L'Osservatore Romano* (December 26-27, 1927).

69. Pius XI, *Motu proprio,* Commission for Russia is separated from the Sacred Congregation for the Oriental Church and is constituted *sui juris, Inde ab inito Pontificatu,* (April 6, 1930), *AAS*, XXII, 153-54.

70. Pius XI, *Motu proprio,* Concerning the Commission for Russia and the publishing of the liturgical books of the Slavic Rite, *Quam sollicita animi,* (December 21, 1934), *AAS*, XXVII 65-67.

71. Pontifical Commission for Russia, Decree *Fidelium Russorum,* (May 20, 1928), *AAS*, XX, 366-67.

72. Pius XI, *Motu proprio, Nostra animarum a Christo,* (October 28, 1932), *AAS*, XXIV, 353-54.

73. Pius XI, Apostolic Constitution, *Quam curam,* (August 15, 1929), *AAS*, XXI, 577-81.

74. Pius XI, Letter to their Eminences Alexander, Cardinal Kakowski, Archbishop of Warsaw and Augustus, Cardinal Hlond, Archbishop of Gniezno and Poznan, concerning the restoration of the week of study on the union of Christian dissidents, *Laeto iucundoque animo,* (January 6, 1933), *AAS*, XXV, 23-24.

75. Pius XI, Apostolic Constitution, *Apostolica Sedes,* (October 26, 1937), *AAS*, XXX, 213-16.

76. Sacred Congregation for the Oriental Church, Decree *Cum data fuerit,* (March 1, 1929), *AAS*, XXI, 152-59.

77. Sacred Congregation for the Oriental Church, Decree, *Graeci-Rutheni ritus,* (May 24, 1930), *AAS*, XXII, 346-54.

78. Pius XI, Apostolic Letter, *Archiepiscopali in urbe,* (March 10, 1929), *AAS*, XXI, 592-93.

79. Sacred Congregation for Extraordinary Ecclesiastical Affairs, Dispatch, n. 1215/31, (May 26, 1931).

80. Pius XI, Sermon, (September 14, 1936), at Castel Gandolfo to Bishops, priests, religious and faithful, refugees from Spain. *La vostra presenza, AAS,* XXVIII, 373-81.

81. Pius XI, Encyclical on Condition of the Catholics in Mexico, *Firmissimam constantiam,* (March 27, 1937), *AAS*, XXIX, 189-99.

82. Pius XI, Letter to the Rev. William Gier, Superior General of the Society of the Divine Word, concerning the seminary for Negroes shortly to be

inaugurated, *Admodum gaudemus,* (April 5, 1923), *AAS,* XV, 216 ff. in which the Supreme Pontiff wrote among other things: "Since by institution the Church of God is Catholic, does it not follow to be opportune that every race or nation have their priests who have the same origin and character, the same feelings and customs? Besides, are not these because they have a more easy approach to their own, able more efficaciously to attract them to the Faith, to make them more stable in it than those priests of different origin gathered elsewhere? . . . For there are in the United States of America many more than 10 million people of different races to be provided for with native missioners as well as pastors as soon as it can be possible." *loc. cit.,* p. 217 f. As to the persistent desire of the Church for the Negroes, cf. *supra,* p. 6.

83. Sacred Consistorial Congregation, *Regolamento per i Direttori dei Cappellani di bordo e per i Cappellani di bordo,* (November 15, 1932), (Vatican Press, 1932).

84. Sacred Consistorial Congregation, from the audience of September 21, 1927,and the Circular letter to the Bishops, (November 10, 1927), n. 1998/12.

85. Sacred Consistorial Congregation, Communication on providing those emigrating from Italy with cards of identification from ecclesiastical authority, *Expedit ut,* (January 26, 1923) *AAS,* XV, 112-13.

86. Pius XI, Letter to His Eminence Raphael Charles Cardinal Rossi, Secretary of the Sacred Consistorial Congregation on the 50th anniversary of the founding of the Pious Society of St. Charles, *Iucundo sane animo,* (June 1, 1937), *AAS,* XXIX, 303.

87. Sacred Consistorial Congregation, Decree *Pia Societas,* (August 15, 1936).

88. Sacred Consistorial Congregation, From the Audience of His Holiness (May 30, 1942), n. 334/40.

89. *L'Opera di pace della Santa Sede e l'Italia, Appunti,* (Vatican Press, 1945).

90. St. Ignatius of Antioch, *Epistola ad Romanos*: Migne, *PG,* V, 685.

91. Allocution, (November 29, 1945), to the Jewish refugees returning from captivity after the hardships of war, *La vostra presenza, AAS,* XXXVII, 317 f.

92. Relief Committee, Cf. *L' attivita' della Santa Sede dal 15 Dicembre 1943 al 15 Dicembre* 1944 (Vatican Press), 107-9; 1946, 107-10; 1947, 105-11; 1948, 97-101.

93. *Vatican Information Office,* September, 1939 to October, 1947. It is useful to recall the particular sections of this office: "1. Correspondence received, 2. Correspondence sent out, 3. Radio, 4. English language prisoners, 5. German and Slavic language prisoners, 6. Prisoners in Russian hands, 7. Prisoners and international political internes, 8. Repatriation." *L'A.d* S.S. 1945, 111-4; 1946, 95-103; sections established later: "9. Special cases; 10. Deceased": L'A d. S.S. . . . 1947, 99-105; *Apercu sur l'oeuvre du Bureau d' Informations Vatican,* 1939-1946 (Vatican Press, 1948).

94. Pontifical Commission of Assistance to Refugees set up April 18, 1944. cf. *L'A d. S.S.* 1944, 118-23.

95. Pontifical Commission of Assistance, set up January 23, 1945, cf. Pastoral instruction to the pastors of Rome and preachers in the Holy Season of Lent: on the Sacraments *In meno di un anno, AAS,* XXXVII, 43; *L'A. d. S.S.* 1945, 124-32; 1946, 111-12; 1948, 102-14.

96. These missions began as follows: the first one June 12, 1945; the second July 2, 1945; the third more extensive and longer, October 29 of the same year; Concerning the affairss and activities of each, cf. *L'A. d. S.S.* 1945, 119-24; 1946, 105. Pontifical mission in Germany (in Kronberg i. T.); 1947, 125-35.

97. Office of Migration. From the Audience of His Holiness May 30, 1946, and November 13, 1946. This office had two sections, one called *natural migration,* the other *refugee migration.* For this last one worked the *Bishops Resettlement Council* (U.S.A.); *Catholic Committee for Relief Abroad* (Great Britain); *Catholic Committee for Aid to Immigrants of Canada; Vaican Mission in Kronberg.* cf. *L'A. d. S.S.* 1947, 125-35; 1948, 115-27.

98. International Catholic Migration Commission, founded Geneva, 1951; Letter of the Secretariate of State to Mr. James J. Norris, provisional President of the International Catholic Migration Commission, Geneva (Switzerland), *Le sono ben noti gli imperiosi motivi,* (April 12, 1951), n. 226960/MSA.

99. On the activities of Our Nuncios, Internuncios, Delegates and Vicars and other ecclesiastics sent for this: *Europe:* Albania, Bulgaria, Czeckoslovakia, Romania, Finland, France, Germany, Greece, Switzerland, Ireland, Spain, Holland, Hungary, Italy, Portugal, Great Britain, Malta, Poland, Rhodes, Thrace, Turkey; *Africa:* Egypt, Ethiopia, Algiers, (office for receiving and sending messages attached to the house of the Missionaries of Africa, set up by Our Secretariat of Maison Carrée), French West Equatorial Africa, South Africa, Belgian Congo, Eritrea, Kenya, Madagascar, Somaliland, Sudan, Tripoli; *North America:* Canada, United States of America, Mexico; *Central America:* Costa Rica, Cuba, Guatemala, Republics of Haiti, Honduras, El Salvador and the Dominican Republic; *South America:* Ecuador, Argentina, Bolivia, Brazil, Chile, Colombia, Peru, Uruguay, Venezuela; *Asia:* India, Batavia, Iran, Iraq, Japan, Palestine, Philippine Islands, China, Syria, Thailand; *Oceania:* Australia, New Zealand. cf. *L'A. d. S.S.,* 1944, 112-17; 1945, 114-19; *Apercu sur l'oeuvre du Bureau d'Informations Vatican,* 1939-1946.

100. As to Catholic Committees for Emigrants, erected almost everywhere: cf. *L'A, d. S.S.,* 1947, 131-35; 1948, 115-27.

101. Pastoral Sermon to the pastors of Rome and preachers for the Holy Season of Lent, *Ci torna sempre sommamente gradito,* (March 16, 1946), *L'Azione caritatevole AAS,* XXXVIII, 183 f. Of the numerous undertakings by the bishops, by Catholic Action, (established and promoted by trustworthy men), it is proper to recall here at the least: War Relief Services—NCWC; *Aumonerie des Prisonniers de Guerre,* which was followed first by *Comité International de l'Aumonerie Catholique,* later *Comité Catholique de Secours,* and finally *Secours Catholique; Mission Catholique Suisse,* cf. *L'A. d. S.S.,* 1944, 112-17; ... 1945, 119-22; 1947, 122-95.

102. Sacred Congregation for the Oriental Church, from the Audience of His Holiness (April 9, 1949); Pontifical Mission for Palestine, *Le Pape et la tragédie palestinienne* (Beirut, 1950); Michel Gillet, S.J., *L'Aide Catholique aux enfants palestiniens réfugiés au Liban* (Beirut, 1950).

103. Cf. *Act. Ap.,* XI, 27-30 and *Rom.* 15:25-28.

104. Catholic Near East Welfare Association.

105. Radio Address given to the world, (June 29, 1941) Feast of Sts. Peter and Paul, on the guiding of Divine Providence on events of human society,

In questa solennitá, AAS, XXXIII, 319 ff. Radio Address, (December 24, 1942) on the eve of the Nativity of Our Lord, given to the world, *Con sempre nuova freschezza, AAS,* XXXV, 9 ff.; Radio Address, (December 24, 1943) on the eve of the Nativity of Our Lord, given to the world, *Ancora una quinta volta, AAS,* XXXVI, 11 ff; Radio Address, (September 1, 1944) fifth anniversary of the breaking out of the present war, given to the world, *Oggi, al compiersi del quinto anno,* AAS, XXXVI, 249 ff; Radio Address given to the world, (April 4, 1946) to solicit mutual aid among the nations lest the needy perish from hunger, *Stretto il cuore da intima angoscia, AAS,* XXXVIII, 165 ff.; Encyclical on the care for needy children to be taken up with more alacrity today, *Quemadmodum,* (January 6, 1946), *AAS,* XXXVIII, 5 ff.; Radio Message to the pupils of Catholic schools of the United States given to ask charity for the needy children of Europe and eastern Asia lest they perish from hunger, *Our loving greetings to you,* (February 19, 1947) *AAS,* XXXIX, 127 ff.; Radio Address to the faithful of the United States collecting aid for needy nations, *Another winter is approaching,* (November 23, 1947) *AAS,* XXXIX, 630 ff.; Radio Address to the clergy and people of the Republic of Argentina, on their outstanding aid to needy nations, *Una vez más la voz,* (February 1, 1948) *AAS,* XXXX, 85 ff.; Radio Address to the pupils of Catholic schools in the United States, given to ask charity for the needy children of other nations, *Dear children,* (March 2, 1949) *AAS,* XXXXI, 179 ff.; and here and there.

106. Allocution to the pastors of Rome and preachers of the Holy Season of Lent: on the precepts of the Decalogue, *L'inscrutabile consiglio divino,* (February 22, 1944) *AAS,* XXXVI, 69 ff.; Allocution to their Eminences the Cardinals offering good wishes on the occasion of the Feast of St. Eugene I, Pope, *Ancora una volta,* (June 2, 1947) *AAS,* XXXIX, 258 ff.

107. Encyclical calling for public prayers for a conciliatory peace among the nations, *Communium interpretes dolorum,* (April 15, 1945) *AAS,* XXXVII, 97 ff.; Letter to His Excellency John De Jong, Archbishop of Utrecht, and to the other Dutch Bishops, *Dum post innumeros* (May 15, 1945) *AAS,* XXXVII, 186 ff.; Letter to their Excellencies Archbishops, Bishops and other Ordinaries of places in Poland, *Per hos postremos annos,* (June 29, 1945) *AAS,* XXXVII, 205 ff.; Letter to His Eminence Michael, Cardinal von Faulhaber, Archbishop of Munich and Frisings, and to the others, their Excellencies, the German Archbishops, Bishops and Ordinaries of places in Germany, *Vixdum vobis licuit,* (November 1, 1945) *AAS,* XXXVII, 278 ff.

108. Letter to their Eminences Michael, Cardinal von Faulhaber, Archbishop of Munich and Frisings, Joseph, Cardinal Frings, Archbishop of Cologne, Conrad, Cardinal von Preysing, Bishop of Berlin and to the other Archbishops, Bishops and Ordinaries of places in Germany, *Disertae admodum litterae,* (December 20, 1948) *AAS,* XXXXI, 216 ff.

109. (April 15, 1949) *AAS,* XXXXI, 162.

110. Letter to His Eminence Samuel, Cardinal Stritch, Archbishop of Chicago, happily marking the twenty-fifth anniversary of his episcopal consecration, *Proximo exeunte mense Novembri,* (October 16, 1946) *AAS,* XXXIX, 33 f.; Letter to their Eminences Joseph, Cardinal Frings, Archbishop of Cologne, Michael, Cardinal von Faulhaber, Archbishop of Munich and Frisings, Conrad Cardinal von Preysing, Bishop of Berlin and to the other Archbishops, Bishops and Ordi-

naries of places in Germany, *Commoti valde sumus,* (December 1, 1947) *AAS,* XL, 544 ff.; "Your letter is a great source of consolation to Us for We perceive from it that following your example, priests and religious have, with admirable diligence and at great labor, dedicated themselves totally to the care of the faithful. They have been especially solicitous for those who, tormented by a more bitter fate, were expelled from their homes, and live now dispersed in other lands.

The Gospel-inspired workers are equal to the task in valor, but not in numbers. For this reason We earnestly remind those who through their ability and age are able actively to engage in this work, that the most appropriate place for the ministers of God is where there is the greatest suffering. Convinced of this, may they go to their unfortunate brothers, and there earn great merit that God will reward with ample favors." *loc. cit.,* 545; Allocution to the distinguished *Nicholas* C. Accame, Ambassador extraordinary and plenipotentiary, bearer of credential letters from his Government, *En la cúspide misma,* (March 6, 1948) *AAS,* XL, 112 ff.; Letter to His Eminence Emanuel, Cardinal Suhard, Archbishop of Paris on the twenty-fifth anniversary of his priesthood, *Opportunum sane,* (November 20, 1948) *AAS,* XXXXI, 27.

111. Letter to His Excellency John T. McNicholas, Archbishop of Cincinnati and Chairman of the Administrative Board of the National Catholic Welfare Conference: because of the aid providentially given to immigrants and other unfortunates by his board, *In fratres caritas,* (December 24, 1948) *AAS,* XXXXI, 69-71.

112. "Nor in recalling your good works should We fail to mention the spirit of Christian charity which opened the doors of your country to welcome so large a number of the dispossessed victims of the war and of those constrained to emigrate by unemployment and the pressure of surplus populations. Especially would We commend the splendid organization which you, Venerable Brethren, so painstakingly established throughout the Australian nation to ensure that the Catholics amongst those new Australians should not lack for religious assistance and as so often happened as a result of the spiritual neglect of the emigrant, be lost to the Faith. This example of Catholic Action is worthy of high commendation." *L'Osservatore Romano,* (April 28, 1951).

113. Radio Address (December 24, 1944) on the eve of the Nativity of Our Lord Jesus Christ given to the whole world, *Benignitas et humanitas apparuit Salvatoris nostri Dei, AAS,* XXXVII, 10 ff.; Letter to the distinguished Charles Flory, President of the Conference of Catholic "Semaines Sociales" in France, *Nous avons pris,* (July 14, 1945) *AAS,* XXXVII, 210 ff.; Allocution (December 24, 1946) on the eve of the Nativity of Our Lord Jesus Christ, to their Eminences the Cardinals and their Excellencies the Bishops and Prelates of the Roman Curia, *Vi fu mai nella storia, AAS,* XXXIX, 7 ff.; Allocution to the distinguished Conrad Traverso of the Republic of Argentina, Ambassador extraordinary and plenipotentiary presenting the credential letters from his Government, *En virtud de la misión,* (January 12, 1947) *AAS,* XXXIX, 56 ff.

114. Encyclical on promoting Catholic missions, *Evangelii praecones,* (June 2, 1951) *AAS,* XXXXIII, 518; statement by Ourselves, handed to the Honorable G. I. van Heuven Goedhart, United Nations High Commissioner for Refugees, upon receiving him, (May 27, 1952); "Among the many painful and distressing problems created by the war there is one which, despite the organized efforts made in recent years to solve it, remains a source of grave preoccupation. It is

that of the refugees, those of our fellowmen who under pressure of political events, have been forced to abandon their homesteads and country and seek hospitality and a livelihood in foreign lands. If we plead their cause, it is to give a renewed expression to the abiding interest which We have ever taken in their lot and to pledge the continued support of the Holy See for the praiseworthy work being accomplished by international organizations for the alleviation of their pitiable condition. In this regard We warmly commend the recent initiative of the United Nations High Commissioner for Refugees which has as its objective the establishment of a fund for the purpose of providing for the essential human needs of the many refugees who, by reason of their extreme poverty, are unable to maintain themselves while awaiting resettlement. Our earliest solicitude for these sorely afflicted members of the human family urges us to exhort government authorities as also social service and charitable associations to co-operate wholeheartedly in fostering this very laudable initiative and to contribute generously to this most timely appeal. In doing so, We feel confident that We are voicing the sentiments of all those who, because they dearly cherish the Christian values and freedom for which, in such great part, these refugees are suffering, can not remain unmoved by their present adversity nor be indifferent to their future destiny." *L'Osservatore Romano,* (July 18, 1952).

115. Chirograph of March 3, 1949: "To Our dear sons who have been forced by the vicissitudes of life to seek their work and bread under alien skies, We repeat, for their temporal and eternal happiness, the advice of the old Tobias: 'All the days of your life, have God on your mind, and remember not to consent to sin and not to transgress the precepts of the Lord our God.' For them personally, for their families and for their future, We implore the Divine assistance, and We bless them with all our heart. Pius XII".

116. Radio Address on the Feast of Pentecost, (June 1, 1941) to the whole world, on the fiftieth anniversary of the Encyclical, *Rerum novarum,* by Leo XIII, *La solennità della Pentecoste, AAS,* XXXIII, 203.

117. Radio Address of December 24, 1942, the eve of the Nativity of Our Lord Jesus Christ, given to the whole world: *Con sempre nuova freschezza, AAS,* XXXV, 16-17; for the Latin version, cf. *AAS,* XXXXIII, 518-19; Allocution to the members of the International Congress on Social Studies, *Nous vous adressons,* (June 3, 1950) *AAS,* XXXXII 485 ff.; "In the fullest sense one must face up to the duty of giving to innumerable families in their natural, moral, juridical and economic unity, an equitable living space equal in however modest a manner to at least the demands of human dignity." *Ibid.,* 485-86.

118. Cf. Note 111, *AAS,* XXXXI, 69-70.

119. Sermon on the eve of the Nativity of Our Lord Jesus Christ to their Eminences the Cardinals and their Excellencies the Bishops and Prelates of the Roman Curia, *Negli ultimi sei anni, AAS,* XXXVIII, 15 ff.

120. Allocution of February 20, 1946 to their Eminences, the newly created Cardinals, *La Elevatezza e la nobilità dei sentimenti, AAS,* XXXVIII, 141, ff; "Man, as God wants him and as the Church accepts him, will never consider himself as firmly fixed in time and space if stripped of secure property and traditions . . . The long experience of the Church as educator of peoples confirms it; accordingly she is careful in every way to join the religious life to national customs and is particularly solicitous of those whom emigration or millitary service

keeps far from their native land. The shipwreck of many souls justifies, alas, this maternal apprehension of the Church, and increases the conclusion that the security of property and attachment to ancient traditions, which are indispensable to the healthy integrity of man, are also fundamental elements of human society. However, it would evidently be equivalent to nullifying the beneficient effect of this postulate and converting it into its contrary, if one were to use it in order to justify the repatriation of men against their will and the refusal of the right of asylum in regard to those who, for grave reasons, wish to fix their residence elsewhere." *op. cit.*, 147.

121. Allocution II, (February 25, 1946), to the most noble words with which His Excellency, Antonio Carneiro-Pacheco, distinguished Portuguese Ambassador, as Dean, expressed to His Holiness the sentiments of devotion and gratitude of the diplomatic representatives present, on the recent Consistory of the Holy Father, His Holiness graciously replied in these words (L'élévation des pensées), *AAS*, XXXVIII, 152, ff.: "Such a peace will not be the work of one day; it will require considerable time, considerable effort. If you ask Us how the diplomatic representatives may foster it, apart from their official duties, it seems to Us possible to point out to their good will two spheres of activity. The first is in the practical order; it aims at immediate goals. Now that the war is finished, diplomats have many opportunities to facilitate, as far as possible, intercourse and friendly relations between nations. At present millions of respectable, hard-working people wait with anxious impatience the moment when they can return to their homelands and their families, from which they have been separated for, perhaps, many years. Others sadly seek a new homeland, to live a new life in new occupations. What a work of charity and of peace one does by going to their assistance!" *op. cit.* 154 f.

122. Allocution to their Eminences the Cardinals offering good wishes on the Feast of Pope St. Eugene I, (June 1, 1946), *Ancora una volta, AAS*, XXXVIII, 253 ff.

123. Radio Address on the eve of the Nativity of Our Lord Jesus Christ, 1948, before their Eminences the Cardinals, their Excellencies the Bishops and Prelates of the Roman Curia, *Gravi ed ad un tempo tenere, AAS*, XXXXI, 5, ff.

124. "Yet it is not surprising that changing circumstances have brought about a certain restriction being placed on foreign immigration. For in this matter, not only the interests of the immigrants, but the welfare of the country must also be consulted. However, it is not too much, We are sure, to expect that in the process of restriction, Christian charity and the sense of human solidarity existing between all men, children of the One Eternal God and Father, will not be forgotten. Immigration can help in solving one of Europe's saddest human problems—a problem which is being aggravated inhumanely by the enforced transfer of helpless, innocent populations." *L'Osservatore Romano*, (March 14, 1946).

125. "One further and controlling observation, dictated by the sacred trust committed to Our charge, you will not fail to understand. Political, economic and even social dangers are involved in a policy of further delay of exaggerated caution. But these dangers, real and serious though they be, are derivative and secondary. Our prime anxiety—as We are sure it is yours deep down in your hearts—touches the judgment of history and of history's Lord on the fulfillment of that gravest duty of man to man and of nation to nation, which calls for

respect for the image of God in even the weakest and most abandoned of His children. No reason of State or pretext of collective advantage, as We had occasion to emphasize once more only a few days ago, can avail to justify the contempt of that human dignity and the denial of those elemental rights which the Creator has imprinted on the soul of each of His creatures." *L'Osservatore Romano,* (October 3-4, 1949).

126. "But We dare say the further question has risen more than once in your minds, if not to your lips: is the present immigration policy as liberal as the natural resources permit in a country so lavishly blessed by the Creator and as the challenging needs of other countries would seem to demand? Your travels will afford much data for the answer to that question." *L'Osservatore Romano,* (October 23, 1949.)

127. "Your country is broad and rich. But its immense territory will be advantageous in the measure that it becomes the happy dwelling place of an ever growing number of physically and morally healthy families. Just as your lands and fields are great and wide, so must your hearts be big and open to receive those who want to come and find a new home among you, where they may live honorably with their families." *L'Osservatore Romano,* (July 21, 1952).

128. Allocution, (July 2, 1951), *Soyez ici les bienvenues,* AAS, XXXXIII, 554, ff.

129. "We do not need to tell you that the Catholic Church feels she has a very serious obligation to take an interest in migrat... .fairs. That is, it is a question of relieving immense wants. There is the lack of space, the lack of means of existence, because the old homeland can no longer provide the livelihood for all her sons, and the excess population forces some to emigrate. Then, the misery of refugees and expellees, who have been forced by the millions to leave the countries of their birth, now lost to them, and to go far off to find and build up another homeland. The Church feels these afflictions the more as they concern in great part her own children." *L'Osservatore Romano,* (October 19, 1951).

130. *Mark* 8:2.

131. Allocution, (March 12, 1944), to those in Rome, refugees from the miseries of the war and to other people in the square of St. Peter's, *Nella desolazione,* AAS, XXXVI, 97 ff. "In 1950, in co-operation with the Central Committee for the Holy Year, the I.R.O. and the War Relief Services, NCWC, there were organized seventeen pilgrimages for alien refugees. Participating in them were residents of the Italian camps, people of various nationalities: Russian, Ukranian, Polish, Hungarian, Albanian, Romanian, Bulgarian, Croatian, Slovenian, Serbian, German, Armenian, Czech, Slovak, and Lithuanian, as well as Romanians residing in Germany, Austria and France. A total of 1500 refugees made that Jubilee." *L'A.d.S.S.,* 1950, 413.

132. Letter to His Eminence Michael Cardinal von Faulhaber, Archbishop of Munich and Frisings, and to their Excellencies the other Archbishops and Bishops of Bavaria, *Laetitiam cepimus,* (August 15, 1945), AAS, XXXVII, 249 ff: "So in order to befriend your people as much as possible, We have not neglected to continue Our intercession with the allied nations, England and the United States, despite the many difficulties that usually hinder the completion of such affairs. Because We are eager to provide assistance and comfort for your nation

as the difficult circumstances permit and require, We are especially intent on aiding your prisoners, so that now at least they can receive news of their families, and send back news of themselves." *Ibid.*, 251.

133. *Motu proprio*, calling for the Holy Sacrifice of the Mass and public prayers for the present necessities of human society on November 24, 1940, *Norunt profecto*, (October 27, 1940,) *AAS*, XXXII, 385-86, Sermon at the Mass celebrated on November 24, 1940 in the Vatican Basilica, to the people praying for the present necessities of human society. *AAS*, XXXII, 531 ff.; Allocution, (March 12, 1944), to the faithful refugees in Rome on account of the miseries of the war and to others of the people in St. Peter's Square, *Nella desolazione*, *AAS*, XXXVI, 97 ff: "Thou Who in the arms of Thy Most Holy and most sweet Mother Mary and under the watchful care of Thy most pure foster-father Joseph, while still a tender infant, didst will to be a refugee, grant to those who go along, wanderers without a roof, that unchanging conformity to the Divine Will which at that time elevated and sanctified the sufferings of Thy exile and that of Thy Family."*Ibid.*, 100; Letter to His Eminence Michael Cardinal von Faulhaber, Archbishop of Munich and Frisings and to their Excellencies the other German Archbishops, Bishops and Ordinaries, *Vixdum vobis licuit*, (November 1, 1945), *AAS*, XXXVII, 278 ff: "Therefore We implore the Divine Mercy in Our prayers for all your nation and for those especially who to the number of many thousands, indeed, wander everywhere, unhappily driven out of their domestic hearths. Now in the past months We have not wished to pass over any opportunity which would allow Us, within Our powers, to mitigate the fate of you and yours, especially concerning food. Also at the moment, this one earnest desire possesses Us, namely, that with Our paternal hopes and prayers, a happy result may come to that which We have undertaken in your behalf." *loc. cit.* 283.

134. Proclamation of the Holy Year, 1950, *Iubilaeum Maximum*, (May 26, 1949), *AAS*, XXXXI, 260.

135. *Katholieke Centrale Emigratie-Stichting;* cf. Pius Almanak (Adresboek van katholier Nederland), 1952, 762.

136. Sacred Consistorial Congregation Circular Letter to their Excellencies, Most Reverend Ordinaries of Italy, *Facendomi interprete*, (October 24, 1951), *AAS*, XXXXIV 231.

137. *Obra de Cooperación sacerdotal Hispano-Americana*, founded March, 1948.

138. Sacred Congregation for Religious, Decree of Praise, (April 22, 1950.)

139. Apostolic Constitution, *Inter praecipuas*, (June 22, 1946) *AAS*, XXXIX, 84 ff.

140. Apostolic Constitution, *Omnium cuiusvis ritus christifidelium*, (March 3, 1948), *AAS*, XXXX, 287 ff.

141. Apostolic Constitution, *De Ruthenorum*, (March 19, 1951), *AAS* XXXXIII, 544 ff.

142. L'Osservatore Romano, (May 2-3, 1952).

143. Sacred Congregation of Seminaries and Universities, Decree, *Feliciter peracta*, (May 1, 1948), *AAS*, XXXX, 298 f.

144. Apostolic Letter, *Quod sanctorum patronatus*, (March 27, 1943), *AAS*, XXXV, 63 f.

145. Decretal Letter, *Spiritus Domini*, (July 7, 1946, *AAS*, XXXIX, 41 f.

146. Apostolic Letter, *Superiore iam aetate*, (September 8, 1950), AAS, XXXXIII, 455 ff.

147. Cf. *Luke* 10:20.

TITLE II

1. Sacred Consistorial Congregation, Decree *Magni semper negotii*, concerning priests emigrating to some specific country, (December 30, 1918), AAS, XI, 39-43.

2. *Ibid.* III, 16, AAS, XI, 43: "Priests, who without observing these laws, rashly and arrogantly emigrate, are *ipso facto* suspended from sacred functions; if any (God forbid) notwithstanding, dare to perform such functions, they incur an irregularity; and they can be absolved from these penalties only by this Sacred Congregation."

3. Sacred Consistorial Congregation, Notification in respect to the institution of a Prelate for Italian Emigration, *Esistono in Italia*, (October 23, 1920), AAS, XXI, 534-35.

4. Pius X, *Motu proprio, Iam pridem*, (March 19, 1914), concerning Italians emigrating to foreign lands. AAS, VI, 173-76.

5. *Ibid.*, 174.

6. Sacred Consistorial Congregation, Communication, (January 23, 1923), AAS, XV, 112-13.

7. Sacred Consistorial Congregation, Circular Letter to the Most Reverend Ordinaries of Italy concerning the spiritual care of emigrants, (December 6, 1914), AAS, VI, 699 f.

8. Sacred Consistorial Congregation, Letter to the Most Reverend Ordinaries of America, (February 22, 1915).

9. Pius X, *Motu Proprio,Iam pridem, op. cit.*, 173 ff. Sacred Consistorial Congregation concerning the Pontifical College for Italian priests for Italians emigrating to foreign lands, Notification, *Sacerdotum Collegium*, (May 29, 1921), AAS, XIII, 309 ff.

10. Sacred Consistorial Congregation, *Collegio de' Sacerdoti per gli emigranti Italiani, Regolamento Generale*, (June 24, 1914).

PART II

TWO COMMENTARIES BY
JOSEPH CARDINAL FERRETTO

HISTORICAL — JURIDICAL
COMMENTARY ON "EXSUL FAMILIA"

Spiritual Assistance to Migrants

PREFACE

AT Montallegro, perched 700 meters above sea level on a spur of the mountains encircling Tugullio, is the famous shrine dedicated to the Blessed Virgin. The shrine is small, but seems a jewel set there to enrich the beauty that the wise and loving hand of God has lavished on this place as well as over all our Italy.

Following the single pathway that leads to the left around the apse, the wayfarer meets with a perpendicular face of rock which has been cut away to make room for the Sanctuary. A steep path skirting the crags leads still higher, but it soon divides and follows opposite directions. The goals to which each branch leads, their altitudes and distances, are indicated on the rock-face in colored signs. At this fork the wayfarer who wishes to continue in search of ever more beautiful panoramas must perforce make a choice of goal, and follow the signs that lead to it.

Anyone who presumes to write briefly concerning the activity of His Holiness Pius XII finds himself of necessity in the same situation: he must choose one single theme and follow the signs pointing to it. As our theme we have chosen the spiritual assistance to emigrants, and the signpost which will guide us on our way is the Apostolic Constitution *Exsul*

Familia, concerning the Spiritual Care of Migrants, promulgated on August 1st, 1952.

Thus it happens that the reader who wishes to follow us in our chosen theme will emigrate with us in spirit from Egypt to Canada, from Australia to the Philippines, from Armenia to France and England, by land and sea routes and even by air, with all the rapidity proper to such voyages. We may here recall the Church's maternal concern for those whose way lies through the skies: Benedict XV confided all such to the protection of the Blessed Virgin of Loreto (*AAS,* XII, 175), and His Holiness Pius XII extended to those priests who travel by plane the same regulations sanctioned in the Code of Canon Law: "For those making a journey by sea" (*AAS,* XXX, 17 and XLIV, 670).

May it be granted that, after such far-flung travels, we shall return to our own lands not only safely, but also with increased love for the Holy Church and her august Head.

This is one of the benefits which it is hoped will result from the present work, a study which originated in the address which we had the honor of giving in the *Aula Magna* of the Pontifical Lateran Atheneum on March 2 of this year, during the solemn program given to celebrate the fifteenth anniversary of the elevation of His Holiness Pius XII to the Supreme Pontificate.

The theme developed on that occasion was "His Holiness Pius XII: Provident Father of the Exiled and Wise Legislator of Spiritual Assistance to the Emigrant." The text of this address substantially furnished the content of these pages (cf. *L'Osservatore Romano,* March 12, 1954, pp. 4-5). An additional chapter has been devoted to the natural right to emigrate; passages appropriate to the different sections of the discussion have been quoted; and, of greatest value, documents emanating from the Holy See after March 2, 1954, representing a further demonstration of the constant solicitude of the Church for migrants, seafarers and seamen, have been appended.

May the Christ Child bless this undertaking. Even before the flight into Egypt, in the manger of Bethlehem, He experienced and shared with His Virgin Mother Mary and with Saint Joseph, His foster father, the pilgrim's wretchedness and bitter weariness: "There was no place for them in the inn."

Rome, on the Day of the Birth of Our Lord, 1954.

Chapter I

GENERAL PREMISES AND DIVISION
OF THIS ESSAY

A BRIEF chapter, the third of Title One, explains the motive which gave rise to the Apostolic Constitution: namely, the urgent need to provide as adequately as possible for spiritual assistance to an ever growing number of refugees and emigrants. Leaving their homelands, they travel now not only to certain regions of Europe and America, but also to Australia and the Philippine Islands.

This chapter also explains the fundamental and informing principle of the new laws. The *Exsul Familia* has in no way relieved the bishops of their responsibility for devoting to the care of migrants the same attention given to the care of the other faithful. It simply offers means better adapted to the fulfillment of the aim.

This is clearly stated in the conclusion of the first part of the papal document: "For We were eagerly awaiting an opportunity to draw up suitable regulations for the bishops, which would provide them with proper authority to offer aliens, whether immigrants or travellers, the religious assistance appropriate to their needs, and not inferior to that available to other Catholics in the dioceses. These regulations were not to conflict with the provisions of the Code of Canon Law, but rather to conform faithfully both to its spirit and practice."[1] "We congratulate the bishops of those diocesan agencies outside Italy, in Europe as well as overseas, who, through national or diocesan agencies and commissions, have tried to provide every alien with spiritual and moral help: receiving them, though they are strangers, as members of their own flocks."[2]

Further substantiation of this same point may be found in the repeated references to the "local Ordinary" and to the "local pastor" in Chapter IV of the quoted Title Two.

The new legislation is designed to constitute an organization for the spiritual assistance of the migrant which will guarantee to him in the foreign country for which he is bound—whether for a temporary stay devoted to work or study, or as an exile or refugee from his native land—the same religious comforts that each one of the faithful finds in his own country.

Particular attention is given to the delicate problem of bringing the special functions of the Missionary to the migrants into a more effective harmony with the extant local ecclesiastical organization. It is intended that the migrant who settles definitely in the country of immigration shall be gradually included within the parochial family, by means of norms which, though new, do not conflict with canonical law, but rather, conform to its spirit and usages.

Herein lies the novelty of the *Exsul Familia*. For the rest, as will be seen, it is mainly devoted to codifying, unifying, confirming, perfecting—at times by modification, at times by clarification—above all, of extending the norms which had already come into being through more or less limited usage.

This new approach was called for by the urgent and unique needs of the migrant. Ignorant as he is of the language, different as he is in his customs, culture, ways of thinking and of expressing himself, the immigrant in a new country is subject to deep nostalgia for his homeland. He cannot but feel himself, especially at the beginning, a stranger even in the very House of God which he enters to pray. The Pope's great heart sensed his need and provided for it.

These norms constitute another step forward on the path already so clearly marked out by heroic pioneers in this vast and precious domain of the apostolate.

Everyone knows that the Constitution opens with the incomparable vision of the Holy Family from Nazareth fleeing into Egypt before Herod's persecuting fury.

The Divine Redeemer, "the first-born among many brethren,"[3] made "in all things like unto his brethren,"[4] had hardly come among us that he must set out on the sorrowful road of exile. With him, sharing in his sufferings, were Blessed Mary and Saint Joseph: "Thou followest the refugee into the strange land of Egypt," chants the Liturgy on the feast day of Saint Joseph, and "Emigrant from the farthest banks of the Nile . . . the Child returns, having already suffered greatly,"[5] on the Sunday in the Epiphany octave.

The Holy Family is the mild and sweet example that the Church offers to refugees, exiles and migrants of every condition, every age and every land. In the name of that Holy Family, She herself, with her priests, strives to be their refuge.

This She has always been.

What infelicity ensues, when the exiled are deprived of the holy ministers' assistance! Saint Augustine shudders at the thought of those who die "unbaptized or chained by sin," at the thought of the sometimes blasphemous laments uttered by survivors, in whom unallayed fear of temporal ill may by great misfortune become the source of eternal woe. "If the ministers are present," the catechumen is baptized, the sinner reconciled with God, the body of the Lord distributed; all are consoled, exhorted, invited to prayer.[6]

In troubled modern times the comfort of the Church has been extended to the fugitives from the French Revolution under Pius VI and Pius VII;[7] to the Negroes under Leo XIII, Benedict XV, and Pius XI;[8] to the fugitives from the first World War and the Mexican Rebellion under Benedict XV and Pius XI; and, under Pius XII, to countless refugees from the second atrocious World War, and to emigrants of every nation.

A brief historical and critical commentary, the proposed scope of this essay, permits only the sketchiest approach to a theme whose importance, vastness and richness merit quite other treatment.

The Apostolic Constitution is divided into two Titles: one devoted to a historical résumé, the other to the norms to be established.

The first develops as a chronological review of facts and documents which evince the Church's maternal solicitude for emigrants. "This appeared necessary," may be read at its conclusion, "in these days when the provident work of the Church has been untruthfully impugned, slighted and disputed on the very grounds of that charity which she has been the first to disseminate, and which she has all too often been left to cultivate alone."[9]

Unfortunately, the historical material can be discussed here only insofar as it serves to reveal the origin of some institutions recommended by the *Exsul Familia*, and in particular those concerned with the spiritual assistance which the emigrant receives from the Bishop and from the parish priest in his native place. These will be reviewed first in chronological order, so that the constant concern of the Church may be seen in greater relief.[10] The assistance to the migrant in the place of immigration will then be dealt with, illustrating the norms contained in the second Title of the Constitution.

It would be impossible to omit mention of Saint Ambrose, who broke the sacred vessels to ransom those carried off after the defeat of Valens at Hadrianopolis, thus saving them not only from material harm, but from spiritual ill graver than death itself. The fearless Archbishop of Milan admonishes us not to treasure up riches when their expenditure may save a man from death, a woman from barbarian molestation, a youth or babe from idolatry: "It is far better to save souls for God than gold."[11]

How much might be said of the resolute efforts that were made in his era to draw into Christian civilization the very barbarian oppressors who had invaded and devastated flourishing Christian communities; of the heroic zeal displayed by the Orders established to liberate prisoners taken into slavery; of the devoted spiritual assistance later lent to the colonizers of the New World!

Particular mention should be made of a characteristic element in the spiritual assistance offered to pilgrims: through many centuries it has always been exercised by priests of the pilgrim's own nationality or language.

Such was the case in Pilgrims' Halls which were established near the sepulchre of Saint Peter in the Vatican as early as the eighth century for the Saxons (whence the appellation "Street of the Saxons," and the name still given to the Church of the Holy Spirit *in Saxia*), for the Lombards, the Franks and the Frisians. Priests of these nations lived permanently in the Halls, offered hospitality there to their co-nationals, and lent them every kind of aid, even, in the case of death, caring for the graves in the cemetery adjoining the church. The Cemetery of the Germans and Belgians is clearly a vestigial example of such Halls.

Later arose monasteries with hospices for pilgrims from Abyssinia, Hungary and Armenia. The many "national" confraternities and churches in Rome are a more recent demonstration of the Church's continuing usage in this respect.

The Fourth Lateran Council, in 1215, made of this custom a general obligation upon Bishops in whose dioceses there were groups of the faithful of differing languages and rites:

> In most regions may be found mingled together in the same cities and dioceses people of differing languages, who, though bound by one Faith, have varied rites and customs. Therefore we strictly enjoin that the Bishops of these cities or dioceses provide the proper men, who will celebrate the Divine Services according to the different rites and languages. They will administer the Sacraments of the Church and instruct their people both by word and by deed.[12]

In instituting the norms for the formation and establishment of parishes of various languages or nationality groups, the Code of Canon Law adheres to these same principles. (Can. 216, 4)

Many "national" parishes have been established in the United States of America, the greater number dating from the turn of the 19th century. Those in Canada are more recent. Lately, a Chinese parish has been founded in the Philippines, an Italian parish at Nairobi in Kenya and another at Saint Peter's Church in London. This parish was created through the urging of the Roman priest Blessed Vincenzo Pallotti [13] and the blessing of Pius IX. Two Italian, one Spanish and five Polish parishes have also been set up in France.

There are numerous Ordinariates of the Oriental Rite.

On behalf of the many Ruthenian lay faithful and priests who emigrated to North America, Saint Pius X created a Ruthenian Bishop in the United States of America and another in Canada, whose relationship with the Latin Clergy he also defined and regulated. He approved an association that had sprung up in Toronto for the Ruthenians' spiritual defense. As a sign of benevolence he donated to the Rumanian Episcopate the Church of the Most Holy Redeemer on the Vicolo delle Coppelle in Rome.

Benedict XV promoted spiritual assistance to the Greco-Ruthenian emigrants to South America, and established in the Monastery of Grottaferrata a seminary for Italo-Greek boys. For the faithful of the Greek Rite who had fled to Italy from the Turkish persecutions in Epirus and Albania, he created the Diocese of Lungro in Calabria.

Pius XI entrusted refugees of the Slavonian Rite first to the Commission for Russia, then to a Section expressly established under the Congregation for the Oriental Church. For the faithful of the same Rite he erected an Ordinariate in China: *Harbinensis Russorum*. In Rome he assigned to them the Church of St. Anthony the Hermit on the Esquiline, and founded the Russian Seminary. It should also be remembered in this connection that he exhorted the bishops of Poland to take care of refugees from the eastern areas, without distinction of language or confession, and made generous donations for this purpose.

For the faithful of the Byzantine Rite he erected in Sicily the Eparchy of *Piana dei Greci*.

He proposed valuable measures for the improvement of

the Greco-Ruthenian Ordinariates in the United States of America and in Canada.

In the time of the Holy Father Pius XII, a diocese has been created in Cairo for the Maronites who fled from Lebanon into Egypt; four Ruthenian Exarchates have been established in Canada, and quite recently Oriental Ordinariates have been created in Brazil and in France.

Chapter II

THE WORK OF THE CHURCH UNDER LEO XIII

IT is a well-known historical fact that in the nineteenth century masses of laborers in search of work emigrated from Europe, and especially from Italy, to America.

Leo XIII, a vigorous defender of the worker's dignity and rights, was not slow in attending to their needs. In 1878, the first year of his pontificate, he approved and commended the Society of St. Raphael (*St. Raphaels-Verein zum Schutze katholischer Auswanderer*), founded on September 13, 1871, by the Bishops of Germany for the purpose of assisting German emigrants. This Society, which had offices at the ports of embarkation and debarkation, later devoted itself to the assistance of emigrants from other countries as well: Belgians, Australians and Italians.

In 1887 he encouraged the Servant of God, John B. Scalabrini, then Bishop of Piacenza, to bring together in an Institute those devoted priests who, like Scalabrini himself, intended to dedicate themselves to the spiritual assistance of the countless Italian emigrants to America. The result was the Institute of the Missionaries of Saint Charles in Piacenza. Since 1914 it was authoritatively suggested that they be bound to the Consistorial, because of the "specific purpose of their Congregation," and be considered as "dependent" on and under the "direction" of that same Congregation. In the words of the Audience of February 20, 1914, the Missionaries of Saint Charles were to consider themselves as "the official assistants to the emigrants." [1] Their status under the Sacred Consistorial Congregation was accepted in full in 1924 by the Sovereign Pontiff Pius XI.[2]

The Pious Society now numbers 542 Religious, of whom 372 are priests, as well as 45 novices and 590 candidates. It has 128 houses distributed in 7 religious provinces; two missions *sui iuris;* with hospitals, schools, orphanages, shelters for migrants and their children, and emigration committees. There are 10 seminaries; three novitiates in Italy, the United States and Brazil.[3]

The missionaries assist migrants in France, Luxembourg, Switzerland (in which nations they have the direction of all the Missions), Belgium, Great Britain, the United States, Canada, Brazil, Argentina, Chile and Australia.

The Consistorial Congregation has placed a Scalabrinian Missionary as the head Director of Emigration Work in Italy, which has its headquarters in Rome, and another as the head Director of the Chaplains on Board, with an office in Genoa equipped by the Sacred Congregation. The Holy Father has entrusted to them the Pontifical College of Priests for Italian Emigration, and thus they have assumed charge of the preparation of missionaries to Italian emigrants.

The Immortal Pontiff's famous letter of December 10, 1888, *Quam Aerumnosa,* to the Archbishops and Bishops of America, aroused many others to good works. Priests and members of religious orders of both sexes dedicated themselves to the assistance of the immigrants. Sodalities and protectorates were established for the assistance of refugees from Ireland, Australia, Hungary, France, Switzerland, Belgium, the Low Countries, Spain and Portugal.

On June 19, 1900, with a Circular of the Secretariate of

State to some of the Italian Archbishops, Leo XIII initiated the work of setting up norms to guide the spiritual assistance to those emigrating only temporarily to other countries of Europe. The Bishop of Cremona, Bonomelli, then established the Institute for Assistance to Italian Emigrants in Europe, through the influence of which there sprang up Catholic Missions, concentrated for the most part in Switzerland, Austria, Germany and France, which devoted themselves to a combined work of charity and instruction. At the death of Bonomelli, Pope Benedict XV entrusted the Missions to Bishop Rodolfi of Vicenza, and Pius XI finally placed them under the Sacred Consistorial Congregation.

There are at present 86 of these Missions, excluding that in Algeria. Of the 138 Missionaries—51 in France, 30 in Belgium, 33 in Switzerland, 9 in Great Britain, 6 in Germany, 3 in Sweden, 2 in Luxembourg, and one each in Holland, Denmark, the Saar and Algeria—61 are of the diocesan clergy, 49 are Scalabrinians, 6 Friars Minor, 4 Salesians, 4 Pallotines, 3 Capuchins, 3 Clerics Regular of the Mother of God, 2 Conventuals, 1 Combonian, 1 Jesuit, 1 Priest of the Sacred Heart of Jesus.

At the head of all these Missionaries and their respective Missions, which the *Exsul Familia* has declared dependent on the local Ordinary, according to the common law, are five Directors.

The spiritual state of the Missions—I do not speak of their material state—is gratifying for the zeal and spirit of sacrifice displayed by the Missionaries. His Eminence, Cardinal Piazza, in the emigration sector, as in all others, a ready instrument of the Holy Father's generous resolutions, has had personal experience of this. For the better part of two years he has devoted himself to often arduous and sometimes dangerous visits to Missions in Switzerland and France. Everywhere acclaimed the "Cardinal of the Emigrants," he has brought the Church's maternal warmth to emigrants even while they are engaged in hard labor in mines or in the depths of wet and fearful excavations, where he wept and prayed with them for one of their companions who had perished tragically but shortly before.

It was again Leo XIII who pointed out to Mother Frances Xavier Cabrini the Western path rather than the Eastern. From the zeal of this Saint sprang up, especially in America, many institutions for the support and education of sons and daughters of Italians, hospitals, shelters for aged immigrants (one at Vitry in Paris Banlieu). For here work she was proclaimed by Pius XI "Mother of Italian Emigrants," and by Pius XII "Heavenly Patron of all Emigrants."

Chapter III

SAINT PIUS X, FOUNDER OF THE OFFICE FOR THE SPIRITUAL ASSISTANCE OF CATHOLIC MIGRANTS OF LATIN RITE

CREDIT for the first all-inclusive and organic plan for spiritual assistance to migrants must be given to a man who, as parish priest of Salzano, had already shown deep concern for his migrant parishioners. Raised to the See of Saint Peter, he assumed a name often invoked today—Pius X.

His ardent zeal is evinced by the many Acts concerned with migrants that he promulgated. Among them may be mentioned his letter to the Archbishop of New York (February 26, 1904) regarding the establishment of a seminary for clerics who were sons of Italian immigrants; a speech to the Argentine pilgrims (November 18, 1908); his letters to the Archbishops and Bishops of Brazil (June 6, 1911), to the Superior of the Missionaries of Saint Charles, to the Director of the Pious Antonian Society and to the Rector of the Catholic Society for Immigrants in Canada.

In 1905 he approved the Society of the Missionaries of Emigration of Saint Anthony of Padua, founded by a Turinese priest, Father John James Coccolo. This Society, described by the Secretary of State, Cardinal Merry del Val, in 1908 as "a highly praiseworthy undertaking," had as its two-fold object "the assistance of the emigrant on shipboard" and the assistance of the emigrant at the ports of embarkation and debarkation, where he is often most in need of help.

The Chaplains on Board were provided by this Society. In 1923 Pius XI entrusted the Chaplains on Board to the Rector of the Pontifical College of Priests for Italian Emigration. They have now been placed directly under the Sacred Consistorial Congregation, and through the benevolence of the Holy Father, have received official recognition in the *Exsul Familia*,[1] in which their juridical status and duties have also been clarified and delimited.

Today twenty-eight Italian ships ply the seas and oceans with permanent Chaplains on board: silent but incomparable pre-eminence, which must certainly draw down on Italy's sons the benediction of the Star of the Sea.

The norms of the *Exsul Familia* are finding their intended application in other nations as well: in Holland, Germany and Portugal.

Saint Pius X promoted the founding in Italy of Diocesan Committees and charitable institutions for emigrants. These organizations are prescribed in the *Exsul Familia* in the chapter, "Concerning the Spiritual Assistance to be Provided Migrants by Italian Bishops." Among the duties of the Diocesan Committees are the catechetical preparation of the migrant and the continuation spiritual assistance to him even beyond the confines of his native country.

Regarding other countries of immigration the text reads: "Where there is a lack of adequate spiritual assistance for Catholic immigrants of other nations, in such places the bishops may, without question, provide this assistance if they follow carefully the methods used for Italian immigrants, adopting only those modifications necessitated by the place and circumstances."[2]

Many invaluable organizations have been set up in other countries: In Germany, the Society of St. Raphael (*St. Raphaels-Verein zum Schutze katholischer Auswanderer*), approved by Leo XIII, which has had two Protectors—The Archbishop of Cologne and the Bishop of Osnabruck, and the Society of the Holy Angels, encouraged by Pius XI; in Poland, with the Archbishop of Gniezno as protector, the Society of Christ for Migrants, established in 1932 and approved in 1950; in Spain, the Hispano-American Institute for Priestly Cooperation (1948); in Holland, the Catholic Agency for the Care of Migrants.

Work has been begun in Portugal. Especially worthy of note is the excellent project of a monthly magazine, through which the Sisters of the Sacred Heart founded by Father Dehon keep the immigrant in touch with his mother country. Quite lately Japan has made an appeal to the Consistorial on behalf of emigrants, both Catholic and non-Catholic, bound for Brazil.

Pius X issued an instruction through the Sacred Congregation of the Sacraments, regarding the certificate of free status and the declaration of contracted marriage, to obviate difficulties which might easily arise from the immigrant's less strict observance of the norms regarding matrimony to his resultant grave spiritual detriment. But the most important act of Saint Pius X was the institution of a special Office under the Sacred Consistorial Congregation, for the spiritual care of Catholic Migrants of the Latin Rite.

The Holy See's clear-sightedness in confronting a most vexatious problem is apparent in a document of June 13, 1912:

The number of Catholics who meet with the shipwreck of their Faith through the deceptions of the Protestants, socialists and free-masons, as well as through the dangers present in large cities, is frightening . . . the problem is great; the questions difficult and complex, but urgent . . . We must act. But how? The project of simply establishing a Congregation for the Preservation of the Faith is too fine to be translated immediately into practice . . . .

Putting aside, at least for the moment, the idea of a Congregation for the Preservation of the Faith, we repeat that it is urgently necessary to do something that is neither vague nor vain. All agree upon some central institution which, without infringing on the jurisdiction of the established Hierarchy as to Catholic immigrants (i.e., those Catholics who are under a lawful superior both in the place from which they leave and in the place for which they are bound), should provide when the forementioned Hierachy cannot do so. Hence, surveillance, counsel, exhortation, aid, and if need be, even commands to these priests, in order that they shall interest themselves in the immigrant as much as they do concerning the other faithful confided to their care.

Without discarding the possibility that a Congregation may eventually be established for this purpose, a provisional organization shall be set up here in Rome. It shall not yet undertake to emit orders which, owing to the inexact and incomplete knowledge now obtainable concerning the emigrants' conditions and needs, might not result beneficial. A single person would be insufficient to cope with the problem, and therefore a nucleus of competent persons shall be established immediately, who shall, in order that they may have legal authority, be dependent on the Congregation most naturally indicated; namely, the Sacred Consistorial Congregation. They shall form a true Section of the same, which shall be called, since the good issue of an undertaking so often depends on the name first given it, the Spiritual Assistance of Catholic Migrants.

It shall undertake—without neglecting the Catholics of Oriental Rite for whom it shall make some arrangement with the Propaganda, although for them the need is not so urgent—to procure information concerning the situation of migrants of Latin Rite, principally of the Italians, who constitute the majority of migrants. For this purpose it shall send detailed "questionnaires" to the Ordinaries from whose dioceses the migrants leave, and to those for whose dioceses the migrants are bound, as well to all institutions which occupy themselves with migration. The replies will give some picture of migrants' material and moral conditions, of their more or less urgent needs, whether permanent or fluctuating, and of the financial and moral means which have been available to the individual centers of migration up to the present time. On the basis of this information the new Section of the Consistorial will plan its project for the Spiritual Assistance of Catholic Migrants.[3]

On June 14, 1912, the Sovereign Pontiff Pius X decreed that "an outline of *Motus Proprii* regarding this matter be prepared," and on the 15 of August he issued the *Motu Proprio: Concerning the Migration of Catholics to Foreign Countries*.

Two years later the matter was again brought up:

The figures are alarming. An evil which is already great threatens every day to assume even vaster proportions. Because of the numerous defections of Italian emigrants and of their fellow-countrymen whom they infect upon their return, one cannot but fear a sad future for religion in Italy.

What has been done up to now through the work of private and individual efforts is good and praiseworthy, but it no longer suffices.

It is necessary that such efforts be not only reinforced, but also concentrated and disciplined. The Consistorial Congregation shall therefore study a vast, over-all plan, serious and efficacious, to be evolved little by little. A clear and precise program shall be developed to deal with questions of permanent and temporary, European and transoceanic migration. Such a plan must absolutely be based on a concentration of organization around the Holy See, from which all work on behalf of migrants must stem.

The Catholic institutions which have occupied themselves up to now with migrants (the Agency of Assistance and the Italica Gens are referred to) shall necessarily be abolished or, in perfected form, be incorporated into those which the Sacred Consistorial Congregation shall see fit to institute or encourage.[4]

A further note from the same document reads: "and as a guarantee of good proper procedure on the part of the priests who assist the emigrant in Europe, also the norm established by the Congregation of the Council shall be applied: *i.e.*, that none may be assumed as missionary for the work of assistance, except with the consent of the Holy See."[5]

Thus the authority over emigrating priests and over those dedicated to the spirtiual assistance of Italian migrants, which had formerly devolved upon the Congregation of the Council, passed from the Council to the Sacred Consistorial Congregation. Their discipline was provided for by the Consistorial Decrees *Ethnographica Studia* of March 5, 1914, and *Magni Semper Negotii* of December 30, 1918, which adapted the earlier decree to the Code of Canon Law.

The norms established by the Consistorial Congregation have remained in effect up to our day. However, in the forty years that have passed since their promulgation, new situations have arisen, and in consequence some deficiencies have become apparent.

The quoted documents excluded from the competence of the Consistorial Congregation the migrant faithful of

Oriental Rite, both the laity: ". . . without prejudice, however, to the rights of the Congregation for the Propagation of the Faith regarding emigrants of the Oriental Rite, for whose care this Congregation may provide according to its purpose;"[6] and the ecclesiastics ". . . without superseding the law of the Congregations for the Propagation of the Faith and for Matters of the Oriental Rite, concerning the emigration of priests of this rite."[7] The ecclesiastics remained subject to the jurisdiction of the Congregation for the Propagation of the Faith and to the Congregation for the Oriental Church.

It is true that the Congregation for the Oriental Church issued norms regarding its subjects in this matter, but at times the Orientals, upon emigrating, found themselves without the assistance of the priests of their own rite, especially when going to territories of Latin Rite. The question then arose as to what provision should be made for them. Similarly, if a priest of Oriental Rite emigrated into Latin territories, was he to consider himself, simply because he was of the Oriental Rite, exempt from the ecclesiastical laws in force in that place?

In his *Mostu Proprio Sancta Dei Ecclesia* of March 25, 1938,[8] Pius XI considerably extended the competence of the Sacred Congregation for the Oriental Church, which now obtained full and exclusive jurisdiction over certain regions of Europe and of Italy also, and not only over the faithful of Oriental Rite, but also over the faithful of Latin Rite living in those regions.

Who should provide for the Latin faithful and priests migrating to Latin territories not subject to the Sacred Congregation for the Oriental Church?

The Consistorial Congregation in practice limited itself to the spiritual care of the flow of transoceanic emigration leaving from Italy and from a few other Mediterranean nations, and bound for the Americas and the Philippine Islands. The Sacred Congregation for the Propagation of the Faith on the other hand, had stepped in to regulate the influx of clergy which was bound for Australia and New Zealand from European dioceses.

The Consistorial Congregation had reserved directly to itself the application of norms governing the emigration of Italian clergy and had entrusted the regulation of the clergy of Spain and Portugal to the Pontifical Representatives stationed in those countries.

According to the *Magni Semper Negotii*, the Consistorial Congregation required the consent of the Ordinary to whose territory the emigrant priest went only if the stay were to be longer than six months, but after 1947,[9] by request of the Bishops of the United States, it exacted such consent also for a shorter period when one of those dioceses was the destination.

Finally, in the matter of spiritual assistance to emigrants, only Italian priests needed the permission from the Holy See.

The disparity in the handling of various aspects of the same problem becomes obvious. In order to do away with these conflicts and to re-establish that uniformity which provides a good basis for the maintenance of discipline, this, in brief, is what the *Exsul Familia* established:

The care of migrants of Latin Rite is the exclusive duty of the Sacred Consistorial Congregation, whatever the place of immigration. However, the Sacred Consistorial

Congregation will proceed in accordance with the Sacred Congregation for the Oriental Church, or with the Sacred Congregation for the Propagation of the Faith, if the territory of immigration is subject to one or the other of those Congregations.

The Sacred Consistorial Congregation is bound to an equivalent duty towards the migrants of Oriental Rite— in agreement, it is understood, with the Sacred Congregation for the Oriental Church—in the case of migrants who are transferring to territories not subject to that Congregation, and where there is no priest of their Rite who can assist them. This would be the case, for example, for Oriental migrants bound for the Philippine Islands, who are obliged to sail on a boat which has only a chaplain of Latin Rite on board.

All priests of Latin Rite who wish to emigrate must submit to the norms of the Consistorial Congregation, even though they are subject to the Congregation for the Oriental Church (as the priests of the Eparchy of *Piana dei Greci*, for example), or to the Sacred Congregation for the Propagation of the Faith (as those of Sweden, Norway, etc.), unless they are transferring to territories subject to one or the other of those Congregations.

Oriental priests emigrating to territories not subject to the Congregation for the Oriental Church must comply with the laws that bind Latin priests. Accordingly, they must secure the consent of the Bishop to whose territory they go, and may not devote themselves to the spiritual assistance of a group of co-nationals of Latin Rite without providing themselves in advance with the permission from the Consistorial Congregation. (Such would be the case for a Greek priest of the diocese of Lungro, should he wish to assist his Calabrian countrymen of Latin Rite.)

Priests emigrating from Europe and from the Mediterranean coast and bound overseas, for whatever continent or for whatever length of time, even for a very brief or indefinite stay and for the purpose of incardination, must have in advance, under pain of incurring the canonical penalties threatened in the *Magni Semper Negotii,* the permission of the Sacred Consistorial Congregation. This shall be granted either directly, as is done for Italians and for refugees of the countries behind the iron curtain, or through the Pontifical Representatives of each individual European nation.

The members of religious orders are not exempt from this law unless they are furnished with the permission from their respective Superiors and are bound for houses of their own Institute: much less so in the case of the exclaustrated or secularized.

The consent of the Bishop to whose territory the priest goes is always required for every permission, which, if obtained for one diocese, is not valid for another. A new appeal must be made to the authority which made the original concession.

Likewise, all priests, whatever their nationality, who dedicate themselves to the spiritual assistance of emigrants, even on ship board, must be authorized for this particular ministry by the Sacred Consistorial Congregation. This holds true, for example, for the Poles in Australia and for the Chinese in the Philippines.

The last act of Saint Pius X was the foundation of the College of Priests for Italian Emigration, in Rome. The

Sacred Consistorial Congregation had raised the question of "whether an institute should be founded to prepare willing young priests for assistance of Italian emigrants abroad." This was the reply:

> There will be practical and above all material difficulties to overcome, but the idea of an institute in Rome for the purpose of preparing good priests to assist Italian immigrants in America is excellent. Such an insitute would do great honor to the Holy See, and make apparent to the world the Church's serious concern with the new dangers to which so many of her children are exposed.
>
> Besides this, well-chosen young priests trained for this purpose, that is, priests with the spirit of missionaries and with a knowledge of the language, customs and laws of the countries to which they are destined, would undoubtedly become valuable workers. Furthermore, the power of the Sacred Congregation to reward, recall, transfer, or employ them in other offices should they be disabled for the missions would be of great value to the cause.
>
> The project should be seriously studied, therefore, in order that it may be translated into actuality.

In approving this resolution the Pope said more specifically that the institute should be formed as "a kind of Academy of orientation, with instruction in the language, in the laws, etc., and instruction to fortify the priest in his piety, etc., over a two-year period: it being established that each priest shall remain attached to his diocese, and shall return to it either after the two-year training period, if he does not leave to assist the emigrants, or after his mission among the emigrants is completed." [10]

The *Motu Proprio, Iam pridem,* regarding the foundation

of the College, is dated March 19, 1914. In the archives of the Consistorial Congregation is a jealously guarded proof of the printed Statutes of the College, which has been corrected and annotated by the hand of Saint Pius X, then near his happy death.

Chapter IV

BENEDICT XV AND THE SPIRITUAL ASSISTANCE TO PRISONERS AND REFUGEES OF THE FIRST WORLD WAR

BENEDICT XV continued with plans for the College notwithstanding the harassing worries of wartime. He assigned to it for its headquarters part of the Building of Saint Apollinaris, which had for so long resounded to the vital life of our Roman Seminary, the Pius Seminary and this glorious Lateran Atheneum.

> His glorious Predecessor had given the Roman Seminary and Pius Seminary the use of a new building inside the Lateran enclosure, near the Basilica of the Most Holy Redeemer, and their old building in the center of the city was vacant. A document of October 16, 1914, in his own hand, directs that after the necessary repairs, it shall become the abode of the College for emigrants, as the deceased Pontiff had intended." [1]

Benedict XV was also prompt in assuring the means necessary for the economic functioning of the College. He assigned to its use a part of the regular income, and sent letters to the Ordinaries in America and Italy to encourage collections for it. He invited these Ordinaries to "establish in all the parishes of their dioceses an annual collection for the work of assistance to Italian migrants."[2]

The College could not be opened until after peace had returned. It was inaugurated on Epiphany in 1920, and its direction was entrusted to the Prelate for Italian Emigration, an office created in that same year.

Nineteen hundred and forty-nine marks the year in which it was revived. In the 17 sessions held since then there have participated 191 priests; some destined for the office of Ship Chaplains, some bound for European missions, or for Latin-American dioceses.

The above mentioned annual collection for the work of assistance to Italian migrants gave rise to a "National Emigrants' Day," which has been celebrated in Italy on the first Sunday of Advent for some years. It was authoritatively comfirmed in Art. 48 of the *Exsul Familia*.

The august Legislator has extended this disposition beyond the confines of Italy: in Art. 49, he addresses not only the Bishops of Italy but also the Bishops of those place to which Italians have immigrated: "We desire of them, that in the Italian parishes, or at least where the Italian population predominates, an annual 'Emigrants' Day' shall be celebrated as it is in Italy."

He likewise suggests that the same should be done for migrants of other nationalities also; ". . . so that an Emigrants' Day may be celebrated throughout the entire Catholic world at one and the same time, that is, on the first Sunday in Advent." Thus, the National Emigrants' day has become a "World" day.[3]

The World Emigrants' Day has already become a gratifying reality in nations from Argentina to Canada, from Australia to Chile and Brazil.

Benedict XV, promoted yet other measures in connection with Italian emigration.

He earnestly recommended to the Archbishop of Sao Paulo and to the Bishops of Brazil that an active vigilance be exercised to keep Italians who had already immigrated overseas from abandoning their Catholic faith. He praised the Bishop of Trenton in the United States of America for having built a church for the Italian colony there, and expressed the wish that Italian emigrants to the United States might everywhere find such comfort (December 10, 1920).

For Italians on the point of leaving he prescribed the establishment of emigration Secretariates and Protectorates.

He also promoted another form of spiritual assistance directed to the alleviation of conditions brought about by the so-called internal migration, which comprises thousands upon thousands of women seasonal rice-workers.

In order to provide financial support for the activities of the Secretariates and Committees, also for the assistance to the rice-workers, he ordered that the parish priests of the regions most involved (Sardinia, Calabria, the Abruzzi and Molise; Lombardy, Emilia, Liguria and the Piedmont) should apply a Mass for the faithful according to the intentions of the Supreme Pontiff (January 2, 1918 and December 6, 1918). This prescription was extended by Pius XI to Sicily on behalf of the Palermo *Emigrant's House* (December 6, 1923). It was later confirmed and further extended to other Regions of Italy (Veneto, Basilicata, Beneventano, Campania, Etruria and Romagna), though no longer for a specific purpose, but more generally "for the work of migration." (December 14, 1928).

This general disposition has also been confirmed in Art. 50 of the *Exsul Familia*.

Some notion of the stage which has been reached in the development of religious and moral assistance to the rice-worker (whom the Holy See has also endowed with

Trailer Chapels) may be derived from a passage in the report on the 1953 work season by the National Delegate, Father John Balduzzi.

As a consequence of the establishment of Diocesan Committees for migration, the Bishops in the dioceses of immigration have been able to unite under their personal authority all the activities devoted to the assistance of the rice-worker. These activities have been carried on mainly by the Catholic Action, the Catholic Association for Italian Workers, the Italian Women's Center, the Association for the Protection of Young Women, and the National Agency for the Religious and Moral Assistance of Workers.

The results of charitable assistance to the many thousands of rice-workers have been truly gratifying.

In order that the work of assistance done by our "Visitatrici in cascina" (Field-visitors) should be more effective, we began this year for the first time, with a "Five Days" workshop in Vercelli, and a "Three Days" workshop, Novara, before the work began. The initiative was taken by the Catholic Association for Italian Workers, in economic collaboration with the Italian Women's Center. Lectures on charitable assistance, organization, hygiene and sanitation, discipline, morals and religion, were given by competent persons.

The many facets of the assistance offered to the mass of migrant rice-workers reflect a program built up through the experience provided by our thirty years of apostolate in rice-fields. The program includes moral, spiritual and disciplinary preparation for the placement of the migrant squads in the respective dioceses and parishes of migration; assistance during the journey; care and assistance in the canteens for the groups travelling by train; daily visits to the centers in which the workers are concentrated(farms and villages), as well as to the dormitories and the places of overnight stay; tutelage of the workers in morality; religious functions; adaptation of the religious day to the rice-worker's day; Rice-Workers' Masses (held in many places in the afternoon as well); general Holy Communions; recreation meetings; care of hygiene; assistance to the ill; distribution of relief; repatriation of the needy, etc. Through these activities our Visitors, the Sisters and the hard-working Priests are offered many opportunities for intensifying that work of moral and spiritual salvage of which the rice-workers stand in constant need.

We are pleased to point out in this connection the activity and the zeal of the most reverend bishops, many of whom have come from their sees to the regions of immigration in order to comfort the rice-workers from their own dioceses with the Pastoral presence and assistance. The bishops of the dioceses of immigration also deserve mention: The Most Reverend Bishop of Vigevano insisted on going to the rice-fields every evening, travelling to hundreds of places in which rice-workers were concentrated and carrying to them everywhere his paternal word.

Relations with the state and local officials in the provincial Bureau of Labor, the Labor Inspection Department and in the prefectures have always been good, and their support has been generously given at our request. Our assistance has been favorably viewed, and appreciated, by the Labor Ministry.

The diocesan committees for migration, in collagoration with the National Headquarters are organizing assistance to other categories of internal migration: the shepherds, olive, and grape pickers, tobacco workers and so on.

Special note should be made of Benedict XV's efforts on behalf of the prisoners and their families, and the refugees, who were victims of the first World War.

With regard to the prisoners, particular mention must be made of the Act with which the Pope recommended to the Ordinaries in whose dioceses there were prisoners of war, that the prisoners' care should be assigned to priests familiar with their language. This Act, entitled: *De Cura Captivorum a Clero Habenda,* issued by the Congregation for Extraordinary Ecclesiastical Affairs on December 21, 1941, is signed by a name dear to all of us: Eugene Pacelli, Secretary.

For the refugees who fled to Italy, Benedict XV established a Common Ordinary (September 3, 1918). He also urged upon the attention of the Bishop of Germany and Central Europe the grave problem presented by the countless refugees in other countries, and he encouraged the activity of the Society of St. Raphael, which had already done much good work. In 1921 he named the Archbishop of Cologne as Patron of the "agency of the Religious Assistance of Catholic Germans." This agency at first worked only with German Catholics in Italy, later included German Catholics in all of western Europe, and finally, under the guidance of the second Patron, the Bishop of Osnabruck, included those in eastern Europe and in areas outside the boundaries of Europe as well.

Refugees in the United States of America—bishops, priests members of religious orders, and the faithful who had fled from Mexico where persecution was rife—found in Benedict XV an effective protector, as attested by a letter to the Bishop of San Antonio (November 25, 1914), and another to the Archbishop of Baltimore concerning a seminary for young Mexican aspirants to the priesthood (March 17, 1915).

CHAPTER V

PIUS XI AND THE CARE OF MIGRANTS OF ORIENTAL RITE

IN matters concerned with migration, Pius XI's earliest and most affectionate care was devoted to the Orientals. His provisions for them has been described earlier, and in this chapter it will suffice to recall a heart-warming episode that occurred on December 24, 1922.

The Sacred College of Cardinals was gathered for Christmas wishes. In these moving words the Pope announced that he had taken the Armenian orphans into the Papal Palace at Castel Gandolfo: "We have, then, a true gift from God; an entire people of children come to gather about Us. More than 400 little orphan girls have come from the Far East, sent to Us by the Holy Child; representatives of a people which has experienced suffering to the point of bloodshed and death."[1]

Among his provisions for the migrants of Latin Rite, those relating to the Poles and the Germans have already been mentioned. The Spaniards who fled to Castel Gandolfo from the Communist persecutions, bishops, priests and members of religious orders of both sexes, experienced on September 14, 1936, all the tenderness of Christ's Vicar. The same may be said for the Mexicans who emigrated to the United States of America, and for the Negroes. Pius XI hailed with pleasure the opening of a preparatory seminary for these last by the Society of the Divine Word; "For there are in the United States more than two million inhabitants of various races for whom it is necessary to provide as soon as possible their own missionaries and their own pastors."[2]

A note must be added regarding a further provision that Pius XI made for Italians. He prescribed, and the *Exsul Familia* has confirmed it, that every migrant shall be furnished by his own parish with an appropriate ecclesiastical identification card.[3]

Chapter VI

HIS HOLINESS PIUS XII: PROVIDENT FATHER OF EXILES

FROM this point on, our attention will be dedicated exclusively to the work of Pius XII.

It has not yet been forgotten that the moment in which Pius XII was assumed to the Supreme Pontificate was one of increasing discord among nations. The insane determination of certain nations to occupy the territories of others, the restrictions placed on the emigration of some peoples and the forced removal of others, resulted in serious disorders and unspeakable suffering. Under Pius XII the Church once more bestirred herself "to preside over all works of charity":[1] comforter of those who wept, refuge for the persecuted, homeland for the exiled. The Pope offered asylum even to the refugee Jews.

Up to the last moment he gave generously of his time and effort in the attempt to avert war. The world, alas, was deaf to his heartfelt appeal for peace, and flung itself brutally into a ferment of hatred, drawing countless innocent victims into the vicious whirlpool, and stained itself with blood. But the Angelic Pastor continued to have thoughts of peace for all.

Never before had history offered to a Pope such a tremendous heart-rending picture of stricken children of God. Pius XII held out his hand to every one of them, to the smallest and weakest, and from his lips rang the Apostle's cry, "Who is weak and I am not weak?"[2]

Ardent and generous, tireless and unsleeping, he built up stone by stone that gigantic Work of Charity which was destined to allay the sufferings brought upon humanity by the atrocious scourge. Ingratitude and calumny will never be able to touch his work of charity, which has become a part of history.

This essay will only deal with deportees, refugees, and prisoners.

The war broke out, and distress followed close behind it. Many works were begun: The Commission for Assistance; the Office of Information; the Pontifical Commission for Assistance to Refugees, the Pontifical Commission for Assistance (still active under the name Agency of Pontifical Assistance), and the Missions in Germany and Austria.

Armed conflict had scarcely ceased when the Office of Migration was established. It was subdivided into two Sections—Natural Migration and Refugee Migration—and was linked with similar institutions which had originated in the work of the Bishops in the United States, Canada and Great Britain, and with the Vatican Mission at Kronberg. An observer was sent to the Emigration Office at Geneva, and an International Catholic Migration Commission was established there.

The list may be completed by noting the activity of the Nuncios, Internuncios and Apostolic Delegates; of the bishops, priests, associations of Catholic Action; of all those belonging to other forms of the apostolate; and finally, the work of the willing and generous faithful, who formed committees and commissions which carried out the Pope's charitable projects in all parts of the world.

In 1948 the war in Palestine broke out, with its resultant piteous exodus of hundreds and thousands of peaceable citizens who, bereft of everything they possessed, were forced to take refuge in Jordan, Syria, Lebanon, Egypt and in the Gaza region. The Pope came promptly to the assistance of the Palestine refugees, forming the Pontifical Mission for Palestine. This Mission still distributes relief, which the Catholic Near East Welfare Association collects from the entire Catholic world, to those unfortunate Arab populations who dwell in flimsy tents or in primitive huts outside the city walls, or in the desert.

At this point it will be appropriate—and perhaps gratifying to the reader also—to recall with gratitude, and in the very words of the Constitution, the generous work of the Defender of the City during one of the most difficult moments of trial:

> While the monstrous war raged, there converged on Rome with each hour a vast throng of people—children, women, the sick and the aged—to seek from the common father of all a place of safety and refuge. They came from the towns and villages which had been laid waste by the invading enemy, particularly from devastated areas of Italy. We then enlarged still further the scope of our charity, for the cries of so many exiles and refugees touched our heart. Moved by that pity we were forced to repeat Our Lord's words: "I have compassion on the multitude." For this reason the doors of all our buildings were opened wide; at the Vatican as well as at the Lateran, and at Castel Gandolfo especially; at the Roman Basilicas and also at the religious houses, seminaries and ecclesiastical colleges of Rome. While almost the entire world flamed with bitter hatred, and the blood of brothers flowed, the Sacred City of Rome, and these buildings, became centers and houses of charity.[3]

After such an introduction it does not seem surprising

to hear on the august lips of Pius XII a phrase such as this: "We have left nothing undone, in the attempt to offer some help to our sorrowing children."[4] The words seem almost a concise description of the work carried out by the Pope on behalf of "those misery-stricken multitudes of refugees of every age and condition, forced by the horrors of war to flee their lands."[5] The Holy Father even provided Visitors for each different nationality. A complete and detailed picture, in so far as it would be possible to compile it, of the innumerable provisions adopted and the abundant means employed in that exquisite work of charity, would be highly useful and of incontrovertible apologetic value.

This brief and all too inadequate summary of the gigantic work of Pius XII cannot be concluded without recalling at least one among the many testimonials of his singular benevolence towards the refugees of eastern Europe: the creation of the College of St. Casimir for the refugee clergy and priests from Lithuania, completed May 1st, 1948.

We must also share in the Pope's sorrowful reflections regarding a limited category of exiles, refugees and prisoners: those who are suffering in the "Church of Silence." His thoughts were expressed in 1952, but unfortunately, they still describe a present reality:

> With grieving heart we recall again and again most beloved sons, the Bishops, priests and nuns dragged unjustly from their homes, and all those who, condemned to prison or to forced labor, have been kept in absolutely inhuman living conditions. All these hapless wanderers have been a constant source of anguish to us. In order that these uprooted peoples may be revived through heavenly gifts and comforts, we have prayed ardently and continually on their behalf to the Eternal Father and to Our Most Loving Redeemer, Source of every consolation.

> We constantly beseech God that the refugees, the prisoners and the deported who have been carried far from their native borders, may return to their own beloved countries as soon as possible.[6]

Perhaps it was not without significance that the Pope dated the *Exsul Familia* on the first day of the feast of St. Peter the Apostle in Chains. On that day the Church reminds us that while "Peter was in prison, the Church prayed to God for him without ceasing."[7]

May our unceasing prayer, strengthened by that of the most pious Vicar of Christ, prevail, so that once again the Angel of the Lord shall descend among us to lighten the darkness of so many prisons. And may every one of those heroic confessors soon repeat: "Now I know for certain that the Lord has sent his angel and rescued me from the power of Herod."[8]

CHAPTER VII

HIS HOLINESS PIUS XII, WISE LEGISLATOR OF SPIRITUAL ASSISTANCE TO MIGRANTS

A BRIEF examination must now be made of the norms established by the *Exsul Familia,* regarding the organization of spiritual assistance to the emigrant during his ocean voyage and in his place of immigration.

This very simple organization is characterized by the fact that, though it evolves in part in immediate dependence on the Holy See, in part it is entirely dependent on the diocesan regulations established by the common law, though still under her vigilant eye.[1]

At the head of the organization are: a) the Supreme Council on Migration; b) the National Directors, each one Secretary of a National Episcopal Commission; c) the Director of the Missionaries and of the Chaplains on Board; d) the Migrants' Missionaries, with or without care of souls, and the Chaplains on Board.

The Migrants' Missionaries and the Chaplains on Board constitute a body of priests, diocesan and regular, who volunteer to place themselves at the disposal of the Holy See, and who come prepared for their apostolate through the Sacred Consistorial Congregation, whose competence it is also to approve, appoint and assign them. To these two categories must be added the Chaplains of the Apostolate of the Sea.[2] The appointment to the Chaplains on Board and the Apostolate of the Sea may also be made by the Pontifical

Representatives in the respective nations, if they be duly and properly authorized by the Consistorial Congregation.

The appointment of the Migrants' Missionaries is officially communicated to the Ordinary *a quo* (from whom they depart) and the Ordinary *ad quem* (to whom they go).

What effect does this appointment produce?

The terms of the Constitution are unequivocally clear: "This effects no excardination from a diocese. Nor does it offer exemption either from the priest's own bishop or religious superior, or from the bishop of the place in which the work is done."[3]

The same is true for Chaplains on Board and for the Directors of both Missionaries and Chaplains.

With this appointment, the missionary is enabled: a) to receive from the bishop of whatever place he shall be sent the necessary faculties to exercise his ministry among migrants, including the care of souls;[4] b) to benefit, in the field assigned to him, from the special Norms and Faculties issued by the Consistorial Congregation for priests who have been entrusted with the spiritual care of emigrants, namely, for Missionaries of Emigrants and the Directors of Missionaries, on order of Pius XII on December 10, 1954, on the Feast of the translation of the Holy House of the Blessed Virgin Mary.

In order to avoid any possibility of misunderstanding, the words of Pius XII to the missionaries to Italian emigrants in Europe (in an audience: August 6, 1952), should be kept in mind:

> Make the migrants understand that yours is an extraordinary spiritual assistance, which, among other things, will offer them the opportunity of going to confession in their mother tongue

> when that is not possible with the indigenous priest; but that in the meantime they must make it a point to attend services on Holydays together with the faithful of the country. Encourage them to accustom themselves to the religious life of the locality, and above all to make contact with Catholic organizations there, especially with those of the workers and the young people.[5]

To this form of extraordinary assistance, to which the entire fourth part of Title Two of the Constitution is dedicated, recourse must be had "unless it seems inexpedient, for one reason or another, at the discretion of the Ordinary, to make recourse to obtain permission for establishing parishes for various language or nationality groups."[6]

Keeping in mind what has been said previously regarding the national parishes, we may conclude that the legislator's intention is that the local Ordinaries shall provide adequate assistance for the establishment of "national parishes" in those places where the immigration has become stabilized, and shall institute "missions with the care of souls" where the immigration is still in its fluctuating early stages.

In either of these cases the Ordinary, in accordance with what is prescribed in Canon 216, 4 of the Code of Canon Law, must obtain permission from the Sacred Consistorial Congregation for the purpose of establishing either a national parish for immigrants[7] or a national mission with the care of souls.[8]

Such a mission necessarily has its own characteristics, which derive from the peculiar circumstances under which the ministry among immigrants must be conducted. This is especially true in the case of places where the need is seasonal, as in the miners' encampments in Belgium or the Saar.

> Not even the minimum plant is required for the establishment of a mission; not even a chapel of its own. If there is no chapel the Bishop will provide with the apposite norms so that the missionary may be enabled fully and freely to exercise his ministry in some church of the locality, even if it be the parish church.[9]
>
> The Bishop must, however, clearly circumscribe the territorial boundaries of the mission.[10]

Only immigrants and their first generation descendants in the direct line may be subjects of the missionary. They may remain with the missionary even though they are naturalized.

The reckoning of descendants is made for each immigrant as such, the degree of consanguinity thus having no importance among the members of a family of immigrants, ascendants and descendants included, as long as each of them finds himself in the same condition of immigrant or pilgrim. In effect, it may be said that each immigrant is a founder of a family.

Thus, for example, if Titius and Caia immigrate to France together with their old parents, Sempronius and Kunegunda, and their children Siegfried and Elizabeth, all find themselves in the same condition as immigrants, and all benefit from the law in equal measure, from the aged Sempronius and Kunegunda, to the very young Siegfried and Elizabeth, as do the possible first generation descendants in the direct line born of each in the place of immigration.

Since we are dealing with a favorable law, it is obvious that *advena*, and *peregrinus*, should be given the broadest possible interpretation. The said subjects, however, are still at liberty to choose between the missionary pastor and the local parish priest.[11]

In the exercise of his functions the missionary pastor is equal to the parish priest, with due reference to the particular position of each, of course.

As established in the norms of the *Declaratio de Missionariorum Officiis*,[12] and within the boundaries of the territory assigned to him, he may administer the Sacrament of Confirmation to subjects who are on the point of death, according to the decree of the Congregation of the Sacraments, *Spiritus Sancti Munera* of September 14, 1946,[13] and may assist validly at the marriage of the faithful of the same language or nationality even if they are not domiciled, nor even quasi-domiciled in that territory. As regards liceity, he must abide by the disposition of Canon 1097, 2 of the Code of Canon Law: "In every case it shall be the rule that the marriage is to be contracted before the pastor of the bride unless a just reason excuses an exception, and also when only one of the two contracting parties is his subject."

For the verification of the status of the contracting parties the missionary must follow the special norms given by the Sacred Congregation of the Sacraments in the Instruction: "Concerning the Norms to be observed by a Pastor in administering . . . ," of June 29, 1941. He must keep in mind numbers 4 and 10 in particular.[14]

In the event that the missionary with care of souls must absent himself from the mission, or should he become ill and unable to carry out his proper duties, he must give the co-operating missionary a general delegation for marriage.[15]

He is not, on the other hand, obliged to apply the Mass for the people (Can. 446) prescribed for rectors of true parishes, since the missionary has no territory of his own distinct and separate from that of the parish, nor has he exclusive powers.

The power which the missionary possesses is personal and cumulative with that of the pastor of the territory,[16] just as that possessed by the rectors of the parishes for different language and nationality groups is personal and cumulative with that of the Ordinary and the pastor of the locality.

From this derives the wise regulation according to which the missionary, who is expressly obliged to keep the parish books discussed in Canon 470, must, at the end of the year, send a copy to the local parish priest and another to the Director of the Missionaries.[17]

It is self-evident that what has been said concerning the Missionary cannot apply to the Chaplain on Board. The faculties which the latter has in the exercise of his functions may be summarized thus:

a) Those which the common law accords to priests making an ocean journey.

b) Those necessary for the exercise of the care of souls, except in matrimonial matters.[18]

c) Those which pertain to a rector of the church, if there exists a legitimately established oratory on board ship.[19]

d) Those other faculties which, envisioned in the *Exsul Familia*,[20] are contained in the *"Norms and Faculties for priests concerned with the spiritual care of seafarers,* namely, for Chaplains on Board and for the Directors of Chaplains issued on March 19, 1954."

The Consistorial Congregation confers such faculties on

each Chaplain individually by handing over a summary specifically prepared.

The Chaplain on Board is also bound to keep records of those baptised, confirmed, and of the dead, and at the end of the voyage must submit an extract of them to the Director.[21]

With regard to the custody of these books, and the obligation to send authentic copies to the Curia, the Sacred Consistorial Congregation has established procedures as follows:

a) An authentic copy of the books of those baptised, those confirmed and of the dead must be transmitted to the Curia of the diocese where the office of the Director is situated.

b) It pertains solely to the Director of the Chaplains on board, as prescribed in the above-mentioned *Norms and Faculties*:[22]

1) to transmit the copies of the above-mentioned books to the Curia;

2) to send to the Consistorial Congregation and to the Ordinary of the above-mentioned Curia the list of those confirmed on board by the chaplain;

3) to communicate to the priest of the parish in which the persons interested are domiciled the acts registered at the diocesan Curias;

4) to keep the originals in his own archives;

5) to grant testimonials furnished with their own seals.

It is also the duty of the Director of the Chaplains on Board to obtain from the Consistorial Congregation an apostolic indult so that the Holy Eucharist may be kept in the ship's oratory, [23] once this has been legitimately established by the Ordinary in whose territory the boat's home port is situated. [24]

The Directors of both Missionaries to the Migrants and the Chaplains on Board have neither territorial nor personal jurisdiction.[25] However, it is the chief duty of the Director to deal with Bishops, present the Missionaries to them, etc.

It is likewise a function of the Director to direct, watch over, convoke and assist the Missionaries, and to give a report of them at the end of the year to the Sacred Consistorial Congregation, together with the report on the state of the missions.

In other words, the office of the Director may be said to be analogous to that of a Vicar Forane, in conformity with the norms of the common law.

Every nation, according to the norms of the *Exsul Familia,* has or may have its National Director on behalf of emigration. His appointment is made by of the Holy See, on the presentation of the Bishops who generally nominate the Secretary of the Episcopal Commission for Emigration. The establishment of such a commission in every nation is strongly urged by the Sovereign Pontiff.[26]

The activity in which the Director must engage varies according to whether the country in question is one of immigration, or emigration, or of both, in some degree, since internal migration may often be accompanied by immigration from abroad.

In either case the main duty of the National Director may be summed up thus: he must be the constant and working expression of the bishops' zeal in developing and carrying on the work of spiritual assistance to migrants, according to the norms urged by the Holy See.

In order to obtain fuller collaboration between the Consistorial Congregation and the bishops, the Holy Father established under this Congregation a Supreme Office of Migration. It is presided over by the highest prelate of that Congregation, and has as secretary the Delegate for Migration Institutions and as membership, first of all, the Secretaries of the above-mentioned Episcopal Commissions.

Another organization which the *Exsul Familia* established under the Consistorial is the International General Secretariate of the Apostolate of the Sea. Originating in Glasgow in Scotland in 1920, through the zeal of good men who were preoccupied by the truly serious spiritual conditions of so many seamen, and especially of those employed on merchant ships and on the long voyages of the fishing-boats, this form of apostolate among sailors of every category is less well-known than it should be.

In Italy too the spiritual well-being of these workers has been given particular consideration. His Holiness has offered to sea-faring Italians the comfort of Saint Francis of Paula as their patron.

Spreading rapidly and silently in the main ports of the world, the Apostolate of the Sea very soon became worthy of the consideration of the Vicar of Christ. In 1922 Pius XI approved it. In 1942 the Holy Father confided its supreme direction to the Consistorial, and in the following October conceded that the General International Secretariate should have its own office in the Papal Building of Saint Apollinaris.

The houses of the Apostolate of the Sea are all dedicated to the Star of the Sea, for whom they are generally named. It would be difficult to give a complete set of statistics regarding them. Particularly flourishing among the clubs open to seamen are those in the United States of America, in Canada, Australia, New Zealand, France, Great Britain, Italy, Spain, Holland, Ireland, Germany, Belgium and Portugal. The missionary centers are scattered everywhere—from Africa to India, from Central and South America to the Pacific Islands. Among the most recently established centers, that in Antwerp, in which one part is reserved exclusively for sailors from the Congo, and that in Rotterdam, are particularly fine. Another is being set up in Hamburg, and yet another at Genoa, through the zeal of the Archbishop Cardinal of that city. A Club has very recently been inaugurated at Bilbao.

A last word is reserved for the office of the Delegate for Migration, to whom the *Exsul Familia* dedicates an entire chapter. He is the representative through whom the Sacred Consistorial Congregation works in all possible ways to promote the spiritual good of all the migrants—taking the word in its broadest sense—and of all the seamen. He is in constant touch with His Holiness' Secretary of State, with the international, national, diocesan and parish Catholic works, as well as with the civil authorities and organizations, steamship companies, and so on.

As regards his relationship with the clergy, he presides over the activity of the Migrants' Missionaries, the Chaplains on Board and the Apostolate of the Sea, and over their respective directors. Part of his function is also to determine the qualifications of those priests who wish to dedicate themselves to these ministries, and finally he is personally in charge of the celebration of the "World Emigrants' Day."

CHAPTER VIII

HIS HOLINESS PIUS XII: DEFENDER OF THE NATURAL RIGHT OF MAN TO MIGRATE

ONE final point must be included in the discussion of Pius XII's ardent and unceasing efforts to solve the urgent problems of migration: his work as the supreme defender of the inviolable natural right of man and his family to migration, and as the supreme lawgiver in matters regarding the exercise of that right.

For the purposes of this essay the word migration will be taken in its broadest sense. It will be seen to comprise two kinds of migration: that is, "forced migration" and "natural migration."

"Forced migration" includes the migration of all those who are expelled, deported, exiled or constrained in any way to flee their native countries.

Various causes may be assigned for this class of migration: the ambition of nations, the disgraceful tyranny of racism, political conflicts, religious persecution, and above all others, the destructive power and barbarism of war. Powerless before these forces, the exile and the refugee are forced to abandon their native countries, their homes, belongings, wealth, and perhaps even their families and dearest kin. They must flee their own countries and wander over the world, often penniless and without a settled goal.

In our days "natural migration" is not actually free

migration, and therefore we cannot term it so. More often than not, though the migrant freely chooses and arranges in advance the move, he migrates only as the last resource, in the face of destitution.

As has been pointed out in Chapter VI, Pius XII was forced to deal with the first (also called "refugee migration") from the very beginning of his pontificate, when the skies of peaceable human co-habitation were already darkened by menacing portents of a fearful tempest. The problem became increasingly urgent during and immediately after the tremendous world conflict.

The Pope has never ceased to attend to "natural migration," according to the need. He has used both word and deed in his work with migrants of either class. He has been the provident father and defender of the weak, the tireless administrator of charity and defender of justice, a haven for the impoverished and the orphaned, and teacher of the laws which enshrine human rights. He has marked out for man the paths of secure temporal well-being, and has been a watchful custodian of his spiritual welfare. He has interpreted the law given by God to human society, and has championed true peace among men and nations.

Hence, Pius XII is an impressive figure in the field of migration, and he remains so even if our view is limited to his teachings. The precepts which he offered to the world had never before been presented so fully.

These precious teachings are based on an open recognition in the *Exsul Familia* that it is the Church's duty to intervene in the matter of migration: "The Catholic Church feels itself under high obligation to interest itself in the work of migration. A remedy must be found for an immense need. . . . The Church becomes more and more sensitive to this dire distress as its effects strike at a growing number of her own children." [1]

The Apostolic Constitution is rich in passages drawn from allocutions, letters and radio messages in which the Pope has repeatedly urged the bishops, priests, national and international institutions, and the governments, too, to devote themselves to the refugee problem. He has called for "open doors" within which the war victim in his lamentable and uncertain plight may find welcome and assistance. As examples we may cite the Letter to the Bishops of Germany (December 20, 1948),[2] the Encyclical *Redemptoris Nostri* (Apirl 15, 1949),[3] the Letter to the Chairman of the National Catholic Welfare Conference (December 24, 1948) [4] and the Letter in his own hand to the Bishops of Australia (April 28, 1951).[5] In the last two documents the Pope expresses his gratitude for a prompt and generous response to his appeals.

Let us now consider his specific teaching as Pontiff. The Pope reminds us that he has severely condemned "the principles of totalitarianism, of State imperialism and the irrational nationalism of those who, arbitrarily restricting the natural right of men to migration and pacific colonization on the one hand, while on the other, they force entire populations to leave their lands, deporting the inhabitants and barbarously uprooting citizens from their families, from their homes, from their birth-places." [6] This is one of the first and very fundamental pronouncements.

What action did Pius XII take, in his defense of man's inalienable rights against the violations inflicted upon them by the principles which we have already condemned?

First of all, concerning man's natural right to migration, Pius XII undertook the defense without regard to race or religion, speaking alike for Hebrews, Arabs and Japanese.[7] Usually, his was a solitary voice. In radio messages and by other means he repeatedly called to the world's attention "the misery of the refugees and exiles who, uprooted and disoriented, were forced by the millions to renounce their native lands and to seek distant lands in which to create a new home for themselves."[8] And those "who are obliged to live a life of exile in concentration camps, exposed to contagious diseases and to dangers of every kind,"[9] these suffer an even worse fate.

In no uncertain terms, he proclaimed that it was unlawful to allow the nefarious circumstances in which the refugees found themselves to be protracted, and he called upon the sense of justice to bring them to an end: "We cry aloud to those whose responsibility it is, that justice be done for all who have been driven from their dwelling places by war's fury, and who long for nothing more earnestly than for the possibility of resuming their tranquil life of before."[10]

In cases where justice alone would not serve to resolve the refugee problem, in truth one of the gravest which has tormented Europe, Pius XII suggested recourse to charity: "harmonizing the requirements of justice with charitable motivations, for, to many of the injustices that reveal themselves in social relations, charity may bring some relief." However, he adds immediately ". . . that is not enough. It is a prime requisite that justice be in force, be observed and truly practiced."[11]

The Pope described another postulate essential for social justice in these words: "Man, such as God wills him and the Church embraces him, will never feel himself firmly established in space and time without a fixed abode and without traditions."

In this, incidentally, may be recognized one of the Church's reasons for "attempting in every way to integrate the religious life with the customs of the country, showing its particular solicitude to those whom migration or military service detains far from their homeland." [12] "Now experience teaches," said Pius XII on August 6, 1952, to the Missionaries for Italian migrants in Europe, "that man, uprooted from his own land and transplanted into foreign soil, loses not a little of his sense of security, of—one might almost say—his human dignity. On the affective side this disorientation strikes at and enervates his most inward spiritual emotions, and his religious life itself. He needs time and persevering effort in order to settle himself in new and very different circumstances, and, as it were, put down roots for his Catholic Faith, restoring it to its normal vitality...." [13]

"Stability of dwelling place," continues Pius XII, "and attachment to ancestral traditions, elements indispensable to the healthy integrity of the individual, are also fundamental to the human community." [14]

This was the mind of Pius XII when he addressed the members of the Diplomatic Corps accredited to the Holy See, in the Solemn Audience of February 25, 1946. He spoke for millions when he expressed the hope that, in working out the means of achieving a just and secure peace, early consideration should be given to permitting exiles and refugees to return to their home: [15] "Now, at a moment when millions of honest and hardworking men are impatiently longing for the moment of returning to their homelands, to their families, from whom they may have been separated for many long years; when others are wearily seeking a new homeland where they will live a new life amid new concerns, what a work of charity and peace is accomplished in coming to their aid!" [16]

What should be the foundation of such work, and who should be responsible for the administration of the justice he had invoked, Pius XII did not omit to specify when he spoke to the group of United States Senators who had been assigned to European refugee problems. Dwelling on "another authoritative observation" revealed to him through the "sacred trust confided" to his care, he urged that they "discharge that grave duty incumbent upon individuals and nations alike, which imposes respect for the image of God that is reflected in even the weakest and most forlorn of His children." [17]

What has been described to this point by no means concludes the activity of the Church on behalf of the victims of "forced migration," under the Sovereign Pontiff. In some respects the image of the exile or the refugee is inseparable from that of the migrant. A large part of the following, concerning "natural migration," must therefore be duly applied or extended to include the refugee and the exile.

The Pope has specified what shall be the fundamental purpose of "natural migration:" that is, "the most favorable disposition of men over the earth's surface, grouped about agricultural colonies." [18]

The most immediate causes of migration may in fact be recognized as "lack of space" and "lack of means of subsistence; as the old country cannot nourish all her children, and overpopulation forces some to migrate."[19]

In Pius XII's unequivocal words, the paths of migration *must* be opened for those who are "forced by unemployment and hunger to migrate,[20] not only in charity towards human kind, but in recognition of "a law based on the very nature of the earth which men inhabit." [21] The same Pontiff adduces further reasons why this obligation must bind all men when, speaking of the surface of the earth, he affirms that it is "a surface which God created and prepared for the use of all," [22] and when, treating of the purpose of every created thing he writes: "the goods created by God for all must belong to all, in accordance with the principles of justice and charity." [23] Again: "The Creator of the Universe, in fact, created all things in the first place for the use of all." [24]

With these expressions Pius XII reaffirms the principles already propounded by Leo XIII in *Rerum Novarum*. Treating of the common use of private goods and individual owership of the same, *Rerum Novarum* records that "God has given the earth for the use and enjoyment of all mankind," and that "the earth, though divided among private persons, nonetheless remains for the service and benefit of all, there being no man in the world who does not receive his sustenance from it. Whoever has no goods of his own substitutes with work so that it may be truthfully affirmed that the universal means of providing for a livelihood is work. A man may be employed by others, or may cultivate his own land, or he may practice a craft, but the recompense for all work, in the end, derives from the multiple fruits of the earth and is computed in terms of the same."[25]

Afterwards referring to the community of the blessings of nature and of grace, the same immortal Leo XIII affirmed that "all the classes, obeying the evangelical law, know and sense that the blessings of nature and of grace are the common patrimony of mankind." [26]

What, then, is the doctrine of the Church with regard to emigration of the family, which God has willed to be the first natural society?

Leo XIII recognized that the family has a right equivalent to that of the State: "Within the limits determined by its ends, the family has equal rights in the choice and the employment of means necessary to its preservation and legitimate independence." [27] It must be concluded that this applies in the matter of migration also.

Pius XII clearly corroborates this principle. In the radio message given on June 1, 1941, the 50th anniversary of *Rerum Novarum,* may be read: "Though our planet has vast expanses of ocean, sea and lake, though it has mountains and plains covered with eternal snow and ice, and great deserts and inhospitable and sterile lands, there are none the less many life-supporting regions which, though well suited to cultivation by the hand of man, and sufficient to his activities and civic requirements, are left to the vegetative caprices of nature. It is inevitable that families, migrating from here and there, should seek a new homeland in other places. According to the precepts given in *Rerum Novarum,* the right of a family to living space must be respected. Where precepts are adhered to, migration will achieve that natural end which is often confirmed by experience: that is, the most favorable distribution of men, grouped around agricultural colonies, over the earth's surface which God created and prepared for the use of all." [28]

In like manner Pius XII has proclaimed before scholars of Christian social doctrine: "It is necessary to observe carefully, in all its amplitude, the duty of giving to countless human families in their natural, moral, juridical and economic unity, a just living space which may correspond in sufficient, even if in modest manner, to the requirements of man's dignity." [29]

Young married people must not be impeded in any way

when, "seeking to free themselves from the limitations that restrict their growth in the homeland, they find no other remedy than migration. At other times migration is a result of that pressing need to earn a livelihood, which today's misery so often imposes." [30]

Finally, "the intelligent promotion of the migration of the family; of its migration to regions capable of providing its members with what is necessary," is infinitely preferable to the enormous expenditures made in helping refugees.[31]

But human society is not built upon the relationship between individual and family alone. There is a society which is broader than the family: the state. In our time especially, because of materialistic doctrines, the state unfortunately disclaims recognition of man's rights in the matter of migration as in other matters.

However, it cannot be gainsaid that the State must seek the common good in preference to the individual good.

The norms dictated by the supreme ecclesiastical Magisterium are of enormous interest and immediate practicability. They appear even so when it is remembered that the Pope also affirmed that "in this matter one must be concerned not only with the interests of the immigrants but also with the good of the country." Hence, it is not to be wondered at when a State, under certain justifiable circumstances, places restrictions on the immigration of foreigners. [32]

It is self-evident that the principles enunciated by Pius XII do not apply indiscriminately to every State: they require that the condition of the State be considered, in order to establish whether a country may be classed as one of emigration, or of immigration. But there is a fundamental precept applicable to all States: It is their bounden duty to recognize the natural laws established by God. From this springs the other universal duty of "eliminating whatever may impede the birth and growth of a reciprocal trust between the country of emigration and the country of immigration."[33]

The State must carefully avoid proceeding in such a manner that "the natural right of the person not to be impeded in his emigration or immigration" is either "not recognized or practically annulled, on the pretext of a common good falsely interpreted or falsely applied."[34]

No reason of state, no collective advantage, may justify the violation of that human dignity and the denial of those elementary human rights, with which the Creator has stamped the soul of every one of His creatures.[35]

The state may not exaggerate its proper dominion and thereby, for insufficient motives and unjust reasons, prevent needy and honest foreigners from entering. The dictates of public utility must be subjected to the most careful scrutiny.[36]

Such restrictive laws as may eventually seem necessary, exhorts Pius XII, should be applied with the maximum latitude, and in their formation Christian charity and human solidarity must not be forgotten.[37]

The Pope has also noted the factors which should be considered in determining a liberal migration policy: the country's natural resources on the one hand, and the needs of men in other countries, on the other. "Is the present immigration policy, in a country so abundantly blessed by the Creator, as liberal as the complex of natural resources seems to permit, and as liberal as the imperious needs of other countries appears to require?"[38]

From this there follows naturally an invitation to nations rich in territory and sparsely populated, to open their frontiers for the many who tread upon each other's heels in overpopulated lands.[39]

From this also follows the exhortation: "As broad and expansive as are your fields and lands, so great and open may your hearts be, to receive those who wish to find among you a new homeland where they may live honestly in the company of their own dear ones."[40] And again: "the immensity of the territory will be a blessing if and in so far as it shall become the happy dwelling place of an ever growing number of physically and morally healthy families."[41]

The State, finally, cannot: a) arbitrarily restrict the natural right of man to migration[42] and to peaceful colonization;[43] b) deny the right of asylum to those who for grave reasons wish to fix their residence elsewhere;[44] c) constrain entire populations to leave their lands;[45] d) impose forced repatriation.[46]

What are the advantages of an ideal form of migration? These too Pius XII has pointed out to human society. It may be remarked first of all that migration is a means of securing a just and lasting peace. If the mutual communications between peoples are facilitated, the poverty-stricken, unable to find the necessities of life in their native countries, may migrate to other countries.[47]

As a result of this the burden will be lifted from densely populated lands; families will receive land which will serve as their homeland in the true sense of the word; peoples will create new friends in foreign territories; human well-being and human culture will benefit by it.[48]

The Pope has stated that to bring about such advantages is "a merit on the part of both the State which gives, and the State which receives."[49]

Why then, could not some international legislation be

evolved to regulate migration? The world must know that this is a proposal springing from the great heart of Pius XII, a proposal offered at a time which he recognized as "extraordinarily opportune for achieving some form of international regulation in the matter of migration":[50] a proposal made with the highest sense of responsibility and with the most far-reaching beneficent intent.

CLARIFICATION OF THE CONSISTORIAL CONGREGATION ON THE DUTIES OF THE MISSIONARIES TO MIGRANTS

IN order to prevent doubts concering the duties of the Missionaries to Emigrants, which are dealt with in Chapter 4 of the Apostolic Constitution *Exsul Familia*, and in order to establish uniformity in the way of acting, the Consistorial Congregation declares:

1. Concerning the administration of the Sacrament of Confirmation: In accordance with the Decree of the Sacred Congregation of the Sacraments *Spiritus Sancti munera* of September 14, 1946 (*AAS*, XXXVIII, 349), Missionaries of Emigrants to whom, in accordance with Nos. 34-40 of the Apostolic Constitution *Exsul Familia*, the local ordinaries entrusted with the care of souls in thier own dioceses, have the power to administer the Sacrament of Confirmation to their subjects who are at the point of death.

Pius XII, in an audience granted on August 31, 1953, graciously ratified this declaration.

2. Concerning witnessing at marriages: a) In accordance with the Constitution *Exsul Familia*, No. 39, the Missionary of Emigrants to whom the care of souls has been entrusted, all other requirements of law being observed, can, within the limits of the territory entrusted to him, validly assist at marriages if one or the other of the contracting parties is his

subject; b) as regards licit assistance, the prescription of Canon 1097, 2, must be kept, according to which "In any case it shall be the rule that the marriage is to be contracted before the pastor of the bride-to-be unless a just reason excuses therefrom."; c) in regard to the investigations of the status of the contracting parties the Instruction of the Congregation of the Sacraments *De normis a Parocho servandis in peragendis . . ."* issued on June 29, 1941, particularly what is prescribed in Nos. 4 and 10 (*AAS*, XXXIII, 297-307) must be scrupulously observed.

Given at Rome, from the Office of the Sacred Consistorial Congregation, October 7, 1953.

A. J. CARD. PIAZZA, *Bishop of Sabina and Poggio Mirteto, Secretary*

JOSEPH FERRETTO, *Assessor*

COMMENTARY ON THE CLARIFICATION OF THE CONSISTORIAL CONGREGATION

AFTER publication of the Apostolic Constitution, *Exsul Famila,* which concerns the spiritual care of the souls of emigrants, by virtue of the norm of the Decree *Spiritus Sancti munera* (*AAS*, XXXVIII, 349-54) because of the principle of the common law, a doubt was raised whether one could maintain that the missionary of the emigrants, to whom was committed the promulgated care, enjoys the faculty of administering the Sacrament of Confirmation to his faithful, in the cases and under the conditions stated in the same Decree.

In order that a more suitable answer may be given to this doubt, it is necessary, first of all, to consider whether in such case the conditions which are required by the aforementioned Decree exist in the priest. That Decree asserts: "By general indult of the Apostolic See, the faculty to confer the Sacrament of Confirmation on extraordinary ministers (Canon 782, 2) is given only to the following priests: a) to pastors with territorial jurisdiction; hence the personal pastor and family pastors are excluded unless they also have territorial cumulative jurisdiction." Certainly, personal or family pastors are not granted the faculty of administering confirmation *unless they also enjoy their own territory, even if cumulative.*

Pastors, constituted because of the diversity of language or nationality, are usually given the same rights as personal pastors or family pastors, concerning whom see Canon 216, 4. By virtue of the Apostolic Constitution, *Exsul Familia,* Title 2, Article 35, 1, the missionaries of emigrants, to whom the care of souls is entrusted by the Ordinaries of the places, are given the rights of personal and family pastors.

In order that you may well understand, however, whether or not the faculty of administering Confirmation to the faithful be within the capacity of these missionaries by virtue of the same Decree, it is necessary to consider whether in addition to personal jurisdiction, which is dealt with in Article 36 of the Apostolic Constitution, they may also enjoy a territorial jurisdiction even though it may be cumulative with that of the pastor of the place, and therefore does not belong exclusively to the missionaries themselves, as stated in 2 of the same Article.

Everybody knows that the jurisdiction of family pastors, personal pastors, as well as that of the pastors of faithful of different language or nationality may be exercised in behalf of the subjects in every place in which the subjects happen to have domicile or quasi-domicile; so that we have true and distinct parishes with a true rector in care of souls, whose capacity is determined by reason of persons. Such are family or *gens*, personal or national parishes; the first established in behalf of persons belonging to a certain family; the second, in behalf of persons belonging to a certain category, i.e., army; the third, in behalf of persons of the same language or nationality living in the same city or territory.

Sometimes these parishes have no territorial boundaries at all; sometimes, they exist, instead, enclosed within the boundaries of a peculiar territory already governed by its own pastor. In the first instance, jurisdiction is simply personal, restricted by no territory, reaching persons wherever they may sojourn; in the second instance, jurisdiction is territorial according to the general norm in the constitutive organization of the Church, by virtue of which ordinary jurisdiction is limited by territorial competence, reaching only the persons within the limits of that territory.

Also, we should not forget that jurisdiction may be either exclusive or privative, that is, reserved only to family pastors, or cumulative with that of the pastor of the place, in such a way that the faithful may consider themselves subject both to the personal pastor (for instance a military chaplain) and to the national pastor or to the pastor of the place. Consequently, when the missionaries of the emigrants enjoy jurisdiction, not only personal but also territorial, though cumulative with that of the pastor of the place, which is what we have in the present case according to the above mentioned 2 of Article 36, by virtue of the same Decree and by the principle of the common law they have the power of administering Confirmation to their subjects. If this should not be the case therefore, such faculty must be sought through an Apostolic Indult, since one does not have it by law.

In order to solve clearly the proposed question, it will be useful to bear in mind the following: the Consistorial Congregation, in granting permission to erect "a mission in care of souls" on account of difference of language or nationality according to Article 36 of the Apostolic Constitution *Exsul Familia,* adds usually the clause "the boundaries being accurately indicated." From these words, we may doubtlessly conclude that a mission with the care of souls enjoys its own, though cumulative, territory.

It is clear, then, that it is necessary to give an affirmative answer to the proposed doubt, and this answer Pius XII also condescended to confirm and ordered it to be promulgated as decreed in the Declaration of October 7, 1953.

Another doubt was also proposed to the Consistorial Congregation, to wit, which opinion is to be followed concerning the faculty to assist at the celebration of a marriage according to Articles 34, 35, 36 of the Apostolic Constitution, *Exsul Familia*, granted to the above mentioned missionary in behalf of the subjects of the same language or nationality.

In order to answer, it is necessary to consider some specific points. The Decree *Ne Temere* of August 2, 1907, issued by the Congregation of the Council, almost entirely integrated into the Code of Canon Law (Canon 1094, ff.) changed completely the canonical form of marriage. In fact, since the reason of domicile or quasi-domicile of the parties is no longer in force, the pastor and the Ordinary of the place assist validly at marriages of the faithful, at least within the limits of their territory, whether these faithful on account of their domicile or quasi-domicile be their subjects or not. It is within the limits of their territory that they can assist validly at marriages not only of their own subjects, but also of persons who are not their subjects." (Canon 1095, 1, 2⁰).

Undoubtedly, this may be applied also to the missionary of emigrants who has care of souls within the limits of the territory prescribed to him, by virtue of the general reason manifested in the words which make clear the mind of the law-giver promulgating the Apostolic Constitution, *Exsul Familia*.

In fact, after stating that the Supreme Pontiff was entreated many times, "that a new plan of action be decreed according to which the spiritual care of the aliens could be provided with the diocesan set-up," the following is added: "These pleas agree clearly with our feeling; we strongly desired to be afforded an opportune occasion, on which we could provide each Ordinary with suitable norms not discordant, but on the contrary, consonant with the spirit and practice of Canon Law." (*AAS*, XLIV, 692.)

Prompted by these reasons, the lawgiver intends to confer such faculty so that any Ordinary may offer to aliens, whether they have quasi-domicile (*advenae*) or no domicile at all (*peregrini*), spiritual care and assistance neither unequal or inferior to that which the other faithful of his diocese enjoy.

Hence, jurisdiction on the persons of the emigrants and the faculty of assisting at their marriages, which the Apostolic Constitution (Article 39) grants to the missionary of the emigrants, rest upon the same reason, that is territorial, and are upheld by the same general norms, as that of the pastors, properly called, making due allowances. From what we said so far, we may gather that the missionary of emigrants can validly assist at marriages, at least within the limits of the territory prescribed for him by the Ordinary of the place.

We said and stress the words, *making due allowances. In* fact, if somebody should inquire whether all the faithful wishing to contract marriage may indiscriminately approach the missionary of emigrants, it is easy to answer that only those who are subjects of the missionary on account of their language or nationality may do so. Indeed, the Apostolic Constitution, *Exsul Familia* uses these words explicitly, leaving absolutely no doubt: "any alien, whether he has quasi-domicile (*advena*) or no domicile (*peregrinus*), has an unrestricted right to approach the missionary of emigrants of his same language or the pastor of the place concerning Sacraments, matrimony included." (Article 39)

Now recall Cannon 91: "A person is called an *advena* in the place where he has a quas-domicile and a *peregrinus* while he is actually outside the place of his domicile or quasi-domicile which he still keeps."

The emigrants, though they may not have a domicile or quasi-domicile in the territory entrusted to the missionary of the emigrants, may approach the missionary of their own language or nationality in the same way that they may approach the pastor of the place in order to receive the Sacraments, matrimony not excepted; and both the pastor and the missionary may administer the Sacraments to the emigrants since their jurisdiction is cumulative.

To these considerations we must add: "Under the terms *advena* or *peregrinus* for our present purposes are included: all aliens—not excluding those who migrated from the colonies—who are in a foreign land for whatever length of time or whatever reason, including study." (Article 40). By these words, it is evident that there is no further mention of domicile or quasi-domicile, whereas in order to acquire either, according to the norm of Canon 92, *C.I.C.*, it is necessary that the residence be associated with the intention of staying there permanently or to stay there for the greater part of the year or for more than ten years or by actually having lived there for the greater part of the year.

No doubt, therefore, remains that the missionary of emigrants, to whom the care of souls has been entrusted with the same right as that of the pastor of the place (Article 36, 2), may assist at marriages of the faithful of his own language or nationality, at least within the limits of the territory entrusted to him, whether the parties wishing to contract marriages are subjects of the pastor of the place on account of their domicile or quasi-domicile in the parish or are not because they have no domicile or quasi-domicile there.

Validity of marriage, then, is upheld, even though only one of the parties on account of the language or nationality is a subject of the missionary, without prejudice to the prescription of 2 of Canon 1097 concerning its licitness: "In every case is shall be the rule that the marriage be contracted before the pastor of the bride-to-be, unless a just reason excuses therefrom."

After all these clarifications, the Sacred Consistorial Congregation sought to provide for the good of the Sacrament by warning the "missionaries" who are concerned, to take, scrupulously, all the cautions which the discipline in force set up in such a serious matter, advising them to bear in mind the Instruction of the Congregation of the Sacraments: *"Norms to be Observed by the Pastor in Conducting the Canonical Investigations before Admitting the Parties to the Celebration of Marriage."* (Canon 1020), published on June 29, 1941. (*A.A.S.*, XXXIII, 297-307). It is necessary that they be very careful about those points that must be most specially noted concerning the elements of investigations (n.4), and which the priest ought to learn well before assisting at marriage in order that the marriage may not be null because of the nonobservance of the canonical form (n. 10).

JOSEPH FERRETTO

REFERENCES

CHAPTER I

1. *AAS*, XLIV, 692.
2. *Ibid.*, 702.
3. *Romans* 8:29.
4. *Hebrews* 2:17.
5. Hymn at Matins, Holy Family Sunday.
6. St. Augustine, Epistle 228, 8: Migne, *PL*, XXXIII, 1016 ff.
7. XLIV, 654-658.
8. *Ibid.*, 652.
9. *Ibid.*, 691.
10. For the historical part cf.: Ferretto, Giuseppe, "The Apostolic Constitution *Exsul Familia*," part I, in *The American Ecclesiastical Review*, volume CXXX, 73-83.
11. *De officiis ministrorum*, II, 136-137: *PL*, XVI, 148.
12. Mansi, *Sacrorum Conciliorum nova et amplissima collectio*, (Venice, 1778), XXII, 998.
13. *AAS*, XLIV, 658-659.

CHAPTER II

1. Circular Letter of March 26, 1924, prot. 809/20 "...The S.C.C. assumes the direction of this work and Institute."
2. Sacred Consitorial Congregation, *Audience of His Holiness*, February 20, 1914, No. 2283/13.
3. As of January 1, 1962 the Pious Society numbers 727 Religious, of whom 484 are priests. The novices are 46, aspirants 700. The Society has 9 religious provinces in 13 countries with 184 residences. (Editor's note.)
4. Sacred Consistorial Congregation, Audience of His Holiness January 22, 1949, No. 48/49, article 53 of the *Exsul Familia*, *AAS*, XLIV, 703.

CHAPTER III

1. *Titulo altero*, chapter 3, *AAS*, XLIV, 698-699.
2. Article 56, *AAS*, XLIV, 703-704.
3. Sacred Consistorial Congregation, General Congregation, June 13, 1912, No. 503/12.
4. General Congregation of February 19, 1914: Audience of His Holiness, February 20, 1914, No. 2283/13.
5. *Ibid.*
6. *Motu Proprio, Cum omnes Catholicos*, *AAS*, IV, 526.

7. Decree *Magni semper negotii*, I., AAS, XI, 40.
8. AAS, XXX, 154-159.
9. Audience of His Holiness June 21, 1947, No. 106/32.
10. General Congregation of February 19, 1914: Audience of His Holiness, February 20, 1914, No. 2283/13.

CHAPTER IV

1. AAS, VI, 700: Circular Letter to the Most Reverend Ordinaries of Italy, Concerning the Spiritual Care of Emigrants.
2. Sacred Consistorial Congregation: Circular Letter to the Most Reverend Ordinaries of Italy concerning the Spiriual Care of Emigrants: *Sorrow and Trials*, AAS, VI, 699-701:
"To provide for the needs of this college and of the many institutions which have been established for the purpose of assisting Italians emigrating abroad, both to Europe and across the Ocean, and to care for their religious and moral good amid the immense dangers in which they find themselves, this Sacred Congregation, in execution of the orders of the Sovereign Pontiff:
1. Invites the Most Reverend Ordinaries of Italy to take up, in all the parishes of their respective dioceses an annual collection for the work of assistance to emigrant Italians."
3. *Exsul Familia, Tit. Alt.*, 49, Paragraph 2, AAS, XLIV.

CHAPTER V

1. AAS, XLIV, 670-671.
2. AAS, XLIV, 670-671.
3. AAS, XV, 112-113. The motive which pressed Pius XI to prescribe the emigrant's ecclesiastical identity card is evident; namely, the spiritual benefit which the holder may derive from it, in the defense of his faith. In some respects, it may be related to the norm issued with the same purpose by Clement VIII (July 26, 1596): "When, then, Italians leave Italy in order to sojourn or to settle in the aforesaid places (cities, towns or sections where there is no church with a pastor, or priest in charge, or even just a priest) they should notify their Bishops or inquisitors."

CHAPTER VI

1. St. Ignatius of Antioch, *Epistle to the Romans*: Migne, PG. V, 685.
2. 2 *Cor.* 11:29.
3. AAS, XLIV, 687.
4. *Ibid.* 675.
5 *Ibid.* 679.
6. *Ibid.* 688-689.
7. *Acts of the Apostles*, 12:5.
8. *Ibid.* 12:11.

CHAPTER VII

1. For this section cf.: Ferretto, Iosephus, '*In Constitutionem Apostolicam "Exsul Familia" animadversiones*' in *Monitor Ecclesiasticus*, LXXVIII, 7-22;

and by the same, 'The Apostolic Constitution *Exsul Familia;* part II,' in *The American Ecclesiastical Review,* CXXX, 146-162.

2. *AAS,* XXXXVI, 249, 4: "With due reference to the particular position of each one, the same norms as those prescribed by the Apostolic Constitution *Exsul Familia,* in Title Two, Chapter 3, for the maritime chaplains and their directors, hold good for the chaplains appointed either as Chaplains or as Directors of the Apostolate of the Sea Associations." cf. *Ibid.,* the *Norms and Faculties,* published April 2, 1954.

3. *AAS,* XLIV, 679, article 18, paragraph 2.

4. *Ibid.,* 700, article 33.

5. *Ibid.,* 774, no. 2.

6. *Ibid.,* 669-670, article 32.

7. "Only the Sacred Consistorial Congregation can grant an apostolic indult according to the Norm laid down in Canon 216, 4 of the Code of Canon Law, enabling parishes to be erected for the convenience of emigrants of different languages and nationalities." *Ibid.,* 694, article 4.

8. *"Audita Sacra Congregatione Consistoriali:"* *Ibid.,* 700, article 34.

9. *Ibid.,* 700, article 37.

10. *"presse circumscriptis eiusdem Missionis finibus"* are the words used by the Sacred Consistorial Congregation in every rescript concerning the erection of a national Mission with the care of souls—the same that are used in the rescript for the erection of a national parish.

11. *Ibid.,* 700, article 39.

12. *Ibid.,* XXXXV, 748; see the "Adnotationes" edited by Iosephus Ferretto in *Monitor Eccesiasticus,* LXXIX, 215-219.

13. *Ibid.* XXXVIII, 349.

14. *Ibid.* XXXIII, 297-307.

15. For greater clarity we give here in their entirety the following resolutions given by the Sacred Consistorial Congregation (Prot. no. 778/53), regarding certain questions, on March 27, 1954.

1. Whether when these boundary lines have been disregarded which have been assigned by the local Ordinaries in the erection of missions with the care of the souls of the faithful Christian emigrants of different languages and nationalities, the missionary with the care of the souls of the emigrants may validly witness marriages of the faithful of the same nationality or language, who, by domicile or quasi-domicile, are not subject to him.

ANSWER: Affirmative, of course, at least within the boundaries of the missions erected accurately by the Bishop.

2. Whether the Bishop of a diocese where there are many foreigners or emigrants of different language or nationality, who are habitually visited by the Missionaries of the emigrants of the same language or nationality staying in another diocese, may grant to such missionaries in his own territory all the faculties they enjoy in the other diocese. And in so far as it is affirmative, whether the Bishop may use this formula:

"The Missionaries to whom the spiritual care of people of different language or nationality has been entrusted, in missions erected canonically in the diocese of . . . may enjoy the same faculties and powers in our own diocese as they enjoy in the diocese of . . ."

ANSWER: Affirmative to both.

3. Whether the Missionary of the emigrants who, since he has the care of their souls and is equal to a pastor, is obliged to apply a Mass for the people according to the norm of the common law.

ANSWER: Negative.

4. Whether in the case in which a Missionary with the care of souls should be absent from the diocese, or should cease from taking part in his duties because of illness, may generally delegate to an assistant priest the power of blessing marriages of his subjects. And in so far as it is affirmative, whether this faculty may be subdelegated.

ANSWER: To the first, affirmative; to the second, affirmative, but only in individual cases.

16. *AAS*, XLIV, 700, article 36.

17. *Ibid.*, 700, article 35, 2.

18. *AAS*, XLIV, 698, article 25, 1.

19. *Ibid.*, 698, article 25. The Sacred Consistorial Congregation has given the following liturgical norms:

1. In saying Mass and reciting the Divine Office during the ocean crossing, priests on board may use the Calendar of the Universal Church.

2. In the Canon of the Mass, during the crossing, the name of the Pope is said, but there is no mention of any Bishop.

20. *Ibid.*, 698, article 25, 2; and XLVI, 415-418.

21. *AAS*, XLIV, 698, article 25, 3.

22. See *"Norms and Faculties,"* Part II, Appendix.

23. The concession of this indult is made by means of a Consistorial Rescript in which are noted the following conditions: "That the pyx be held fast to an immovable tabernacle, lest it be upset by the raging waves, and be carefully protected by a lock, and lamps, even electric, be kept lit before it continually by day and by night."

It will be of interest to cite the privileges with which the Holy Father Pius XII has endowed these Oratories:

"The Christian Faithful on board, provided that they confess and receive Holy Communion, can obtain a *toties quoties* Plenary Indulgence on August 2, by making a pious visit to the oratory set up legitimately on the ship, where, by an apostolic indult the Most Blessed Sacrament is being kept, and by reciting there with devotion, 6 *Our Fathers*, 6 *Hail Marys* and 6 *Glorys* for the intentions of the Holy Father, during each visit."

"The same Christian Faithful in the same conditions may obtain a *toties quoties* Plenary Indulgence which must be applied to the departed Faithful on November 2, by making a pious visit to the mentioned oratory and reciting there with devotion, 6 *Our Fathers*, 6 *Hail Marys* and 6 *Glorys* for the intentions of the Holy Father during each visit."

Cf. the *Norms and Faculties for priests engaged in the spiritual care of seamen*, Part II, Appendix.

24. *AAS*, XLIV, 699, article 30.

25. *Ibid.*, 697, article 19.

26. In answer to some questions concerning article 6, 1 and 2, Title

Two of the Apostolic Constitution *Exsul Familia,* the Sacred Consistorial Congregation replied on December 9, 1952, as follows (prot. no. 247/52):

"In conformity with the norms laid down in numbers 1 and 2, Chapter 1 of Title Two of the Apostolic Consititution *Exsul Familia,* the President of the Commission for Emigrants in France asks:

1. Whether the Episcopal Commission may be considered among those which have been approved by the Holy Father.

2. Whether the priest who is secretary of the same Commission, at present, John Rupp, Vicar General for foreigners of the Archdiocese of Paris, may assume the title of Director of the Agencies for Foreigners Emigrating to France.

3. Whether it be necessary that this be conferred by decree of the Sacred Consistorial Congregation; whether it be licit to request such a title; whether it be licit to obtain it through the Archbishop of Paris.

ANSWERS:

1. Affirmative.

2. Affirmative.

3. Affirmative to the first part. The second part is licit moreover and is even fitting; affirmative to the third part in so far as the Archbishop of Paris seems to act in the name of the Episcopal Commision for the Assistance of Emigrants or of the Bishops of France."

CHAPTER VIII

1. *AAS,* XLIV, 686, note 129.
2. *Ibid.,* 679.
3. *Ibid.,* 679, ff.
4. *Ibid.,* 680.
5. *Ibid.,* 680.
6. *Ibid.,* 684.
7. *Ibid.,* 675, 678, 685.
8. *Ibid.,* 686, note 129.
9. *Ibid.,* 679.
10. *Ibid.,* 680.
11. *Ibid.,* 681.
12. *Ibid.,* 684, note 120.
13. *Ibid.,* 774.
14. *Ibid.,* 684, note 120.
15. *Ibid.,* 684, note 121.
16. *Ibid.,* 684, note 121.
17. *Ibid.,* 685, note 125.
18. *Ibid.,* 682.
19. *Ibid.,* 686, note 129.
20. *Ibid.,* 683.
21. *Ibid.,* 682.
22. *Ibid.,* 682.
23. Encyclical *Sertum Laetitiae,* November 1, 1939; *AAS,* XXXI, 665, ff.
24. *AAS,* XLIV, 683.
25. *Le Encicliche sociali dei Papi da Pio IX a Pio XII,* (1864-1946), ed. Igino Giordani. Third edition. Rome, Studium Press, 1959.

26. *Ibid.*, 168.
27. *Ibid.*, 161.
28. *AAS*, XLIV, 682.
29. *Ibid.*, 683, note 117.
30. *Ibid.*, XXXXV, 685.
31. *AAS*, XLIV, 685.
32. *Ibid.*, 685, note 124.
33. *Ibid.*, 682.
34. *Ibid.*, XXXXV, 41.
35. *Ibid.*, 685, note 125.
36. *Ibid.*, 683.
37. *Ibid.*, 685, note 124.
38. *Ibid.*, 686, note 126.
39. *Ibid.*, 685.
40. *Ibid.*, 686, note 127.
41. *Ibid.*, l.c.
42. *Ibid.*, 684, note 120.
43. *Ibid.*, l.c.
44. *Ibid.*, 684, note 120.
45. *Ibid.*, 684.
46 *Ibid.*, 684, note 120.
47. *Ibid.*, 684, note 121.
48. *Ibid.*, 682-683.
49. *Ibid.*, 682.
50. *Ibid.*, 686.

II

Commentary On Norms And Faculties For Priests Engaged In The Spiritual Care Of Sea Travellers, Seamen And Migrants

PREFACE

DURING 1954, the Consistorial Congregation published, with Pius XII's approval, several sets of *Norms and Faculties,* supplementing the Apostolic Constitution on the Spiritual Care of Migrants, *Exsul Familia.*

It will be recalled that *Exsul Familia,* in Part II, Chapter 3, n. 25, 2, states: "The chaplains shall be given special norms and faculties by the Consistorial Congregation." New norms have also been given, either to settle doubts perhaps already arisen or that may arise, or else to remove difficulties that have accompanied or will accompany their exercise and use. By means of these norms, Chaplains of the Apostolate of the Sea and their Directors are granted everything that has already been accorded for the benefit of Ship Chaplains and their Directors by the Apostolic Constitution. Finally, for the spiritual good of those of the Faithful who will be benefited, special favors and privileges are provided for missionaries to migrants, ship chaplains, (i.e. chaplains on board ship) and chaplains of the Apostolate of the Sea (i.e. of maritime people).

These *Norms and Faculties* were not however all published at the same time, but in various documents issued after the interval of some months. Most recently, on December 10, 1954, Feast of the Translation of the Holy House of the Blessed Virgin Mary,[1] there appeared the *Norms and Faculties* for missionaries to migrants; on April 2, 1954, the Feast of St. Francis of Paula, Patron of Italian seamen, the *Norm and Faculties* for chaplains of the Apostolate of the Sea,[2] and lastly, on March 19, 1954, the Feast of St. Joseph, Spouse of the Blessed Virgin Mary, there were published the *Norms and Faculties* for ships chaplains.[3]

We will now discuss these three documents together, for the Sacred Congregation used the same plan in preparing all of them. Again, they form, generally speaking, one whole; if there are differences, rather easily noticed by comparison, they arise from the fact that the priest carrying out his sacred ministry lives in various circumstances, now on board ship for the advantage either of travellers or of maritime people, and now on land for the good of migrants. The *Norms and Faculties* seem to point at this special objective, namely: that the priestly ministry that is zealously exercised among the categories of the faithful mentioned may be carried out more aptly and fruitfully.

Having stated this, we believe that it is proper to explain the meaning, in the present context, of certain terms: sailing person, maritime person and migrant.

A *sailing person* means one who is living on board ship for a voyage he has undertaken, for whatever length of time, whether he is just travelling or migrating, for whatever plans or reason. The faithful in this situation remains only temporarily outside the place where he has long resided and, once back in his own country, will again receive the spiritual aid usually offered in one parish, now left behind but to be again sought out.

A *maritime person* is one who habitually, either by reason of his duties or for the sake of work, whether in administration, or performing a service, or engaged in fishing, stays aboard ship. He therefore does not receive spiritual aid, neither in the parish of origin nor in those of the ports of call. Further, the maritime person does not, because of his work, receive the spiritual care that the ship chaplain offers the faithful on voyages, for it is clear that those who are employed at the engines, in the kitchens and in other necesary works are frequently prevented from duly attending the Holy Sacrifice of the Mass celebrated in the morning hours on Sundays or Holy Days of Obligation.

A *migrant* is one who, of his own will or because of necessity, alone or with his family, lives away from his native country, but on land.

Each set of the *Norms and Faculties* that we shall discuss is made up of three sections. First is stated what is required for anyone to be considered licitly installed in the position of ship chaplain or chaplain to maritime people, or missionary to migrants, or Director of chaplains of missionaries. In addition, some new rules are given, for chaplains especially.

Secondly are enumerated the faculties and privileges that Pius XII has deigned to grant the three mentioned classes of priests, during their office and for the competence or varied duties of each.

Thirdly are listed certain spiritual benefits that Pius XII has bestowed on the faithful who are sailing, maritimes and migrants.

There is one exception. In the list for priests engaged in the spiritual care of migrants, these three sections are prefaced by a few lines, in reality taken literally from *Exsul Familia,* on the origin of the work of the Apostolate of the Sea and on the general international Secretariate directing this work.

We shall now discuss each of these sections separately.

A

REQUISITES FOR THE OFFICE OF CHAPLAIN AND MISSIONARY: NATURE OF THESE OFFICES.

AAS, XLVI, 249, 3, 4: 415, 1, 2, 3; XLVII, 91, 1, 2.

In order to fill either of these offices one must obtain a special rescript from the Consistorial Congregation and be duly approved and appointed. However, sometimes when a ship is about to leave port, it may be necessary to provide a chaplain without contacting the Congregation. In such case, all nuncios, internuncios and apostolic delegates outside Italy are given the faculty of appointing, the usual norms having been observed, ship chaplains and chaplains for the Apostolate of the Sea and for maritime people. The appointment of Directors, however, is reserved to the Consistorial Congregation.

Acting in their capacity of pontifical representatives in making such appointments they follow the same procedure as does the Sacred Consistorial Congregation, which provides with a special rescript the priest accepted as a ship chaplain or chaplain of the Apostolate of the Sea and gives him a list of faculties. Only after this rescript has been received does the chaplain licitly and validly use these faculties.

As to duties, there is noted, in a general statement, the duty of conscientiously observing everything in the proper section prescribed by the Apostolic Constitution for ship chaplains and missionaries to migrants and their Directors. These rules, with the proper distinctions, are also to be exactly observed by chaplains to maritime people or chaplains of the Apostolate of the Sea and their Directors, as is expressly noted.

Remarks about the Chaplains

First of all, mention is made of the Delegate for Migration Affairs to whose authority all chaplains of whatever rank are subject. For by virtue of his office, the Delegate is superior to chaplains whether they are secular priests or religious, and their Directors.[4] Besides, by the mandate of the Sacred Consistorial Congregation, he directs all of them, supervises them,[5] assigns them to ships[6] and carfully aids them through their Directors.[7]

All of this, as is readily seen, holds also for chaplains of the Apostolate of the Sea.

Indult for preserving the Blessed Sacrament in a Chapel aboard Ship.

(AAS, XLVI 415, 4.)

This is the doubt first proposed for solution: whether the Blessed Sacrament may be preserved in an oratory aboard ship that has been legitimately erected[8] by the Ordinary of the place in which the home port of the ship is located; or whether there is required a special permission or apostolic indult, in accordance with Canon 1265, 2.

By law, the Blessed Sacrament must be kept in the cathedral and parish churches, and in the church of exempt religious; it may, by *permission of the local Ordinary*, be kept in a boarding school church, and in a main chapel, whether public or semi-public, both of a pious or religious house and of an ecclesiastical college (Canon 1265, 1, 1⁰, 2⁰).

So it is clear that the reply to the second is in the affirmative; it needs no explanation, since it is obvious that a ship's chapel is in no way included among the churches or chapels listed in Canon 1265, 1, 1⁰ and 2⁰, where the Blessed Sacrament must, or by permission of the local Ordinary, may be kept.

Besides, who may be called the "Ordinary" of a ship on a sea voyage?

A doubt arose, however, as to the procedure to be followed in obtaining the Apostolic indult; *i.e.*, which Congregation should be approached?

It is agreed among all that ship chaplains and their Directors perform their functions under the direction of the Consistorial Congregation,[9] which "alone has the authority to seek and procure everything pertaining to the spiritual welfare of migrants of the Latin rite."[10] Presently, to remove any grounds for uncertainty, it was decided that "an Apostolic indult must be obtained from the Consistorial Congregation to preserve the Blessed Sacrament in a licitly erected ship's chapel."[11]

Further, certain conditions are stipulated for such application:

1. Application is not to be made by a ship chaplain, but only by the Director of chaplains.

2. The local Ordinary who is responsible for the erection and blessing of the ship's chapel, is to furnish testimonial letters on the observance of liturgical laws.

These conditions being satisfied, the Consistorial Congregation grants the indult for keeping the Blessed Sacrament in a ship's chapel, directly not to the Director of chaplains, but send it to the above mentioned Ordinary so that he may then confer the privilege, good only during voyages and provided the due requirments of law are met. Therefore, there should be someone on the ship to guard the Blessed Sacrament and a priest who celegrates Mass at least weekly in the ship's chapel. Ship chaplains should ponder all this carefully, since, at the end of a voyage, a ship may be deserted for several days or for a considerable time.

Also the following instructions are to be remembered carefully. The pyx should be attached firmly in the tabernacle, so that it does not move about in heavy seas. The key should be guarded carefully, and a lamp which may be electric,[12] should be kept burning continuously night and day before the tabernacle.

The calendar to be followed and the mentioning of the Pope's name in the Canon of the Mass:

AAS, XLVI, 249, 5, 6 and 416, 5, 6.

Without prejudice to what was previously stated concerning "who, that is, may be called the Ordinary of a ship on a sea voyage," special rules have been published with regard both to the Calendar to be followed and the name of a bishop to be mentioned in the Canon of the Mass.

As everyone knows, the Calendar to be followed in saying Mass and in reciting the divine office must be approved by the Ordinary; furthermore, Mass should regularly agree with the celebrant's office. An exception is made, though, if you are in a church or public chapel other than your own; in that case Mass should regularly agree with the place, not the office of the celebrant. Again, it may happen that a priest has begun a voyage, to extend perhaps through the week, without, for whatever reason, taking a Calendar along. It might be that two priests, belonging to different dioceses, countries and regions, want to say the divine office together.

For these reasons Pius XII has graciously deigned to grant the following: "During a voyage, priests on board ship may use the Calendar of the universal Church in conducting divine services and in reciting the divine office" and "during a voyage, after mentioning the Pope's name in the Canon of the Mass, the name of no bishop is mentioned."

These rules hold aboard ship, whether or not there is a chapel and, especially, for priests who are ship chaplains, or chaplains of the Apostolate of the Sea, actually performing their duties.

Parish records to be prepared and preserved.

(AAS, XLVI, 249, 7, 8, and 416, 7.)

The second rule deals with the parish records, covered in Canon 470.

Here, I believe we should begin with the words of *Exsul Familia:*

"It is the duty of chaplains aboard ships to attend, throughout a voyage, to the spiritual care of all those who for whatever reason are on board. The only exception is the case of marriage."[13] Since this is also stated of chaplains of the Apostolate of the Sea, these two groups, clearly, will have the duty of preparing records of baptism, confirmations and deaths.[14]

A pastor, in addition, has of course, by Canon 470, the

obligation not only of preparing as accurately as possible and carefully preserving all parish records (1), but also of installing files in which the records can be preserved (4), of forwarding an accurate copy of them to the episcopal curia at the end of each year (3) and of using the parish seal (4).

These other items, however, cannot be completely performed by a chaplain. He is often compelled to take care of souls while he is in precarious and special circumstances; he may easily be replaced by another chaplain; and where the ship has a chapel, the chaplain has little space and lacks equipment for safeguarding documents.

For these and other reasons I think I shall omit some remarks which are evident. All the ships subject to the National Director of Ship Chaplains and to the National Director of the Apostolate of the Sea were considered as a specific unity. This unity, however, may not be regarded as a parish moving about at sea, with the archives set up in the National Director's headquarters.

With these things carefully considered, it seemed good to the legislator to divide the duties imposed by the Code on a pastor, assigning some to the Director and others to the chaplain. So, a chaplain has the duty of preparing the records described above, and of handing over these records to his Director at the end of every voyage; nothing else is required of the chaplain. It will be up to the Director, however, to have a file or cabinet in which the said records are kept; he is to forward an accurate copy of them to the Curia of the diocese in which his office is located; he is to use his own seal and to give reference letters to those concerned.

Considering the special condition of the migrant,

whether he is taken generally—for he is forced to live outside his own country—or whether taken singly—for while the voyage continues he may receive Baptism or Confirmation or meet with death—the Consistorial Congregation expressly renews the rules set by the Code for Baptism and Confirmation conferred in the absence of the pastor. For the Code specifies: "If Baptism was not administered by the proper pastor, nor in his presence, the minister should, as soon as possible, inform the pastor of the domicile of the person baptized" (Can. 778), and "if the proper pastor of the person confirmed was not present, the minister of Confirmation shall personally or through another inform the same as soon as possible" (Can. 799).

Extending these to the case of death, if it should occur during a voyage, the Rules state that, observing strictly the requirements in this matter of the sacred canons, after the event is duly entered in the records, the pastor of the domicile of the deceased should be notified by the Director as soon as possible. As to the report of the exercise by chaplains of the office of minister extraordinary of Confirmation, that will be dealt with later, when we speak specifically of this sacrament.

B

THE FACULTY OF ADMINISTERING THE SACRAMENT OF CONFIRMATION.

AAS, XLVI, 250, 9, 1o and 2o and 416, 8, 1o and 2o.)

This faculty, possessed by chaplains on ships and chaplains of the Apostolate of the Sea by virtue of a papal concession, may be distinguished in three ways.

The faculty of administering Confirmation to those in danger of death from serious illness.

By virtue of the Decree *Spiritus Sancti munera,*[1b] the faculty possessed by the minister extraordinary of Confirmation is granted by a general indult of the Holy See, in the cases only and under the conditions listed, to the following priests, and to them only:

a. pastors with their own territories, and excluding therefore personal or family pastors, unless they have their own territory, which may be cumulative.

b. vicars, discussed in Canon 471, and vicars administrators.

c. priests to whom there has been committed exclusively and enduringly the full care of souls in a certain district with a specified church and all the rights and duties of pastors.

Accordingly, while missionaries to migrants with the care of souls may be considered as personal or family pastors with their own territory, even if cumulative,[16] as Pius XII himself has graciously declared, to no class of the priests mentioned above, may ship chaplains or chaplains of the Apostolate of the Sea be held equal.

Therefore, it was most fitting that ship chaplains and the chaplains of the Apostolate of the Sea be endowed, through a special new indult, with the faculty of acting as ministers extraordinary of Confirmation. As a result, travellers on ships, whether or not they are migrants in the strict sense, and maritime personnel can partake of the spiritual gifts the Supreme Pontiff has deigned to lavish, providing better by this means for the spiritual welfare "of the faithful —infants, children, and adults—who on account of serious illness are led to the brink of death, and would certainly die without Confirmation if the provisions of the common law as to the ordinary minister were insisted on strictly."[17] On November 24, 1952, our Holy Father graciously conceded, in behalf of migrants, the aforementioned special indult for two years, through the Congregation of the Sacraments, to ship chaplains, providing though:

"That the Sacrament of Confirmation, in the circumstances described in the aforementioned Decree be conferred on *migrants*, and only while on board ship during a sea voyage, by their own chaplain, if only one has been assigned them; or if several have been appointed to the same ship by the chief among them. However, the chaplain may use this faculty only if no bishop, even titular, enjoying communion with the Holy See, is on board ship. If a bishop is on board, the administration of Confirmation remains reserved to him.

It will, though, be the chaplain's duty, whether the sacrament is administered by him or by a bishop, to record carefully in the journal with which he should be provided, everything prescribed in No. 6 and the following p. I of the above mentioned Decree. The chaplain should besides record any Confirmation administered, with the month, year and place noted, in the so-called *family book,* prepared under the direction of the Consistorial Congregation, in which are registered the families of emigrants, so that whereever they go there will always and in every event be the certainty of their having received the sacraments.

At the end of a voyage, the same chaplain should as soon as possible inform the proper pastors of any confirmations, through authentic documents that should contain all the information described above, so that the pastor can note the

Confirmation in the confirmation and baptismal records, as required by Canons 798 and 799.

But if the ship chaplain, or if there are several, the chief among them cannot personally confirm, no one else, except a bishop, may validly confer this sacrament.

For the rest, the terms and clauses of the said Decree are to be complied with, especially what concerns the "annual Report to be sent to this Congregation."

Later, on August 31, 1953, the Holy Father, retaining the above rules, granted that ship chaplains and chaplains of the Apostolate of the Sea be raised permanently to the status of extraordinary ministers of Confirmation for the faithful under their jurisdiction.

Therefore, ship chaplains and their Directors have, during their term of office, the faculty of administering Confirmation during a voyage to any Christian in serious illness and in danger of death on board. Similarly, chaplains of the Apostolate of the Sea and their Directors have the faculty, in the same circumstances and conditions, of administering the sacrament of Confirmation to any maritime people and to them only.

It is asked whether the words "during a voyage" should be understood in the strict sense, so that while the ship is berthed in any port, although the voyage is not yet finished, the mentioned faculty should be considered suspended.

We should evidently answer no, for the words "during a voyage " mean, we think, the whole sea voyage, which begins when the ship leaves the port from which a voyage begins and ends when it reaches the port at which the same voyage is completed. Besides, obviously, bishops cannot without serious inconvenience board a ship in the ports where, during a voyage, it stops for a while.

It is also asked on which maritime personnel chaplains of the Apostolate of the Sea may bestow Confirmation.

The answer is, I believe, that chaplains of the Apostolate of the Sea may confirm all maritime people. But, and consider this well, only them, and provided that they happen to be within the territorial confines, say in some port preassigned by the local Ordinary.

It is asked, finally, whether the chaplain is also bound to send, personally or through his Director, to the "diocesan" Ordinary an authentic notice of Confirmation administered, adding all the accompanying circumstances in the case,[18] the answer is evident from the following. The Consistorial Congregation has in no way relaxed the discipline laid down by the Congregation of the Sacraments; rather, the Consistorial Congregation insists on it, considering the special circumstances we mentioned above. The Consistorial Congregation requires both the Director of Ship Chaplains and the Director of Chaplains of the Apostolate of the Sea to report on the number of those who, in danger of death from grave illness, are confirmed by chaplains, and on the motive used by them in fulfilling their office as extraordinary ministers. The report for each year is to be sent, at the beginning of the following year, to the Consistorial Congregation and to the Ordinary of the diocese in which the Director's office is established.

We said the Consistorial Congregation insists on observance of the rules issued by the Congregation of the Sacraments. In fact, in requiring that it be shown the report, it is not only able more readily to note conditions, but also to forward the report to the Congregation of Sacraments, in accordance with the directive in n. 9 of the Decree, *Spiritus Sancti.*[19]

The faculty of administering Confirmation during a voyage to any migrant child or adult who has received his first Holy Communion on the same ship.

Pius XII granted ship chaplains and chaplains of the Apostolate of the Sea such a faculty on February 12, 1954. It can be seen from the context that the faculty was given primarily out of consideration for migrants, for this condition among others is stated: "provided it can be foreseen that because of his age, or ignorance of language, or because of local circumstances, the person to be confirmed will receive this sacrament only with great difficulty in the region of immigration."

The faculty of administering Confirmation during a voyage to any migrant.

Granting of the previous faculty was scarcely announced when the question arose of a condition of numerous young people migrating from southern Italy who, after somehow receiving first Communion, followed the bad custom of the region (by Canon 788, a custom altogether out of place) and had not yet been confirmed. Further, either because of ignorance of the language or because of local circumstances, they would receive it in the region of immigration only with great difficulty. When this was reported to Pius XII in an audience of July 4, 1954, he deigned to bestow the same faculty in favor of such migrants that he had already bestowed for migrants who received first Communion on board ship. If you look at the mention of the faculty under discussion in the recently published list of faculties, at the words "who has made his first Communion on the ship," you find added: "especially."

It is clear that these concessions in no way dispense from strict observance of all the requirements of common law, and are only valid when no bishop in communion with the Holy See is on the ship.

As to the rite, however, in this case, you should know that in *AAS,* XXXVIII, pp. 356-358, there is reprinted the rite to be followed by priests in conferring Confirmation by virtue of that Apostolic indult. The rite is contained in the *Roman Ritual,* published in 1925 on the authority of Pius XI, in accordance with the Code of Canon Law.

Concerning numbers II and III, a summary published by the Consistorial Congregation recalls the *Instructions* of the Congregation of the Sacraments as regards the administration, by delegation of the Holy See, of the sacrament of Confirmation by an ordinary priest. The *Instructions* were published on order of the same Congregation on Pentecost in 1934, and consisted of three parts: "I. The need for new Instructions after the promulgation of the Code of Canon Law and after some published modifications regarding the minister of Confirmation and the age of those to be confirmed. II. The discipline, introduced by the Code for the administration of Confirmation by an ordinary priest. III. The Rite to be followed, etc." Everyone can see that all of this is useful for consideration by chaplains.

The privilege of a portable altar

AAS, XLVI, 250, 9, 3o, 417, 3o and XLVII, 91, 3, 1o

Missionaries to migrants, ship chaplains and all chaplains of the Apostolate of the Sea [20] and their Directors have the privilege of a *portable altar.*

It is of considerable interest to inquire into the meaning of the words "portable altar," and under what conditions this privilege has been granted. It is well known that Mass is to be celebrated on a consecrated altar and in a church or oratory that had been consecrated or blessed according to law (Canon 822, 1). Liturgically, altars are divided into two classes: there is the immovable or fixed altar, consisting of an upper table properly joined to stone supports (at least for the sides) and consecrated with them as one whole (Canon 1197, 1, 1⁰); and the movable or portable altar, a sacred stone or portable stone only, which alone is consecrated; or a stone united with a base, which, however, is not consecrated with the stone as one whole.

There is also, in order to gain indulgences, a fixed altar in a less strict sense: an altar that is to some extent fixed, which may be made of wood. Such an altar may be privileged.[21]

A fixed altar is to be consecrated by the Ordinary of the place in which the church is located, provided he has episcopal consecration, without prejudice, however, to the privileges of Abbots and prelates *nullius*. A portable altar may be consecrated by any bishop, without prejudice, however, to the privileges of Vicars or prefects apostolic. In both types of altars, there must be a sepulchre containing the relics of saints, closed with a stone.

As to the preparation and decoration of the altar on which the most holy sacrifice of the Mass is to be offered, the following directives are prescribed in the General Rubrics of the *Roman Missal*: *The preparation of the altar and its decoration.* It is to be covered with three clean cloths, blessed by the bishop or another having the authority. The top cloth at least is to be oblong; and (unless the altar is decorated in another way) it should reach the floor. The two others are to be shorter, or one doubled up. Above the altar, in the middle, there should be placed a cross, with the image of the Crucified, in plain sight, large enough that it immediately comes to the attention of the celebrant and the people,[22] and at least two candle holders with lighted candles, one on either side.

On ships, even if they have oratories, there are generally only movable or portable altars or, at most, altars that are fixed in a loose sense; knowledge of this is useful concerning indulgences. However, we believe it not superfluous to ask whose task it is to consecrate an immovable or fixed altar that might be installed in a ship's oratory. In our opinion, whatever its weight may be, the answer any be drawn analogically from n. 30, Title Two of *Exsul Familia,* and therefore the right of consecrating such an altar belongs to the Ordinary of the place in which the home port of the ship is located.

But a portable altar is one thing in the liturgical sense, and another thing in the canonical sense. It is an altar in the canonical and not in the liturgical sense that would be implied in the faculty given somebody by law or by Apostolic indult of celebrating Mass *anywhere,* always supposing a fitting and decent place, however, and over a consecrated stone, but not at sea or in a bedroom (Canon 822, 3 and 4) and observing the other requirements of law and especially the Rules contained in the *Instructions* of the Sacred Congregation for the Sacraments, *Quam plurimum,* published October 1, 1949,[23] from which we take the following, for the reader's convenience:

"The privilege of a portable altar, or travelling altar, whether for carrying, or for a journey, is similar to the indult for a private chapel, and is broader in scope, for it bestows the faculty of saying Mass anywhere in a decent and respectable place, and on a consecrated altar stone, not however, at sea (Canon 822, 3), hence the celebration of Mass is not limited to a place intended exclusively for divine worship, nor is it necessary for the Ordinary to visit and approve it.

In view of the wider extent of this favor, all the greater are the dangers of abuse as well as of impairing the proper decorum due to the most holy sacrifice of the Mass, which it is feared may happen in two ways: as regards the place, if an unsuitable place for such a Mystery is chosen (e.g., a bedroom) and as regards the person, if such an indult is abused through immoderate use. . . .

Again, this Congregation is wont to grant this privilege on account of real necessity or obvious usefulness and for the exclusive or chief purpose of religious services, to priests only, since they give greater assurance of its proper use.

The main cases, which occur more often, involve priests who have the care of souls among the faithful dwelling in isolated places where churches are widely scattered or non-existent or in regions inhabited by heretics or schismatics (diaspora). It happens chiefly in certain vast areas of Asia and America, where the faithful are thinly settled and widely spread out: they cannot assist at Mass unless it is said outside a holy place or evn outdoors, as for example at harvest time.

The place where a portable altar is set up should be appropriate and decent, or fitting and respectable, lest serious harm and irreverence befall the divine services because of its unworthy and unbecoming character. An appropriate place presupposes security and roominess, so that Mass can be offered safely and conveniently and without any danger of profaning or spilling the sacred species from the chalice. A 'decent place' refers to the nature of the place; thus it requires that Mass be not celebrated in rooms where someone usually sleeps nor in other places unfitted to the dignity of such a sacrifice.

Also with regard to decency, the immediate place, i.e., the table on which the portable altar is placed, should not be dirty nor intended for non-religious use. This table should be of such length and breadth that it can safely hold the stone and accomodate the missal and allow a proper and decent celebration." [24]

As to the conditions laid down by the Consistorial Congregation, although others may be issued for any group of chaplains or missionaries, one in particular is to be considered which makes their privilege distinct from all: i.e., Mass should be said for the benefit of the *faithful entrusted* to the celebrant, or of *maritime people* or of *those travelling by ship,* or *migrants,* rather than for the sole benefit of the celebrant, so that all the faithful who assist at such Mass celebrated on a portable altar may satisfy fully the precept of hearing Mass.[25]

In regard to the other special conditions, we believe these in particular should be considered: ship chaplains should take care, as far as possible, that any danger of spilling the sacred species be eliminated; and if there is another priest on board, he should, dressed in surplice, assist the celebrating priest.

The same rules are prescribed for maritime personnel chaplains, who are likewise given the faculty of celebrating Mass at sea.

Missionaries to migrants need also the consent of the local Ordinary for the repeated use of this apostolic privilege, since a missionary enjoys no exemption from the local Ordinary and should exercise the spiritual care of the faithful of his language and nation under the jurisdiction of that Ordinary.

The faculty of saying Mass outdoors

AAS, XLVII, 91, 3, 20

Missionaries have also, under the same conditions, the privilege of celebrating Mass even outdoors, provided that a tent is set up to protect the altar from the wind, so that no fragments will be scattered, and observing the *Instructions* issued by the Congregation of the Sacraments, October 1, 1949.[26]

Moreover, we want to repeat here a few pertinent lines from the instruction *Dominus Salvator*, of the Congregation of the Sacraments, of March 26, 1929: *"What things are to be avoided and what be followed in offering the Mass and in distributing and preserving the Eucharist."* [27]

> "Another cause of scattering fragments of the Eucharist can easily arise when, in some special circumstance and by Apostolic indult or by the authority given by law to local Ordinaries, Mass is celebrated outdoors—sometimes with the wind blowing. To avoid such scattering, care should be taken that the altar where Mass is celebrated is sheltered by panels on three sides. Or an awning should be raised over the altar, falling down on three sides in the form of a shrine, so that the altar itself is protected from the wind, or that protection should be afforted in some other way consistent with the reverence due to such a great Sacrament." [28]

The privilege of celebrating Mass on Christmas night and on New Year's Eve

AAS, XLVI, 250, 9, 40, 50; XLVIII, p. 92, 40 and 50

For the two circumstances of time, mentioned above, the celebration of Mass is, as everyone knows, subject to rules that bind absolutely unless a special indult from the Holy See should be granted.

The Code of Canon Law decrees that, generally speaking, "Mass should not be begun earlier than one hour before daybreak." Some exceptions however, are allowed. On Christmas, the conventual or parochial Mass alone may be begun at Midnight. In all religious or pious houses having oratories with the privilege of preserving regularly the Blessed Sacrament, one priest may celebrate three Masses or, observing the other requirements of law, only one. (Canon 821, 1, 2, 3).

A Mass celebrated on ship board cannot, according to law, be called parochial, even though some, however, think otherwise because of the words of the Constitution *Exsul Familia*: "It is the duty of ship chaplains, throughout the voyages, to care for souls, except for matrimonial matters." [29] On certain ships indeed there are legitimately erected chapels with the privilege of preserving regularly the Blessed Sacrament, but this does not seem relevant, for it is no question of an oratory in a religious or pious house; nor is the fact relevant that ship chaplains, if there is a legitimately erected chapel on board, are, with due allowances, considered as rectors of churches. [30] For, as we remarked above, it is not the person but the setting that is in question. Thence arises the need for a special Apostolic indult, at least to remove any doubt. This type of indult holds of course for ship chaplains, chaplains of the Apostolate of the Sea, and missionaries to migrants.

The same words may be found in the concession made to ship chaplains and chaplains to maritime people. They bestow the faculty of celebrating Mass on ships, not only where there are chapels, but also on portable altars, provided that some devotions precede Mass by at least half an hour and the Mass is not begun earlier than one half hour after midnight. These conditions, imposed generally by the Congregation of Sacrament, are prompted by special circumstances of time and place, mainly for more certain elimination of any danger of irreverence.

However, missionaries to migrants, whether or not they have the care of souls, possess, in virtue of the Apostolic indult, the faculty of celebrating Mass at midnight, provided they offer the sacrifice for the benefit of the faithful entrusted to them; being careful however, especially if no church or chapel or public or semi-public oratory had been appointed by the local Ordinary for exercising the care of souls, that all danger of irreverence be eliminated and the other requirements of law followed exactly.

On New Year's Eve, all ship chaplains and chaplains of the Apostolate of the Sea, and missionaries to migrants, whether or not engaged in the care of souls strictly speaking, have the faculty of celebrating Mass at midnight, provided they offer for the benefit of the faithful entrusted to them and there be devotions for about two hours, including the time spent in saying Mass. It will be very helpful towards removing any danger of irreverence and fostering devotion of those present, if the celebration of the Mass will take place only on the condition that the above-mentioned prayers be said before and after Mass.

The privilege of saying one Mass on Holy Thursday and of using the short ritual of Benedict XIII

AAS, XLVI, 250, 6o and 417, 6o XVII, 92, 6o.

In the Latin Church private Mass is forbidden both in churches and in chapels on Holy Thursday; for generally, on this and the two following days, Masses not in connection with the functions of the Three Days services are absolutely forbidden.[31]

Nevertheless:

1. Cardinals have the privilege of celebrating Mass on this day or of permitting others to celebrate in their presence;[32]

2. Bishops, whether resident—provided they are not bound to celebrate in the cathedral—or titular, have the same privilege;[33]

3. Likewise one Mass may be read in the oratories of Regulars properly speaking, but not in those belonging to seminaries or pious communities, unless there is an Apostolic indult.[34]

So it is clear that missioaries to migrants, ship chaplains, and chaplains of the Apostolate of the Sea need an Apostolic indult to say private Masses; which indult His Holiness has in fact generously granted to all those wishing to say Mass for the benefit, as is clear, of those entrusted to them.

On the same day, in all churches where the Blessed Sacrament is preserved, and in them only, a solemn Mass is allowed if celebrated by the pastor of the Church, or by the one taking his place.[35]

It is to this solemn Mass that the Code of Canon Law refers in recommending: "On Holy Thursday, it is fitting that all clerics, including priests who do not celebrate Mass on that day, receive Holy Communion at the solemn or conventual Mass."[36]

This accords well with rules contained in the *Caeremoniale Episcoporum:* "A silver or gold chalice should be prepared with many consecrated hosts, for giving Communion to canons and clergy."[37]

In smaller parish churches where the sacred ceremonies cannot be carried out *solemnly,* use may be made of the form in the short Ritual, published by order of Benedict XIII. The above-mentioned small Ritual of Benedict XIII, without special indult may not be followed in those churches that are not parochial (in oratories of Religious, hospitals, prisons, etc.).[38]

Those who make use of this indult, although held to offer the divine services on Good Friday, are not bound to say the office or Mass on Holy Saturday.[39] All of which it is fitting to recall here, since missionaries to migrants, ship chaplains and chaplains of the Apostolate of the Sea have been given, by Apostolic indult of Pius XII,[40] the privilege of using the short Ritual of Benedict XIII during Holy Week.

The privilege of saying Mass two or three times on Sundays and Holy Days of Obligation; and of doing the same on ferial days

(AAS, XLVI, 251, 7 *and* 417, 7; XLVII, 91, 3.)

The Holy Father did not directly grant the priests in question the faculty of saying Mass two or three times on Holy Days of Obligation, but gave the Consistorial Congregation (on June 12, 1953) the authority for conferring this privilege on any missionary or chaplain, observing however the requirements of common law, and under certain conditions.

Now the Consistorial Congregation grants the faculty:

1. In the first place, as often as necessity urges of further-

ing the spiritual good of migrants or travellers at sea or maritime people through the celebration of Mass, since it allows them to fulfill the precept of hearing Mass. Concerning the observance of the Instructions, it is stated: "the Director of missionaries being responsible in conscience for this." However, after examining the letter of concession, and having in mind the purpose of the lawgiver, we add: "the Director of chaplains being responsible in conscience for this," in so far as it is proper for them to take pains that all prudent rules be exactly followed.

2. The danger of any surprise or scandal must be removed.

3. The celebrant is forbidden to accept any offering or stipend for two masses, as specified by Canon 824, 2. He has the duty, however, whether he is a missionary or a ship chaplain (audience with the Holy Father, January 4, 1929, n. 1829) of applying the second Mass for the intention of the Consistorial Congregation and likewise if it is a question of missionaries who celebrate on the mainland.

4. With the consent of the local Ordinary, and

5. The third Mass finally may not be celebrated in the church where the other two were celebrated, if this can be done without serious inconvenience, and

6. Observing the other requirements of law.

The Consistorial Congregation was concerned over the inadequate number of missionaries and chaplains; it took into consideration the unusual circumstances in which find themselves the faithful who are committed to them. It has considered especially the difficulty of calling together to one same place and time the faithful living in remote and sometimes impassable places—"The great size of seaports

(Antwerp, Rotterdam, Hamburg, Le Havre, etc.) is for maritime people," said the Director of the French Work of the Apostolate of the Sea, "a hindrance to the practice of religion. We cannot reasonbly ask them to go three, six, or ten miles to attend Mass. Whence the necessity for the chaplain to be able to celebrate two or three Masses at meeting places where the maritime workers may gather." So the Holy Father was asked to give the Consistorial Congregation the authority to concede to missionaries and chaplains the faculty of saying two or three Masses, even on ferial days.

This favor Pius XII, after having duly considered all circumstances, most graciously deigned to concede, on October 3, 1953, with the same conditions as above. Therefore these lines are found in the list of faculties: "The faculty of saying Mass two or three times on Sundays and Holydays of Obligation, as well as on *ferial* days."

When this was published, someone asked, "which days are to be understood by the word *ferial?* Those days that are described as such in Canon 1639, 1, or rather, the days that are usually called 'ferias', which are also commonly called ferial?"

The answer is found primarily, whatever the common use of the word 'ferial', in the purpose of this concession. By the words "ferial days" are to be understood all the days in the year that do not, for any reason, come under the name of Sunday or Holyday of Obligation.

A further remark on "ferial" will not be unwelcome. The word "ferial day" may be taken in two different senses: the first sense is classic and legal, the second taken from common language, or rather from liturgical use.

It is clear that in the classical sense of *ferial, ferial* days were the same as festive days, on which everyone was supposed to refrain from public cares and business as well as from commercial transactions. In the common meaning, on the other hand, which I would call liturgical, ferial days are understood as "non-festive", or ordinary working days. Such a meaning ties up with what we have in the Roman Breviary for the feast of St. Sylvester, Pope: "With the names of Saturday and Sunday retained, he wanted the rest of the days of the week to be distinct with the name *ferias,* as they were already begun to be called in the Church, in order to signify that clerics, having given up the care of other things, ought daily to attend absolutely only to God."[41]

The Privilege of Mass at evening hours

AAS, XLVI, 251, 8 and 417, 8; XLVII, 92, 7.

The decree of the Holy Office is to remain in effect.

With regard to evening Mass celebrated in missions for migrants and in ports, missionaries and chaplains ought to have recourse to the local Ordinary, according to No. VI[42] of the Apostolic Constitution *Christus Dominus,* on the discipline to be observed in the Eucharistic fast, and to the Instructions of the Congregation of the Holy Office on the Eucharistic fast, *with reference to evening Mass,*[43] where special mention is made of dock workers.

With these promulgated, and considering the admonitions in the above mentioned *Instructions, i.e.,* that the interpretation of the Constitution and of the *Instructions* has to adhere faithfully to the text and has not in any way to enlarge the already very favorable faculties, the, Sacred Consistorial Congregation, intending primarily the spiritual good of maritime workers, who, preparing a voyage, very often can attend Mass neither in the morning nor in the evening, immediately raised a question with the Congregation of the Holy Office as to whether any Ordinary has the faculty of permitting the celebration of evening Mass during a voyage.

For on February 26, 1953, the Consistorial Congregation sent the following letter to the Congregation of the Holy Office:

"In the Instruction on the Eucharistic fast, issued by the Congregation on January 6 of this year, it is stated with regard to evening Mass that by virtue of the Apostolic Constitution 'Christus Dominus,' local Ordinaries have the faculty of permitting evening Mass in their territory, etc. . . . for those workers who must work during the morning hours on feast days, such as dock workers . . . (AAS, XXXV, 50 f.).

Now, since a doubt arose, this Congregation respectfully asks: 1. that, among these listed workers, there be included also those who work on board ships during voyages; 2. that the Ordinary who is competent to bestow the aforementioned faculty be he in whose territory the home port of a ship is located, for he has the right to erect and bless a chapel on the ship, by rule n. 30, Title Two of the Apostolic Constitution 'Exsul Familia' (AAS, XLIV, 699)."

The Congregation of the Holy Office in a letter (404/46) of May 8, 1953 to the Consistorial Congregation returned a favorable answer to both questions.

The Congregation of the Holy Office confirmed this answer and incorporated it into law through the Decree on evening Mass at sea, published May 31, 1953;[44] the *Norms and Faculties* for ship chaplains and chiplains to maritime workers refer to this Decree.

The faculty of absolving, during a voyage, any penitents from the penalty they incur for inducing abortion

AAS, XLVI, 251, 9o and 417, 9o.

A penalty of this type is excommunication automatically incurred, reserved to the Ordinary. It is incurred by those who induce abortion, including the mother, if abortion actually takes place (Canon 2350, 1).

Considering the difficulty of approaching the Ordinary during a voyage, Pius XII has graciously granted to both ship chaplains and chaplains to maritime people or of the Apostolate of the Sea, the faculty that by law belongs to the bishop. The chaplains using this faculty are to impose on penitents the obligation required by law in each case, according to the principles provided by approved authors. However, if there is a question of irregularity arising from procuring abortion, recourse must be had to the Penitentiary for dispensation.

The faculty of absolving, during a voyage, apostates, heretics and schismatics

AAS, XLVI, 251, 10o and 417, 10o.

To correctly understand who it is that, by common law, comes under the name apostate, heretic or schismatic, Canon 1325, 2, it should be recalled, where this is found:

> "If any baptized person, calling himself a Christian, stubbornly denies or questions any of the truths to be believed by Divine and Catholic faith, he is a, heretic, if he turns away altogether from the Christian faith, he is an 'apostate;' if, lastly, he refuses to be subject to the Pontiff or to communicate

with other members of the Church subject to the Pontiff he is a 'schimatic.' "

For a fuller understanding of these things, it helps to add this: heresy is an obstinate error or doubt against the Catholic faith, in one who has received Baptism and faith.

Heresy is distinguished in many ways:

1. In regard to sin, it is *formal,* if anyone obstinately clings to error, *i.e., knowingly* and *willingly,* or *material,* if there is error in the mind, without obstinacy in the will.

2. In regard to an act, it is *internal,* if it remains hidden in the mind; or *purely external* if, while denying the faith orally or by bowing down to an idol, a person still keeps it in his heart, heresy is *external* or *manifest* if it is in the mind and disclosed outwardly.

3. In regard to disclosure, it is *hidden* if no one or only a few know of it; *public* if many know of it and it cannot be concealed.

Apostasy is complete separation from the Christian faith by *one who has been baptized.* Apostasy, however, does not mean a specified type of infidelity but a certain worse condition.[45]

For the crime of apostasy there is not required a profession of some false religion. Therefore, under the name of apostates come also *masons* (or at least very many of them), *nihilists, anarchists, communists,*[46] many *socialists, properly so called, free thinkers, rationalists, deists, pantheists, spiritists,* and in general all those who, after being baptized, wholly leave the Christian faith, even though they do not embrace Judaism or another infidelity.

All apostates from the Christian faith and each and

every heretic or schismatic are under excommunication reserved to the Holy See in a special way. (Canon 2314, 2).

*For heresy, which is punished with canonical penalties,
there is required;*

1. of the *person:* a continued profession of the Christian
religion, and validly received Baptism (for a catechumen
cannot be punished by the Church).

2. of the *intellect:* error or formulated doubting, *i.e.,*
assent or a formulated judgment.

3. of the *will:* obstinacy, by which somebody knowingly
and willfully refuses to submit his judgment to the infallible
teaching Church (which is characteristic of this sin). It is,
however, not necessary that he adhere to such error ten-
aciously and over a period of time.

4. of the *matter:* error against *divine and Catholic faith,*
i.e., against any point of faith explicitly defined by the
Church or proposed for belief as being divinely revealed.

5. of the *act:* that the error be externalized, whether by
deed or by word, revealing the interior heresy.

The censure therefore affects *apostates* and *heretics,* who
sin against faith by interior and exterior act; similarly
schismatics, i.e., those who refuse to be subject to the
Supreme Pontiff, or refuse to communicate with members of
the Church who are subject to him. It does not therefore
follow that they constitute a new religious sect or lend their
names to any sect already organized.

Those converted from heresy. A confessor needs no
special faculty to absolve in confession a heretic converted
to the Catholic faith, if he was only *materially* a heretic;

also, if he was formally a heretic but *ignorant* of the excommunication attached to formal heresy (for excommunication is not incurred by those who act unknowingly) provided, however, he is not a notorious heretic or one enrolled in any sect.

A notorious heretic, or one who has joined some sect, must abjure *in the external form, i.e.,* in the presence of the local Ordinary or his representative, and at least two witnesses.[47]

The absolution of heretics.

Any confessor may absolve penitents guilty of purely interior heresy as well as heretics who incur no censure.

The Roman Pontiff alone can absolve (personally or through a representative) notorious or occult heretics who incurred censure, for this censure is reserved in a special way to the Holy See, as we have already intimated.

Ordinaries have the right, by their usual authority, the requisite abjuration and other requirements of law being complied with, to absolve in the external *forum* heretics, apostates, or schismatics who are under censure, if their offenses have in any way been brought into the court of the local Ordinary, even through voluntary confession. The abjuration is considered juridically accomplished when it is done in the presence of the local Ordinary himself or of his representative and of at least two witnesses. (Canon 2314, 2).[48]

In reconciling heretics, the method of procedure is because of the diversity of cases, distinguished in three ways:

1. If previous Baptism has been judged certainly valid,

only an *abjuration* is received, or profession of faith, which is followed by absolution from censure."[49]

2. If it is certain that a previous Baptism was null, Baptism is conferred *absolutely*. No abjuration or absolution follows, since the sacrament of regeneration cleanses everything;

3. If Baptism is to be repeated *conditionally*, this order is to be followed:

a. The abjuration, or profession of faith, is to be made before two witnesses, and according to the formula prescribed by the Congregation of the Holy Office.

b. Conditional Baptism is to follow; using the *Shorter formula for conditional Baptism*, likewise published by the Congregation of the Holy Office.

c. There is to be given conditional absolution from the censure, according to the formula published by the Holy Office.

d. Sacramental confession is to be made with absolution, likewise conditional, of sins.

As to the manner of absolving from excommunication, chapains concerned should remember what the Code of Canon Law says of this matter.

In the sacramental *forum*, anyone is absolved from censure through the usual form, prescribed in the ritual, for absolution of sins. See the *Roman Ritual*, Tit. III, Chap. 2, published by the order of His Holiness, Pope Pius XI, in conformity with the Code of Canon Law.

In bestowing absolution from excommunication, use should regularly be made, in the non-sacramental *forum*, of the form provided in the same books, *i.e.*, in the mentioned *Ritual*, Tit. III, Chap. 2, which deals with the manner of absolving from excommunication, outside sacramental Confession. The *Pontificale Romanum* prescribes a second form entitled "Manner of excommunicating and absolving," for the use really of bishops, which will also be very useful to the ordinary priest to know, at least so that he can better and more correctly explain the sacred rites of the Church.

This faculty is not absolute, but limited by several restrictions:

Firstly, absolution may not be given to "heretics purposely disseminating heresy among the faithful, whether with no one listening or paying attention or in the presence of others;" whether for reasons readily understood, or whether because the Apostolic Penitentiary itself, conceding this faculty for the internal *forum*, is accustomed to exclude such heretics.

The other requirements usually imposed by the Penitentiary in such circumstances are to be observed; it is clear however, that those things which are imposed in the case by the Penitentiary for the internal *forum* are, generally speaking, to be applied for the external *forum*.

With these outlined, it seems useful to review some of the requirements usually imposed by the Penitentiary: a penitent must not be absolved unless he reports to the Congregation of the Holy Office those teachers, if he knows of any, who intentionally teach heretical doctrines, and ecclesiastics and religious, if he has had any as partners in this affair, either doing this himself, or, by his permission, through the same priest who absolves him. If for just reason, such report cannot be made before absolution, an earnest promise is to be given by him, to make the report as soon and in the best way possible. There is imposed, according to the gravity of the offense, salutary penitence, with frequent use of the Sacraments and the obligation, according to the prudent judgment of the absolver, of retraction among persons before whom he expounded heresy, and of making amends for that scandal.

The National Directors of the Work of the Apostolate of the Sea are given faculty of hearing confessions near the shores of their own nations

AAS, XLVI, 251, 11o.

In regard to the Directors of the Work of the Apostolate of the Sea, it was disclosed to the Consistorial Congregation in 1953 that: "In the course of the unceasing visits that they make along the entire coast lines of their countries, the national chaplains are often requested to hear confessions while there is no time to apply to the local Ordinary for permission. In particular, the priests are happy to take advantage of the passing through of outside priests to make their own confessions." So there was requested for National Directors the faculty of hearing the confessions of any of the faithful approaching them in nearby places along the whole coast of their country.

On August 31, 1953, Pius XII permitted the Consistorial Congregation to concede to National Directors, and to them only, the aforesaid faculty, provided that they have been approved by their own Ordinary for hearing confessions.

The faculty of blessing sacred utensils

AAS, XLVI, 251, 12o and 418, 11o; 47, 92, 8o.

A missionary to emigrants with the care of souls, or a ship chaplain, if there is a legitimately erected chapel on the ship, needs no special faculty for blessing sacred utensils. For in virtue of the Apostolic Constitution *Exsul Familia,* Title 2, art. 35, missionaries with the care of souls are equated to pastors; while ship chaplains, by virtue of art. 26 of the same Constitution, are equated to rectors of churches.

Every pastor has the authority, by virtue of his office, to bless the sacred utensils for the churches and oratories located within the boundaries of his parish, and a rector for his church. These utensils ought by liturgical law to be blessed before being employed in their proper use.

And so since, generally speaking, missionaries to migrants with the care of souls acquire the same faculties as pastors, we may say that such missionaries have, in virtue of their office, the power of blessing sacred utensils within the strictly circumscribed limits of the mission entrusted to them; likewise it is clear that the same faculty belongs, by virtue of their office, to ship chaplains for the chapels aboard ship committed to them.

Now, the Consistorial Congregation in this matter found that was no clear statement concerning missionaries and chaplains, both of those on voyage and of the maritime workers, because they do not find themselves in the condition above described.

After considering also the special circumstances of places and affairs, and since there are usually to be found difficulties that urge the ministry of these men, the privilege has been bestowed on them of blessing priestly vestments, altar cloths, corporals, tabernacles or vessels for preserving the Blessed Sacrament, and other things used in divine worship, using of course, the formulas found in the Roman Ritual, which are all reserved to priests who have the power to do so.

We need not add that missionaries and chaplains possess such privileges only during their term of office within the territory assigned to them. Thus, the national Director is to be regarded as having the mentioned faculty anywhere in the nation, within the limites of his jurisdiction; the missionary or chaplain only within the limits of the mission or port or ship to which he is assigned.

The faculty of blessing rosaries, crucifixes, small statues and medals

AAS, XLVI, 251, 13o and 418, 12o; XLVII, 92, 9o.

All missionaries to migrants, ship chiplains, and chaplains to maritime people are given the faculty of blessing "with the ceremonies prescribed by the Church, with all the indulgences usually granted by the Holy See, rosaries, crucifixes, small statues and medals; furthermore to apply to rosaries the indulgences called of St. Bridget and the Crosier Fathers."

We must consider first the words "with the ceremonies prescribed by the Church." These words are the same as those in Canon 349, 1, 1⁰, in which are recalled the privileges enjoyed by bishops whether residential or titular. For by virtue of Canon 349, 1, 1⁰, bishops, from the time they receive authentic notification of their canonical promotion, have the faculty of blessing everywhere, using the prescribed ceremonies of the Church, with all the indulgences usually granted by the Holy See, rosaries and other devotional chaplets, crosses, medals, statues, etc.

Cardinals alone, have by common law the faculty of doing this with only the sign of the cross. (Canon 239, 1, 5⁰)

So in regard to rite, missionaries and chaplains ought to use the special forms provided in the *Roman Ritual,* as *e.g.,* in the Appendix under nos. 35, 36, 39, etc. These contain formulas for the blessing of beads, whether the Holy Rosary of the Blessed Virgin Mary, proper to the Order of Preachers, or of St. Bridget, proper to the Order of the most Holy Savior.

Secondly you will note that the faculty which missionaries and chaplains possess by virtue of the present concession is not as broad as the faculty of bishops, for the latters' is good everywhere, while a missionary's faculty is confined to the territory where he works.

It remains to explain what should be understood by the words "with all the indulgences usually granted by the Holy See."

In our opinion there are included, besides others, those Apostolic indulgences also that the Supreme Pontiff graciously bestowed on March 12, 1939.[50]

It may be permitted to add a few words on the faculty of granting the indulgences of the rosary called of the Crosier Fathers, since we have already spoken briefly on the blessing of the beads of St. Bridget.

The indulgences attached to rosaries blessed by the Crosier Fathers are to be understood as those which have been applied by the Roman Pontiff to rosaries blessed by the Master General of the Order of Canons Regular of the Holy Cross or by members of that Order; they are, of course, indulgences of 500 days as often as the *Our Farther* or *Hail Mary* is said devoutly on the rosary blessed by the Crosiers. To gain these indulgences it is not necessary to recite the whole Rosary.[51]

C

MIGRANTS, TRAVELLERS ON SHIPS, AND MARITIME WORKERS, MAY SATISFY THE PRECEPT OF EASTER COMMUNION AT ANY TIME DURING THE YEAR

AAS, XLVI, 251, 10, and 418, 9: XLVII, 92, 4.

With His life-giving words "Unless you eat the flesh of the Son of man, and drink his blood, you shall not have life in you" (John 6:54), Christ Our Lord gave men the precept of receiving Holy Communion. Holy Mother Church insists on this divine precept in her laws. With the solemn sanction of the 4th Lateran Ecumenical Council in 1215, she promulgated the famous Canon 21, by which sacramental Confession and Holy Communion are prescribed for the faithful who have attained the use of reason:

> "Each and every one of the faithful, of either sex, who has reached the age of reason, is to confess all his sins at least once a year to his own priest and to strive as far as possible to complete the penance imposed on him, reverently receiving, at least at Easter time, the Eucharistic Sacrament, unless, perhaps, on the advice of his priest, for some good reason he judges he should abstain for a time from its reception." [52]

The Congregation of the Sacraments, in a wonderful Decree of August 8, 1910, *Quam singulari*, on the age for first Holy Communion, gave new and very wise rules that removed abuses. By these rules, children at the age when they are reaching the use of reason, *i.e.*, around seven years, more or less, have acquired the obligation of satisfying the precepts both of Confession and of Communion, so that they may keep to Jesus Christ, even at tender years, live His life and find safety against the dangers of corruption.[53]

Finally, Canon 859 of the Code of Canon Law confirms the precept of the 4th Lateran Council almost word for word in prescribing:

> "Each and everyone of the faithful, of either sex, after reaching the age of discretion, i.e., of the use of reason, should once a year at least at Easter time, receive the Eucharistic Sacrament, unless possibly, on the advice of his priest, for some good reason he judges he should abstain for a time from its reception."

The Easter time is assigned by the Church not for terminating, but for urging the obligation, so that the precept of Easter Communion still binds, even though one has not fulfilled it at the prescribed time for some reason. (Canon 859, 4)

The Easter time for fulfilling the precept begins with Palm Sunday and ends with the Sunday after Easter. However, by common law, "The local ordinaries may, if the circumstances of persons or places require it, extend this time for all their faithful; they cannot, however, start it earlier than the fourth Sunday in Lent, nor end it later than Trinity Sunday." (Canon 859, 4)

Kindly Mother Church has been busied in considering the spiritual welfare of those of her faithful who are migrants, maritime workers or traveling on ships; for after having considered the special circumstances of persons and places, she has granted that these Christians may satisfy the precept of Easter Communion during any time of the year.

For a fuller knowledge of the matter and the concession, it is enough to note only a few things about seamen.

Seamen, because of their duties, whether they are on

merchant vessels or at sea as fishermen, are for the most part cut off from the Church's ministry, not only for years but even for their whole lives. They are seldom in ports on Sundays, for to save expenses ships are often sent to sea on Saturday not to return before Monday. If sometimes, indeed, a ship is in port on Sunday, the men may have to work all day at repairing it, Sunday or not. I need not mention fishing boats, that call at a port in the morning and leave again the following night, or vice versa.

Therefore, using this concession, chaplains and missionaries who are altogether inadequate in number for the needs of souls can, during any time of the year, urge the faithful entrusted to them though they meet them infrequently, to fulfill their Easter duty, using of course, those means of the apostolate and solemnities of ceremony urged by circumstances of time and place.

As to the place in which Easter Communion may be received, the faithful were in past times supposed to approach the altar rail of their own parish, so that the pastor could know more closely the flock entrusted to his care.

In the present altered circumstances, and according to the ecclesiastical discipline in force, the faithful can merely be advised to satisfy this precept in their own parish church. Whoever satisfies it in some other parish should take care to inform his own pastor that he has fulfilled the requirement. (Canon 859, 3)

If these last words are considered carefully, along with those of *Exsul Familia*, Title Two, article 46: "The bishops should not hesitate to urge pastors to keep in contact with their people even after they migrate," you can readily understand that missionaries and chaplains will be a service if they strive to inform the migrants' pastors when these people fulfill their Easter duty.

Actually, what we referred to above does not seem to be the last novelty brought up since it corresponds perfectly to those prescriptions for Italians outside Italy, "in places where free and public worship or the use of the Catholic religion does not exist," which were stated by Clement VIII, as far back as 1596:

> "Since the aforementioned Italians leave Italy to sojourn or to dwell in the mentioned regions, they should inform their local Ordinaries or the Inquisitors, by whom they should be gravely admonished that in those new places they are to lead a devout Catholic life, resolutely retaining and professing the Catholic and true faith. They should honor religiously the Sundays and Holydays, abstinences and holy fasts prescribed by the Church, and flee and avoid every heresy and error, heretics, schismatics and all those who wander from the true faith. At least once a year they are to report to their Ordinaries or the Inquisitors in Italy on their reception of the sacraments of Confession and Communion. We declare this obligatory for the migrating Italians." [54]

Faithful who assist at a Mass said by a missionary as well as by a ship chaplain or by a chaplain to maritime people on a portable altar satisfy the obligation of hearing Mass

AAS, XLVII, 92, 5.

Among the requirements for hearing Mass on Holydays of obligation there should certainly be considered *a proper place*. We deduce from the principles of common law that he fully and properly satisfies the precept of hearing Mass who is present at Mass celebrated outdoors or in any church or public or semi-public oratory, even in any Catholic Rite. (Canon 1249)

To remove any cause of doubt or anxiety, and having considered the privilege of the portable altar, which as we noted above, missionaries or chaplains possess, Pius XII granted and declared that the faithful who attend Mass celebrated by a missionary or chaplain on a portable altar in any place, or even outdoors, satisfy fully the precept of hearing Mass.

Faithful may gain an indulgence "toties quoties" in a ship's chapel and in a mission chapel on August 2

AAS, XLVI, 251, 11 and 418, 10: XLVII, 92, 6.

One firstly ought to know the following about the *Portiuncula* indulgence.

Whoever wants to gain the *Portiuncula* indulgence should confess his sins, and if necessary, be absolved from them, and then receive the Sacrament of the altar. He should visit a church or oratory endowed with the privilege, and offer prayers as usual for the intention of the Holy Father, i.e., at least six *Our Fathers, Hail Marys and Glorys* on each of the visits, which he may make repeatedly for gaining the indulgence.

Local Ordinaries, pastors and rectors of sacred buildings in which the privilege exists have the faculty, if for just reasons they deem it expedient, of substituting the next following Sunday as the day for gaining the indulgence, if August 2 is not a Sunday.[55]

By common law, if a visit to a church or oratory is required for gaining an indulgence attached to any day, it may be made from noon of the preceding day to the midnight that ends the appointed day.[56]

The *Portiuncula* privilege, conceded to ship's chapels and mission chapels or oratories is granted with these words:

> The faithful on board ship, provided they have confessed and received Holy Communion, may gain a plenary indulgence on August 2, as often as they devoutly visit an oratory legitimately established on the ship where the Blessed Sacrament is preserved by Apostolic indult, and there recite earnestly on each visit six Our Fathers, Hail Marys and Glorys for the intention of the Supreme Pontiff. Similarly, the faithful who are migrants, provided they have comfessed and received Holy Communion, gain a plenary indulgence on August 2 as they devoutly visit an oratory or mission chapel where the Blessed Sacrament is lawfully reserved, and there devoutly recite six Our Fathers, Hail Marys and Glorys for the intentions of the Holy Father on each visit."

Faithful may gain an indulgence "toties quoties" to be applied to the dead, in a ship's chapel on November 2

AAS, XXXXVI, 252, 12 and 418, 11.

This type of spiritual privilege seems to require no special explanation; it is expressed in these words:

> "The faithful travelling on ships, provided they have confessed and received Holy Communion, may receive a plenary indulgence to be applied to the dead on November 2, as often as they devoutly visit an oratory legitimately established on a ship where the Blessed Sacrament is preserved by Apostolic indult, and there devoutly recite six Our Fathers, Hail Marys, and Glorys for the intention of the Supreme Pontiff on each visit."

One further note may be added, since in *"The Norms and Facuties for priests engaged in the spiritual care of migrants,"* no mention is found of indulgences to be gained on November 2 for the dead. The reason is that in this matter there are available for migrants the general rules given by Pope Pius XI, which we are glad to recall for the convenience of missionaries:

> "On All Souls day or on the following Sunday there is granted to the faithful as often as they visit any church or public or (for legitimate users) semi-public oratory, in behalf of the dead, a plenary indulgence applicable only to the souls in purgatory, if, besides confession, these faithful receive Holy Communion and recite six Our Fathers, Hail Marys and Glorys for the intention of the Holy Father on each visit."[57]

FOOTNOTES

1. *AAS*, XXXXVII, 91-92.
2. *AAS*, XXXXVI, 248-52.
3. *AAS*, XXXXVI, 415-18.
4. *Exsul Familia*, title II, chapter II, n. 11, 1.
5. *Exsul Familia*, title II, chapter II, n. 11, 2.
6. *loc. cit.*, n. 13, 1.
7. *loc. cit.*, n. 13, 2.
8. *Exsul Familia*, title II, chapter III, n. 30.
9. *loc. cit.*, n. 18, 1.
10. *Exsul Familia*, title II, chapter I, n. 1, 1.
11. *AAS*, XXXXVI, 415, I, 4.
12. *Acts of the Consistorial Congregation*, AM, 3.
13. *Exsul Familia*, title II, chapter III, n. 25, 1.
14. *loc. cit.*; *AAS*, XXXXVI, 249, II, 7.
15. *AAS*, XXXVIII, 349-354.
16. *AAS*, XLV, 758-759.
17. *AAS*, XXXVIII, 351.
18. *AAS*, XXXVIII, 353, VII.
19. *AAS*, XXXVIII, 353,
20. The Congregation of the Sacraments in 1953 to the Archbishop of Mechlin, who had asked for it, granted the faculty of permitting in the port of Antwerp to the priests of the Apostolate of the Sea, during sea journeys, to celebrate Mass and hear confessions.
21. J. B. Raus, *Instit. can.*, n. 332, *Instit. morales Alphonsianae*, 19th ed., title II, p. 172.
22. *Decreta authentica S. Rituum Congregationis*, n. 2621.
23. *AAS*, XXXXI, 493 f.
24. Instruction of the Congregation concerning the Discipline of the Sacraments, October 1, 1949; *AAS*, XXXXI, 501-504, II, 1, 4, 7.
25. Consistorial Congregation, in audience with the Pope, June 12, 1953.
26. *AAS*, XXXXI, 493.
27. *AAS*, XXI, 631-642.
28. *AAS*, *loc. cit.*, 636.
29. *Exsul Familia*, title II, chapter III, n. 25, 1.
30. *Exsul Familia*, title II, chapter III, n. 26.
31. *Authentic Decrees of the Sacred Congregation of Rites* (Rome: Vatican press) nos. 980, 1822, 2465.
32. Canon 239 1, 40.
33. Canon 349 1, 10.
34. *Ordo Divini officii recitandi sacrique peragendi pro clero saeculari romano*, 1954 (Rome: Vatican Library Press), p. 48.

35. *Authentic Decrees of the Sacred Congregation of Rites*, n. 3390.

36. Canon 862.

37. *Caeremoniale Episcoporum*, 1, II, chapter XXIII, 3.

38. *Authentic Decrees of the Sacred Congregation of Rites*, n. 1837, 2099.

39. *Ibid.*, n. 3309.

40. Audience of His Holiness, February 12, 1954, B.

41. Roman Breviary, December 31, St. Sylvester Pope and Confessor, Lesson VI; Cfr. Mononi, *Dizionario di erudizione storico—ecclessastica*, "Feria", Venice, MIDCCCXLIII, 22-23.

42. *AAS*, XXXXV, 22-23.

43. *Ibid.*, 49-50.

44. *AAS*, XXXXV, 426.

45. *Summa Theologica*, II-II, q. XII, a. I, ad 3.

46. *AAS*, XXXXI, 334.

47. *Institutiones Morales Alphonsianae*, Cl. Marc and Fr. X. Gestermann. 19th edition by P. J. B. Raus, C. Ss. R., (Paris: Emmanuel Vitte, 1934) column II, n. 370, n. 1833, 1.

48. *Ibid.*, 283, n. 444, I.

49. Holy Office, June 20, 1859, *Coll. Lac.*, III, 50.

50. *AAS*, XXXI 132, Apostolic Penitentiary (Section on Indulgences). Pope Pius XII in an audience granted to the Major Cardinal Penitentiary on March 11, 1939 graciously bestowed the Apostolic Indulgences upon "those who possess any devotional or religious object blessed by Himself or a priest having the power, if they satisfy the necessary conditions."

51. Decree of the Congregation on Indulgences, May 15, 1884: Collections of the Congregation for the Propagation of the Faith, vol. II, Rome, 1907. p. 200, n. 1616.

52. *AAS*, II, 578.

53. *AAS*, II, 577-583.

54. *Bullarium Romanum*, title X, Augustae Taurinorum, MDCCCLXV, p. 279: "That the Italians going abroad should not settle in places where there is no free and public worship or practice of the Catholic religion." n. 3.

55. *Enchiridion Indulgentiarum*, (Rome: Vatican Press) (2nd ed.) MCMLII, p. 533, n. 698.

56. Canon 923.

57. *Enchiridion Indulgentiarum* (2nd ed.), MCMLII, 455 f.

NORMS AND FACULTIES OF THE CONSISTORIAL CONGREGATION

For priests engaged in the spiritual care of those on ships, i.e., for ship chaplains and Directors of chaplains.

I

1. Those priests are considered lawfully established as ship Chaplains or Directors of chaplains who meet fully the requirements prescribed in Title Two, article 5, of the Apostolic Constitution *Exsul Familia,* and are approved and appointed by the Consistorial Congregation and given a special Rescript.

2. The Delegate for Migration Affairs, who has jurisdiction over ship Chaplains, whether secular or religious, and their Directors, directs all of them, supervises them, assigns Chaplains to ships and carefully aids them, mainly through the Directors.

3. It shall be a sacred duty for ship Chaplains and their Directors to observe scrupulously everything prescribed for ship Chaplains and their Directors in the Constitution mentioned above. (1.c., c. III)

4. An Apostolic indult must be obtained from the Consistorial Congregation if the Blessed Sacrament is to be preserved in alegitimately erected ship's chapel. (*Ibid.,* article 30) Application for such an indult is to be made by the Director of ship Chaplains. In addition, the local Ordinary, who has charge of establishing and blessing ships' chapels,

is to furnish evidence of conformity with liturgical law.

5. Priests on a ship at sea may, throughout the journey, use the calendar of the Universal Church in conducting services and in reciting the divine office.

6. During a voyage, after having mentioned the Pope's name in the Canon of the Mass, the name of any local bishop is omitted.

7. Records are to be kept of baptisms, confirmations and deaths, (*loc. cit.*, article 25, 3) and accurate copies are to be forwarded to the Curia.

In regard to this, the Consistorial Congregation directs that:

a) An authentic copy of the baptism, confirmation and death records, prepared by the ship Chaplain, is to be forwarded to the Curia of the diocese in which the Director's office is located.

b) Such copies are to be prepared by the Director alone for forwarding by him to the Curia.

c) The same Director is to report on the number confirmed by ship Chaplains in virtue of the authority conferred below, and on the motive used by them in performing this function as ministers extraordinary. This report, for each year is to be sent at the beginning of the following year to the Consistorial Congregation and to the Ordinary of the diocese mentioned.

d) The pastor of the domicile of the persons who occur in the records must also be notified by the Director as soon as possible of the acts recorded therein, observing exactly in their matter the norms of the sacred canons.

e) The Director of Chaplains is to use his own seal, and have cabinets or files, where for convenience or necessity the said records can be preserved, together with letters and other documents from the Consistorial Congregation and the bishops.

f) The Director alone is to furnish letters of reference to those concerned.

II

8. The following faculties or privileges, granted to ship Chaplains, are bestowed *for the duration of their term of office.*

a) The faculty of administering Confirmation, in accordance with the Decree *Spiritus Sancti munera,* of the Congregation of the Sacraments, (*AAS,* XXXVIII, 349) to any of the faithful travelling aboard ship who are gravely ill and in danger of death.

b) The faculty of administering the sacrament of Confirmation, during a voyage, to any child or adult, especially to any who has made his first Communion on that ship, provided that no Bishop enjoying communion with the Holy See is present and it may be foreseen that the person to be confirmed, will, because of age or ignorance of language or the circumstances of the place, receive this sacrament only with great difficulty in the region of immigration. The other requirements of law are to be observed, and especially, concerning the ceremonies, the Instructions found in the appendix of the *Roman Ritual,* for the administration of the Sacrament of Confirmation by a simple priest delegated by the Holy See.

c) The privilege of a portable altar, provided that Mass is celebrated for the advantage of the faithful on board, observing well, however, all the precautions on this matter contained in the Constitution *Exsul Familia* and especially Title Two, article 28.

d) The faculty of celebrating the Sacrifice of the Mass

on ships, even though they lack a legitimately erected chapel, at midnight on Christmas, provided that devotions precede the celebration of Mass for a least half an hour and the Mass be not begun until one-half hour after midnight, any danger of irreverence being always removed and observing the other requirements of law.

e) The faculty of celebrating Mass on ships, even though they lack a legitimately erected chapel, on New Year's Eve, with the privilege of beginning Mass at midnight, provided that the devotions last for a period of around two hours, including the time for celebrating Mass; the danger of any irreverence being always removed and other requirements of law being observed.

f) The privilege of celebrating one Mass on Holy Thursday.

g) The faculty of saying Mass two or three times on Sundays and Holy Days of obligation, as well as on ferial days, for the advantage of the faithful travelling on ships, as often as necessity urges providing for their spiritual welfare through the celebration of Mass.

h) With regard to the celebration of afternoon or evening Masses, there continues in effect the Decree of the Congregation of the Holy Office of May 31, 1953. (AAS. XXXXV, 426)

i) The faculty of absolving, during a voyage, the other requirements of law being observed, any penitents from the penalty which, according to Canon 2350, they incur who induce abortion.

j) The faculty of absolving, during a voyage, other requirements of law being observed, as well as others that in such circumstances are usually imposed by the Penitentiary, and in cases in which, according to Canon 2314, 2, the Ordinary himself can grant absolution, any penitents, travelling for any reason by ship, from the censures and penalties to which they are held because of apostasy, heresy or schism (except, however, heretics purposely spreading heresy among the faithful, as well as with no one listening or noticing, as before others) and of receiving their abjuration juridically performed.

k) The faculty of blessing the priestly vestments, altar cloths and linens, corporals, tabernacles or vessels for preserving the Blessed Sacrament, and other things used in the divine services.

l) The faculty of blessing, using the rites prescribed by the Church, and with all the indulgences usually granted by the Holy See, rosaries, crucifixes, small statues and medals and moreover of attaching to rosaries the indulgences of St. Bridget and of the Crozier Fathers.

III

9. Maritime persons may satisfy the precept of Easter Communion at any time during the whole year.

10. The faithful aboard ship, provided they have confessed and received Holy Communion, may obtain a plenary indulgence on August 2, as often as they devoutly visit a chapel legitimately established on a ship, where the Blessed Sacrament is reserved by Apostolic indult, and there reverently recite six *Our Fathers, Hail Marys and Glorys*, for the intention of the Holy Father on each visit.

Given at Rome, from the offices of the Consistorial Congregation, March 19, 1954, on the feast of St. Joseph, spouse of the Blessed Virgin Mary.

A. Cardinal Piazza, Bishop of Sabina and Poggio Mirteto, Secretary,

JOSEPH FERRETTO,
Assessor.

For priests engaged in the spiritual care of Maritime
Persons, i.e., for Chaplains and Directors of the
Apostolate of the Sea.

I

On April 17, 1922, Pope Pius XI, of happy memory, "honored with his own good wishes and enriched with the approval of the Holy See the work of the Apostolate of the Sea. That work was first established in Glasgow, Scotland, in 1920, for the spiritual, moral and social welfare of sailors. When, after numerous congresses and through the approval of bishops, the Apostolate had developed and spread widely, We ourselves decreed on May 30, 1942, that it should in the future have the benefit and advantage of direction by the Consistorial Congregation." (Constitution *Exsul Familia*, Title One, *AAS*, XLIV, 674)

"We establish in the offices of the Consistorial Congregation another agency, the General International Secretariate, to direct the work of the Apostolate of the Sea. The chief function of this Apostolate is to promote the spiritual and moral welfare of maritime people, *i.e.*, of both those who board ships as officers and those who go as crew members, together with those who are employed in ports to prepare sailings.

"The Assessor of the Consistorial Congregation shall direct this Secretariate as its president. The Delegate for Migration Affairs shall be its Secretary.

"The following may be chosen as members of the Secretariate:

1. Those ecclesiastics who in each country have been appointed as Directors of such work.

2. Other priests who, having worked notably in the

development of this work, should be honored by proper recognition." (*Ibid.*, Title Two, article 8: 1, 2, 3; AAS, XXXXIV, 695)

II

Those priests shall be considered lawfully established as Chaplains or Directors—for each country or nation—in the work of the Apostolate of the Sea, who have been nominated by the Ordinaries and approved and chosen by the Consistorial Congregation and given a special Rescript.

The same rules, with due allowances, hold for priests legitimately installed as Chaplains or Directors of the Apostolate of the Sea as are prescribed for ship Chaplains and their Directors in the Constitution *Exsul Familia*, Title Two, chapter 3.

Priests on a ship at sea may, throughout the voyage, use the calendar of the Universal Church in saying Mass and in reciting the Divine Office.

During a voyage, after having mentioned the Pope's name in the Canon of the Mass, no name of any local Bishop is mentioned.

Chaplains of the Apostolate of the Sea are also held to the obligation of keeping records of baptisms, confirmations and deaths, and of sending them to the Director for preservation in the files.

With regard to the preservation of these records and the forwarding of an accurate copy to the Curia, the Consistorial Congregation directs that:

1. An accurate copy of the baptism, confirmation and death records prepared by the Chaplains of the Apostolate of the Sea is to be forwarded to the Curia of the diocese in which the Director's office is located.

2. Such copies are to be prepared by the Director alone for forwarding by him to the Curia.

3. The same Director is to report on the number confirmed, by virtue of the faculty conferred below, by Chaplains of the Apostolate of the Sea, and on the motives used by them in performing this function as extraordinary ministers. This report, for each year, is to be sent at the beginning of the following year to the Consistorial Congregation and to the Ordinary of the diocese mentioned.

In order that the regulations of the sacred canons on this matter may be strictly observed, the Director should as soon as possible report the acts described in the records to the pastors of the domicile of those persons whose names appear in them.

5. The national Director is to use his own seal and have cabinets or files, where for convenience or necessity the said records can be preserved, together with letters and other documents from the Consistorial Congregation and the bishops.

6. The Director alone is to furnish letters of reference to those concerned.

III

The following faculties or privileges, granted to Chaplains of the work of the Apostolate of the Sea and their Directors, are bestowed *for the term of their office.*

1. The faculty of administering Confirmation, in accordance with the Decree *Spiritus Sancti munera,* of the Congregation for the Sacraments, (*AAS*, XXXVIII, 349) to maritime persons who are gravely ill and in danger of death.

2. The faculty of administering the sacrament of Confirmation, during a voyage, to any child or adult, especially to any who has made his first Communion on this ship, pro-

vided that no bishop enjoying communion with the Holy See is present and it may be foreseen that the person to be confirmed will, because of age or ignorance of language or the circumstances of the place, receive this sacrament only with great difficulty in the region of immigration. The other requirements of law are to be observed, and especially concerning the rite the Instructions, found in the appendix of the Roman Ritual, for the administration of the Sacrament of Confirmation by a simple priest delegated by the Holy See.

3. The privilege of a portable altar, provided that Mass is celebrated for the benefit of maritime persons; this privilege may also be used at sea, observing well, however, all the requirements on this matter contained in the Apostolic Constitution *Exsul Familia* and especially Title 2, article 28.

4. The faculty of celebrating the Sacrifice of the Mass on ships, even though they lack a legitimately erected chapel, at midnight on Christmas, provided that devotions precede the celebration of Mass for at least half an hour and the Mass be not begun until one-half hour after midnight, any danger of irreverence being always removed and other requirements of law being fulfilled.

5. The faculty of celebrating Mass on ships, even though they lack a legitimately erected chapel, on New Year's Eve, with the privilege of beginning Mass at midnight, provided that devotions last for a period of around two hours, including the time for celebrating Mass; the danger of any irreverence being always removed and other requirements of law observed.

6. The privilege of celebrating one Mass on Holy Thursday.

7. The faculty of saying Mass two or three times on Sundays and Holydays of obligation, as well as on ferial

days, for the benefit of maritime persons, as often as necessity urges providing for their spiritual welfare through the celebration of Mass.

8. With regard to the celebration of afternoon or evening Masses, there continues in effect the Decree of the Congregation of the Holy Office of May 31, 1953. (*AAS, XXXXV*, 426)

9. The faculty of absolving, during a voyage, the other requirements of law being observed, any penitents from the penalty which, according to Canon 2350, 1, they incur who induce abortion.

10. The faculty of absolving, during a voyage, other requirements of law being observed, as well as others that are usually imposed by the Sacred Penitentiary in such circumstances, and in cases in which, according to Canon 2314, 2, the Ordinary himself can grant absolution, any penitents, travelling for any reason by ship, from the censures and penalties to which they are held because of apostasy, heresy or schism (except, however, heretics purposely spreading heresy among the faithful, as well as with no one listening or noticing, as before others) and of receiving their abjuration, juridically performed.

11. To the National Directors, and to them only, the faculty of hearing confessions, in case of necessity, of any of the faithful who approach them in places near the shores of their own nation, provided that the Director has been approved by his own Ordinary for hearing confessions.

12. The faculty of blessing the priestly vestments, cloths and altar linens, corporals, tabernacles or vessels for preserving the Blessed Sacrament, and other things used in the divine worship.

13 The faculty of blessing, using the rite prescribed by

the Church, and with all the indulgences usually granted by the Holy See, rosaries, crucifixes, small statues and medals; and moreover of attaching to rosaries indulgences of St. Bridget and of the Crosier Fathers.

Maritime persons may satisfy the precept of Easter Communion at any time during the whole year.

The faithful aboard ship, provided they have confessed and received Holy Communion, may obtain a plenary indulgence on August 2, as often as they devoutly visit a chapel legitimately existing on a ship, where the Blessed Sacrament is preserved by Apostolic indult, and there reverently recite six *Our Fathers, Hail Marys* and *Glorys* for the intention of the Holy Father on each visit.

The same faithful may, under the same conditions, gain a plenary indulgence on November 2, to be applied to the dead, as often as they devoutly visit the said chapel and there reverently say six *Our Fathers, Hail Marys and Glorys,* for the intention of the Holy Father on each visit.

Given at Rome, from the offices of the Consistorial Congregation, April 2, 1954, the feast of St. Francis of Paula, patron of Italian seamen.

A. Cardinal Piazza, Bishop of Sabina and Poggio Mirteto, Secretary.

JOSEPH FERRETTO,
Assessor

*For priests engaged in the spiritual care of Migrants,
i.e., for missionaries to Migrants and Directors
of missionaries to Migrants.*

I

Those priests shall be considered legitimately established as Missionaries to migrants or Directors of Missionaries, who meet fully the requirements prescribed in Title Two, article 5, of the Apostolic Constitution *Exsul Familia,* and are approved and appointed by the Consistorial Congregation and given a special Rescript.

It shall be a sacred duty for Missionaries to Migrants and their Directors to observe everything prescribed for Missionaries to Migrants and their Directors in the Constitution mentioned above. (Title 2, chapters 3 and 4)

II

The following faculties or privileges, granted to ship Chaplains and their Directors, are bestowed *during the tenure of their office.*

1. The privilege with the consent of the local Ordinary of a portable altar, provided that Mass is said for the benefit of the faithful entrusted to them, and observing the other requirements of law.

2. The faculty of celebrating outdoors, provided likewise that Mass is celebrated for the benefit of the faithful entrusted to them, and the place fitting and decent and furnished with a tent protecting the altar from the wind, lest fragments be blown away, and having in mind the *Instruction* of the Congregation of Sacraments of October 1, 1949, (*AAS,* XXXXI, 493) the permission of the local Ordinary having similarly been obtained and observing the other requirements of law.

3. The faculty of saying two or three Masses on Sundays and Holydays of obligation, as well as on ferial days, for the benefit of the faithful living in mission territories, provided that permission of the local Ordinary is obtained and that the third Mass is celebrated in a different church from the first two, if this can be done without serious inconven-

ience; there being certainty in each case of the real necessity for a third Mass, the Director of Missionaries being responsible in conscience for this and the danger of an astonishment or scandal having been removed. The celebrant is forbidden to accept stipends for two Masses. He is to observe the other requirements of law.

4. The faculty of celebrating Mass, for the benefit of the faithful entrusted to him, at midnight on Christmas, any danger of irreverence being removed and observing the other requirements of law.

5. The faculty, likewise, of celebrating Mass for the same faithful on New Year's Eve, with the privilege of beginning Mass at midnight, provided that the devotions last for a period of around two hours, including the time for celebrating Mass; the danger of any irreverence being always removed and other requirements of law being observed.

6. The privilege of celebrating one Mass on Holy Thursday.

7. With regard to the celebration of afternoon or evening Mass, there continues in effect the requirements of Chapter 6 of the Constitution *Christus Dominus* of January 6, 1953. (*AAS*, XXXXV, 22)

8. The faculty of blessing the priestly vestments, cloths and altar linens, corporals, tabernacles or vessels for preserving the Blessed Sacrament, and other things used in the divine worship.

9. The faculty of blessing using the rite prescribed by the Church, and with all the indulgences usually granted by the Holy See, rosaries, crucifixes, small statues and medals; and moreover to attach indulgences to all rosaries of St. Bridget and of the Crosier Fathers.

III

Migrants may satisfy the precept of Easter Communion at any time during the year.

The faithful who assist at Mass celebrated by a Missionary to Migrants on a portable altar or outdoors satisfy the precept of hearing Mass on Holydays of obligation.

The faithful who are migrants, provided they have confessed and received Holy Communion, may gain a plenary indulgence on August 2, as often as they devoutly visit a mission oratory or chapel where the Blessed Sacrament is lawfully preserved and there reverently recite six *Our Fathers, Hail Marys* and *Glorys* for the intention of the Holy Father on each visit.

Given at Rome, from the offices of the Consistorial Congregation, on December 10, 1954, the feast of the Translation of the Holy House of the Blessed Virgin Mary.

A. Cardinal Piazza, Bishop of Sabina and Poggio Mirteto, Secretary.

JOSEPH FERRETTO
Assessor

LAWS OF THE APOSTOLATE OF THE SEA

1. The Work of the Apostolate of the Sea for the spiritual, moral, and social welfare of persons given to maritime pursuits, which was first founded in Glasgow, Scotland, in the year 1920 and was approved by the Holy See under the Pontificate of Pius XI, has, by order of His Holiness Pius XII, the benefit and advantage of direction by the Sacred Consistorial Congregation (Ap. Const., *Exsul Familia*, Title I, *AAS* 44-674).[1]

2. Under the name of persons given to maritime pursuits, in this connection, are included all who are engaged in navigation or fishing, either in positions of command or in service, and are obliged to live permanently in ships and so can only rarely and with difficulty have the benefit of the ordinary care of a pastor, or who are attached to ports for the work of preparing maritime voyages.

3. a) In the same Sacred Consistorial Congregation there is established a special organization or General International Secretariate to govern the Work of the Apostolate of the Sea.

The Head or President of this Secretariate is the Assessor of the Sacred Consistorial Congregation; the office of Secretary is held by the Delegate for Works of Emigration.

b) In this Secretariate the following may be members:

1⁰ Those ecclesiastics who in their respective districts or nations are appointed by the Bishops as Directors of this work;

2⁰ Other priests who have served well in the promotion of this same work, and who are recommended by appropriate testimonials (*Exsul Familia*, Title II, art. 8, a, b and c).[2]

4. From among the ecclesiastics who belong to the General International Secretariate of the Apostolate of the Sea, one is elected by this Sacred Congregation as International Promoter, and another as Executive Secretary.

5. a) According to norms recently issued by the Holy See, in every nation or district a special group or Commission of Bishops shall be established for the purpose of promoting, advancing, and governing the Apostolate of the Sea in that place.

b) If in any nation this Episcopal Commission cannot be established, the Bishops should appoint at least one, in the first place if possible the Bishop of a diocese whose seat or the greater part of whose territory is on the coast, who shall work zealously to promote the Apostolate of the Sea.

6. The Episcopal Commission or the Bishop especially chosen as Promoter must present to the Sacred Consistorial Congregation the name of a priest, as indicated in art. 3, b) 1⁰, so that the Sacred Congregation may by its authority approve him and confirm him in the office of Director of the Apostolate of the Sea for that entire nation or district.

7. a) For the office of Chaplain of the Work of the Apostolate of the Sea, those priests shall be regarded as lawfully chosen who, after being presented by the Ordinaries, are approved and nominated by the Sacred Consistorial Congregation and receive a special rescript (*Norms and Faculties for Chaplains, Apostolate of the Sea*, II, 3).[3]

b) Nuncios, Internuncios, and Apostolic Delegates

who have received for their respective territories the necessary faculties from the Sacred Consistorial Congregation, can by a special rescript approve and appoint to the office of Chaplain of the Work of the Apostolate of the Sea, priests presented by their proper Ordinary, so that these priests may, according to the norms issued by order of the Supreme Pontiff Pius XII on the 2nd of April, 1954 (*AAS,* 46-248- to 252)[4] licitly and validly exercise their office.

8. For priests legitimately appointed to the office of either Chaplain or Director of the Work of the Apostolate of the Sea, the same provisions shall be valid, with due allowances, as those which are enacted for Chaplains of Ships and their Directors in the Apostolic Constitution *Exsul Familia,* Tit. II, Chapter III (*Norms and Faculties,* II, 4).[5]

9. Chaplains of the Apostolate of the Sea and their Directors do their work under the direction of the Sacred Consistorial Congregation through the Delegate for Works of Emigration (*Exsul Familia,* Tit. II, art. 11).[6]

10. The office of Chaplain of the Apostolate of the Sea and that of Director do not produce excardination and do not confer any exemption, either from one's own Ordinary or regular Superior or from the Ordinary of the place where the chaplain happens to be (*Exsul Familia,* Tit. II, art. 18, b).[7]

11. Directors of Chaplains in the Apostolate of the Sea cannot in virtue of their office exercise any jurisdiction either territorial or personal, except as mentioned below.

12. It is especially the right and duty of the Director:

a) To make arrangements with the Bishops of his country regarding all matters which concern the spiritual welfare of maritime persons.

b) To have charge of the Chaplains of the Apostolate of the Sea, without prejudice to the rights of the Ordinaries (*Exsul Familia*, Tit. II, art. 20).[8]

c) To make all preparations and carefully see to it that, even though there is no chaplain and the ship has no legitimately erected oratory, priests who journey by sea be provided with everything that is needed to celebrate the Holy Sacrifice of the Mass according to liturgical laws.

13. Therefore the Director of the Work of the Apostolate of the Sea should inform himself:

a) Whether the chaplains are conducting themselves according to the sacred canons and diligently performing their duties;

b) Whether they duly observe the decrees that are issued by the Sacred Consistorial Congregation and by the local Ordinary;

c) Whether proper care is taken for the elegance and neatness of the churches or chapels or oratories and of the sacred furnishings, especially in regard to the custody of the Most Blessed Sacrament and the celebration of Mass;

d) Whether sacred functions are celebrated according to the prescriptions of liturgical laws and the decrees of the Sacred Congregation of Rites; whether ecclesiastical property is diligently administered and whether the obligations attached thereto, especially those of Masses, are duly fulfilled; finally, whether the parish books mentioned below are properly kept (*Exsul Familia*, Tit. II, art. 21, a).[9]

14. In order that the Director may the better perform all these duties, he should frequently visit the headquarters of the Apostolate of the Sea, especially those that are named after the Star of the Sea, and also the ports and the ships.

15. The Director may, with the consent of the Episcopal

Commission or of the National Promoter, call together as occasion demands all the chaplains or the entire nation, especially for the purpose of making the spiritual exercises together or attending conferences on the more effective fulfillment of their ministry.

16. a) At least once a year he shall report faithfully to the Episcopal Commission or to the National Promoter on the conduct of the chaplains and the condition of the centers of the Apostolate of the Sea, stating not only what has been well done during the year but also whatever defects may have crept in, what remedies were applied to cure them, and whatever seems to be indicated for the improvement of the Work of the Apostolate of the Sea.

b) The Chairman of the Episcopal Commission or the National Promoter shall examine this report, express his own conscientious judgment on it, and send it to the Sacred Consistorial Congregation.

17. a) The spiritual care of maritime people should not be entrusted to any priest who has not been properly prepared to do this special work creditably and been pronounced to be fit for it.

A Chaplain of the Apostolate of the Sea must therefore be marked by an upright life, zeal for souls, prudence, learning; he must be a capable speaker, enjoy sound health, and as far as possible be assigned exclusively to the care of maritime people.

b) Those who are assigned to this work should as far as possible be assigned to it permanently, which however does not prevent their being removed from it for a reasonable cause.

18. Chaplains of the Work of the Apostolate of the Sea

attend to the spiritual care of maritime persons under the jurisdiction of the local Ordinary.

19. It is the proper charge of Chaplains of the Work of the Apostolate of the Sea to have the care of souls, except as regards marriage.

20. Without prejudice to Canon 883 of the Code of Canon Law, the Chaplains are provided with special norms and faculties by the Sacred Consistorial Congregation, as hereinafter explained.

21. A Chaplain of the Apostolate of the Sea is bound in virtue of his office to exercise the care of souls in houses which are named after the Star of the Sea, in nautical academies, and in hospitals for maritime persons.

He should also serve with generous charity maritime persons who are ill, even though they are staying in other hospitals.

22. He should strive to prepare mentally and morally some men and women, especially from Catholic Action groups, to become efficient and earnest helpers in the Apostolate.

23. As far as possible the chaplain should abstain from assuming the financial administration of Stella Maris houses, but he should entrust it to a prudent man who is capable and well recommended, with the obligation of giving an account to the Council, of which the chaplain himself is the chairman.

24. During a sea voyage if the ship chaplain is for any reason absent, the care of the maritime people and of all persons on board shall pertain to the Chaplain of the Apostolate of the Sea.

Consequently—remembering, of course, that he is assigned to maritime people—he shall on all Sundays and feasts of obligation celebrate one Mass for the persons making the voyage and another for the maritime people; this last-mentioned Mass must be celebrated at a convenient hour, in a proper and suitable place, after timely consultation with the master or captain of the ship.

25. Chaplains of the Apostolate of the Sea are also bound to keep registers of baptisms, confirmations, and deaths, and to deliver them to the Director to be kept in the archives.

26. As to the keeping of these books and the sending of authentic copies to the Curia, the Sacred Consistorial Congregation prescribes:

a) Authentic copies of the registers which the Chaplains of the Apostolate of the Sea have kept of baptisms, confirmations, and deaths, shall be sent to the Curia of the diocese in which Director's office is located.

b) It is the duty of the Director alone to make out these copies and send them to the Curia.

c) It is the duty of the same Director to send to the Sacred Consistorial Congregation and to the Ordinary of the said diocese at the beginning of each year a report for the year just past, on the number of persons who were confirmed by the Chaplain of the Apostolate of the Sea in virtue of the faculty mentioned below under n. 29, a, and of the reason which they, as extraordinary ministers, had for performing that function.

d) The pastor of the domicile of the persons who occur in the books must also be notified by the Director as soon as possible of the acts recorded therein, observing exactly in this matter the norms of the sacred canons.

e) The National Director should use his seal and have a depository or archive in which the said books are to be kept, together with the letters of the Sacred Consistorial

Congregation and of the Bishops, and such other documents as it may be necessary or useful to preserve.

f) It pertains to the Director alone to give testimonial letters to persons who are entitled to them.

27. In performing sacred functions and in reciting the divine office during a sea voyage, the priests who are on board may use the Calendar of the Universal Church.

28. In the Canon of the Mass during a sea voyage, only the name of the Pope is mentioned, without that of any Bishop.

29. The Chaplains and Directors of the Apostolate of the Sea are given the following faculties or privileges during the term of their office:

a) The faculty of administering the sacrament of Confirmation according to the Decree of the S. C. of the Sacaments, *Spiritus Sancti munera* (*AAS* 38-349)[10] to maritime persons who are in danger of death from grave illness.

b) The faculty of administering the sacrament of Confirmation during a sea voyage to any child or adult who receives Holy Communion for the first time on board ship; provided there is present no Bishop who is in communion with the Holy See and it is foreseen that the person, either because of his age or his unfamilarity with the language, or because of local circumstances, will not be able without great difficultly to receive this sacrament in the country of immigration; observing the other provisions of law and especially as regards the rite, the Instruction for a simple priest administering the sacrament of Confirmation by delegation of the Holy See, which is found in the Appendix of the Roman Ritual.

c) The privilege of a portable altar, provided the Mass has to be celebrated for the convenience of the maritime persons; this privilege can be used also at sea, observing well however the precautions in this matter which are mentioned in the Apostolic Constitution *Exsul Familia,* especially Tit. II, art. 28.[11]

d) The faculty of celebrating the Sacrifice of the Mass in ships, even though they have no legitimately erected oratory, on the night of the Nativity of Our Lord, and of beginning the Mass at midnight; always removing all danger of irreverence and observing the other requirements of law.[12]

Inasfar as this can be done, the Mass should be preceded by prayers lasting at least half an hour.

e) The faculty of celebrating Mass in ships, even though they have no legitimately erected oratory, on the night between the 31st of December and the following 1st of January every year, with faculty of beginning the Mass at midnight, provided the prayers last for about two hours including the time of the Mass; always removing all danger of irreverence and observing the other requirements of law.

f) The privilege of celebrating one Mass on Holy Thursday.

g) The faculty of celebrating twice or three times on Sundays and feasts of obligation and on week days for the convenience of the maritime persons, whenever it is necessary in order to advance their spiritual welfare by celebrating Mass.

h) As regards the celebration of Mass in the evening or at a late hour, the common law is to be observed. But the Ordinary of the diocese in which the ship usually docks is competent to grant the faculty of celebrating evening Mass during the sea voyage for the benefit of the persons on board, according to the Decree of the Holy Office of May 31, 1953 (*AAS* 45-426).[13]

i) The faculty of absolving, during the sea voyage, any penitents from the censure which is incurred according to Canon 2350, 1 of the Code of Canon Law by persons who procure an abortion; observing the requirements of law.

j) The faculty of absolving, during a sea voyage, observing the requirements of law and the other conditions which the Sacred Penitentiary usually imposes in these circumstances, and in cases in which according to Canon 2314, 2 the Ordinary himself could absolve, all penitents who are on board for any reason, from the censures and penalties which they may have incurred because of apostasy, heresy, or schism, with the exception however of heretics who purposely spread heresy among the faithful, whether they did so outside the hearing and notice of any third person or in the presence of others, and to receive their abjuration made according to law.

k) For National Directors only, the faculty of hearing in case of necessity, the confessions of any of the faithful who come to them in places near the shore of their country, provided the Director has been approved by his own Ordinary for hearing confessions.

l) The faculty of blessing priestly vestments and altar cloths and linens, corporals, ciboriums or vessels for conserving the Most Blessed Eucharist, and other articles which are destined for the service of divine worship.

m) The faculty of blessing with the rites prescribed by the Church, with all the indulgences which are usually granted by the Holy See, rosaries, crosses, little statues and medals; and moreover of attaching to rosaries the indulgences of Saint Brigid and of the Crosier Fathers.

30. Maritime persons can fulfill the precept of paschal Communion at any time during the entire year.

31. The faithful on board ships, provided they go to confession and receive Holy Communion, can gain a plenary indulgence on the 2nd of August as often as they piously visit an oratory legitimately established on the ship, in which by apostolic indult the Most Blessed Eucharist is kept, and there devoutly recite in each visit six *Paters, Aves,* and *Glorias* according to the intentions of the Holy Father.

32. The same faithful, on the same conditions, can gain a plenary indulgence applicable to the faithful departed, on the 2nd of November, as often as they piously visit the said oratory and there devoutly recite in each visit six *Paters, Aves,* and *Glorias* according to the intention of the Holy Father.

Given at Rome, from the office of the Sacred Consistorial Congregation, the 21st of November, 1957, feast of the Presentation of the Blessed Virgin Mary, Star of the Sea.

1. Cf. *Canon Law Digest,* 3, p. 84; 4, p. 116.
AAS 44-695; *Canon Law Digest,* 3, p. 88.
3. *Canon Law Digest,* 4, p. 116.
4. *Ibid.,* 4, pp. 115-120.
5. *Ibid.,* 4, p. 116.
6. *Ibid.,* 3, p. 89.
7. *Ibid.,* 3, p. 90.
8. *Ibid.,* 3, pp. 90-91.
9. *Ibid.,* 3, p. 91.
10. *Canon Law Digest,* 3, p. 303.
11. *Ibid.,* 3, p. 92.
12. This is an enlargement of the faculty previously granted in the *Norms and Faculties for Directors and Chaplains of the Apostolate of the Sea,* Apr. 2, 1954, *AAS* 46-248, III, 9, 40. Cf. *Canon Law Digest,* 4, p. 118.
13. *Canon Law Digest,* 4, p. 283.

Editor's note: The English translation of this document has been taken from *The Canon Law Digest,* 1958, kindness of the Bruce Publishing Company, Milwaukee.

PART III

TWO OUTSTANDING HISTORICAL COMMENTARIES ON "EXSUL FAMILIA"

REFLECTIONS ON THE APOSTOLIC
CONSTITUTION *"EXSUL FAMILIA"*

by Joseph Ahltmayer (Austria)

IN writing down these reflections the author is able to
base himself only on the official text published in the
Acta Apostolica Sedis (Vol. XLIV; September 30, 1952)
and on the German translation of the second part of the
Constitution published *pro manu scriptu* by the Catholic
Foreign Secretariate, Beuel/Bonn. The article by Dr. Adolf
Kindermann, Koenigstein/Taunus is also very valuable.
It was published by installments in the *"Mitteilungen fuer
die heimatvertrebenen Priester aus dem Osten"* (1953,
numbers 1, 3 and 4), edited by the Priesterreferat, Koenigstein. Unfortunately I did not have at hand other inter-
pretations.

I want to stress here briefly a few principal features of the
Constitution:

1. The papal document contains two parts, one longer
and historical, the other shorter and normative. The historical part is not only instructive for the understanding of the
past, but it is above all basic for the understanding of the
spirit of the norms enforced in the second part for present
day practice. What the Church has done in its long history
and in numerous ways with motherly care, corresponding
to the demands of every period, shall also be done in adaptation to the needs of the present for the good of the migrants.
One cannot therefore correctly understand the present norms

for the spiritual care of the migrants without knowing about past activity.

2. The Constitution uses many expressions and terms for those being cared for, *emigrantes,* refugee, *peregrini, advenae, navigantes, emigrati*) and these make us see, that the Constitution is not only interested in a definite group of migrants, but in *the migrating men in general.* It is at first irrelevant whether these men have left their homes by their own free will, whether they were banished or expelled or have fled from it. All these migrants are endangered in a special degree compared to residents and therefore are the objects of the motherly care of the Church.

3. The dangers of migration appear so great to the Church that it extends its care not only to those actually in the act of migrating, but also to those who have decided on migration, in preparing them for it—and to those who have technically reached the goal of their emigration—by helping them with patient sympathy to get slowly acclimated in the new environment. It is very important for the right understanding of the Constitution to see and to distinguish clearly these three stages of migration, because we modern men are inclined to see and treat human beings simply as pawns on the chessboard of the globe, that is we understand the technical resettlement as the main thing and we underrate the psychological questions in this procedure of sinking new roots in foreign soil.

4. Language is the first means of approach to a human being in spiritual danger, indeed at first the language of the heart, but in the normal and complete way the mother tongue. That the Constitution does not think here only of language as a means of rational understanding can be seen

by the synonymous use of *"sermo"* and *"natio."* The Constitution demands therefore spiritual care in the mother tongue. It seems to us that this is an admonition to caution those who insist that the main purpose in sermon and religious teaching is the understanding of the words by the listener, even if they are not spoken in his mother tongue. Only he who understands something of the wealth of significance of the native language, will be able to imagine and measure the rational and purposive poverty and paleness of a foreign language barely learned. Based on the age-old experience of the Church, the Constitution puts therefore such great value on the spiritual care of the emigrant or immigrant in his own language. In this respect the Constitution is worldwide and catholic. It wishes a spiritual care of the immigrant, and emigrant in his mother tongue, wherever the immigrant is in foreign surroundings. This is just as valid for Italians in Belgium as for Dutchmen in Canada and so on. What is pointed out in Chapter 4 of the second part stating that even seasonal workers and students in foreign language countries are covered by the ruling of the Constitution, proves that the Church takes this care very seriously.

5. According to these reflections although it is a new and strange thing to many persons, it is only logical that the Constitution provides the creation of national—and language—parishes and that it gives to the missionaries of the immigrants or emigrants the faculties of a pastor of a personal kind equal to those of the local pastor (but restricted only to the immigrants).

It is very clear that the ruling of the Constitution is opposed to the policy of rapid "melting down", so frequently practiced, which has become the fashion in this age of extravagant nationalism. When in the Constitution the Holy Father opposes with full consciousness this "National policy" which has frequently become the fashion even in religious circles, then he must have been moved by very good reasons.

6. As main points for securing this kind of spiritual care for the foreign language immigrants in the sense of the Constitution appear to me:

a. The convention of the bishops' conference for foreign immigrants to the country in question, praised by the Holy Father and its referee for these questions and

b. the directors or moderators for foreign language Catholics who have to provide the spiritual care of their countrymen in accord with the bishops of the diocese.

Ending these reflections I still want to give some clarifications illustrating them with two often-used and typical objections:

1. Many believe to get rid of the disagreeable rules of the Constitution by declaring that these rules were only made because of the emigrating Italians. The confirmation to this assertion is that of the 6 chapters of the second part, 2 whole chapters, i.e., a third are intended for the Italians. On this point I want to say the following:

a. It is true that 2 of the 6 chapters of the second part are intended for Italian emigrants. But whoever studies the text of these two chapters carefully will easily recognize that the Holy Father describes more thoroughly and establishes as a norm the spiritual care of the Italian immigrants organized earlier by St. Pius X, because it can and should serve as a model to all other nations.

b. Nobody in his senses can deny it to the Holy Father

that he as the Bishop of Rome cares especially for the needs of his country. This is easily understood, because Italy is, so to say, one of the classically overpopulated countries and therefore is predestined for emigration.

c. A no less important reason is that the Holy Father wanted to insert and adapt the spiritual care of the Italian immigrants which had been organized up to now in its own way into the worldwide frame of the Constitution and therefore visible to the entire world.

2. Not a few people use the argument again that the Constitution should not be taken as seriously as the text demands, or that the norms are valid only for definite countries (the so-called classical immigration countries).

In objection to this I want to point out that several encyclicals of the last century had been commented on and put aside in a similar manner—to the greatest damage of those countries that had the audacity and the levity of thinking in this manner. In this connection I only want to recall the basic social encyclical *Rerum Novarum* of Leo XIII and the surprisingly clear and uncorruptible Encyclical *Divini Redemptoris* of Pius XI (against communism). How much damage could have been avoided if the contemporaries to whom they were addressed had taken seriously at the right moment the teachings and norms of the highest teacher of Christianity! In following the papal norms the main point is always and everywhere whether the children of the Church who naturally are at the same time children of their time and of the spirit of their time, are able and willing to obey God more than to obey men, *i.e.*, to subordinate to the *Cathedra Petri* their conceptions which have become so dear to them through custom and habit of their time. One can see how seriously the Holy Father takes the purpose of the Constitution, because in July of this year he recommended the spiritual care among the emigrants to the whole of Christianity as the intention of the Apostolate of Prayer.

THE CARE OF MIGRANTS

by Rev. C. Henkey-Honig, D.D., Ph.D.

THE new Apostolic Constitution[1] issued at Castel Gandolfo on August 1st, 1952, is the first step of the Holy See towards giving not only particular instructions in a special case, but general rules and a juridical basis for the pastoral care of Catholic emigrants. By these are meant all voluntarily or otherwise leaving their homesteads and countries and conducting a more or less settled life either in groups or scattered in foreign countries. Up to now, the making of necessary arrangements in such cases was left to the pastoral zeal and good sense of the bishops. But after the second world war such vast numbers of people were forced into exile, so many millions were becoming not only homeless but also stateless, that the brief reference in the Code of Canon Law dealing with the pastoral care of aliens was completely inadequate.

The heterogeneous elements, amounting to national islands or island nations, formed by refugees in the different countries could not be adequately provided for by parishes territorially constituted; and the arrangements the bishops were forced to make in very many cases seemed to stretch policy to the limits. The Holy See was fully aware of the delicateness of the matter, and it took more than five long years before it decided to lay down rules and to give a basis in law for this new kind of pastoral care.

I intend to give first a short summary of *Exsul Familia* (I); then I shall trace the reasons which led the Holy See to these decisions (II); and lastly I shall try to show the

importance of this Constitution for the further development
of international Catholic life (III).

Being a refugee myself, perhaps I am somewhat overestimating the weight of *Exsul Familia* for the Catholic
life of the universal Church. But the enormous sufferings of
millions driven out from their homes, torn away in so many
cases from their families, and wandering through the world,
cannot mean merely punishment for a sinful past. The apostles asked Our Lord: who sinned, this man or his parents,
and we know Our Lord's answer. The man's blindness had a
different positive meaning in the plans of divine providence.[2]
So I trust I do not err in supposing that the dire sufferings
of the refugees, too, are not only fruitless severe retributions
for faults and sins of nations and individuals, but that they
have a very positive and constructive value for the future
of the universal Church.

I

After a short introduction, in which the Holy Father
compares all the homeless ones to the Holy Family during
their exile in Egypt, follows a long and highly instructive
account of what the Church has done in the course of her
history for pilgrims, exiles and emigrants. So we learn about
the hospices for pilgrims in Rome and at other sacred places
in the Middle Ages; how the French refugees during the great
revolution were received and assisted; what care the Church
took to assure proper ecclesiastical aid for overseas emigrants, mainly for Italians, towards the end of the last and
at the beginning of this century; how she did her utmost
during the first world war for the prisoners of war and after
it for the masses of Russians, for the persecuted Armenians
and Mexicans; what she did for Spain during the civil war
and religious persecution. So it was also just "going her own

way," when recently, during and after the second world war, the Holy See not only expressed sympathy but took all the possible means to assist the persecuted nations and individuals and the millions drifting without hope in Europe, driven out by fear and force from their native countries.

In the second part, as is explicitly emphasized, exact and detailed norms and instructions are given for the organization of pastoral care for aliens and wayfarers (Apostolate of the Sea) in full accordance with the Code of Canon Law.

The main points of these regulations are:

The exclusive competency of the Consistorial Congregation is maintained and the rights of the Congregation *de propaganda fide* and the Oriental Congregation in the territories and over the persons under their jurisdiction.[3]

In the Consistorial Congregation there is instituted a "Supreme Council for Emigration" as well as the "General International Secretariate for the Apostolate of the Sea"—the presidents of both being assessor of the same Congregation.[4]

Both of these organs have the same secretary, the Delegate for Migration, who, although without jurisdiction either over priests or faithful, surveys the work done by and for them.[5] For every language or nation represented by the Delegate, a Director is appointed in order to survey the work more closely and to discuss with the bishops the measures to be taken to assure a proper pastoral care for the aliens. Here also are given minute rules for naval chaplains.[6]

The main persons under whose immediate authority the work is carried on are the bishops. In practice it is they who execute these provisions. It is they who are to provide for the alien priests of their own language and give to them the necessary faculties.[7]

The priests engaged in this work (*missionarii*) by the

bishop in whose territory they are working are subject to him in their person and also in their ministry. They have the same rights and obligations as the parish priests (*congrua tamen congruis referendo*). Their jurisdiction is full (including also the right to assist at marriages) but only personal, and their faithful are free to approach the local clergy as well for the sacraments.[8]

Here is given also a canonical definition of the persons for whose benefit *Exsul Familia* was drawn up. Aliens are: (1) all foreigners, also immigrants from the colonies independently of the time or length of time, and of the reasons why they reside abroad; (2) all their descendants in the first grade of direct line, even if then they have already acquired the new citizenship.[9]

Chapters V and VI are of more particular interest, dealing exclusively with the problems of Italian emigration, prescribing for the Italian hierarchy and faithful what they are to do[10] and laying down regulations for the Papal College of Priests for Emigrants.[11]

II

Reading *Exsul Famila* with attention, one is struck by the very careful wording used by the Holy See. The expression 'nationalities,' which could easily be misunderstood in the political sense of national minorities creating so many difficulties chiefly in eastern Europe, is never used. The Constitution speaks always of different languages or nations (*sermo, lingua, dicio seu natio*). This sufficiently emphasizes that the problem which alone occupies the Holy See is pastoral care; and one chief means to that is the language used in religious life.

But on the other hand, to insist only upon the difference of language would mean ignoring the problem in its full extent. There are two equally just claims to be reconciled: that of the aliens and that of the countries giving hospitality to them.

Before proceeding further, we should remark that the word 'alien' is used in the most general sense, including refugees who were forced to leave their country, emigrants who left voluntarily but for good, and also aliens who happen to live abroad for some reasons or other for a longer or shorter time. Our discussion is concerned mainly with the situation of refugees; the contrast being sharpest in their case, we can best see the problems of aliens.

It was mainly the case of refugees which urged the Holy See to reconsider the problem and to give it a preemptory solution on a canonical basis, and so I feel justified in arguing from their situation. A Church law must be always broad enough to cover all the possible situations; but the extreme cases always shed a strong light on the necessities which the ordinary cases do not call to our attention sharply. Having met in advance a possible objection, let us now consider the situation from the point of view of the refugees.

Refugees want to preserve not only their own language which they are in any case forced to do because of their ignorance or very imperfect knowledge of the language of their new country, but also their national feelings, traditions, in short everything they were able to save when escaping; and this is but natural. They were forced to leave their countries, and they would return to them if they could. It would be inhuman and unjust to find fault with them for that way of thinking and feeling. Everybody knows, as they also do, that with time a change will come and the second generation will be perfectly acclimatized and will feel the new country is their home. But this change of mind cannot be forced upon the first generation.

Refugees are and feel themselves to be members of their suppressed nation and no country offering refuge to them can ask from them as a reward to give up these feelings. Nowhere are national feelings so strong and delicate as in refugees. They feel the strongest and suffer the most under the antagonism of losing country and retaining nationality. The reality of life is opposed by emotional forces. Inwardly they know that the case is hopeless; these national feelings so dear to them cannot be perpetuated. But the more they feel the hopelessness of their case the more sensitive they are about it. These exaggerations of nationalistic feelings in refugees are perhaps somewhat too exactly and critically observed by their hosts. If they could understand (as the Holy See does) that just claims are here mingled with morbid manifestations they could more easily pardon these much suffering ones their lack of balance. They try honestly to be grateful and loyal, but nobody should demand of them that they forget their past. Even if they were to try to give up everything and start a wholly new life, there would be in it a violence against nature and also a certain lack of sincerity.

The Church understands this terrible strain under which the homeless ones are suffering. Therefore she will not push them and force the process of absorption. This development takes a generation, and it cannot without loss be brought about in a month or a year. Especially is this true in the very delicate terrain of religious feelings. So the Church insists upon Catholicism being preached and fostered in them in their own language, by priests of their own nationality, and she does not object to the national character of such an effort. She does not foster nationalism in the political sense of national minorities, but she acknowledges the right-eousness of patriotic feelings.

Therefore *Exsul Familia* carefully avoids the use of the word "nation" by itself. It could be dangerous. Nationality and citizenship are different terms in political theory, but in everyday life they have the same meaning. It would be unjust towards the countries giving hospitality to refugees to envisage any conceding of portions of their territory to a foreign people living their own separate national life. They expect with right that the refugees will become nationalized. They expect them to become members not only of the state, but also of the nation. And this claim not only does justice to the rightful interests of the receiving country, but also coincides with the interests of the refugees themselves. They must be rescued from an impossible situation: living in a foreign country, regarded as foreigners, as different from everybody else. Criminologists well know what living outside the community and not having its moral support means. Having been chaplain to refugees for longer than three years, I can confirm this with numerous practical examples, and I can tell how these people suffer through loneliness and being strangers. It is a pity, too, that they are sometimes hurt by tactless people, but such grievances would not matter at all if they were not already wounded by being uprooted from their native soil. These wounds cannot be healed except through repatriation or assimilation. Both being impossible now and for this generation, what else remains for the Church to do for them, but to assure at least proper spiritual assistance for refugees through priests of their own nationality?

We cannot but marvel at and appreciate how tactfully and considerately the Holy See treats this delicate problem.

It concedes nothing to the national political aims either of the refugees or of the receiving countries. It insists only that the refugees must not be handicapped in their religious life also by the fact of exile.

By giving canonically precise definition of those in question (all aliens living in a foreign country no matter for how long or why they reside there, and all their descendants in the first grade of direct line, without regard to the fact of having got or not got their new citizenship) she fundamentally acknowledges the rights of refugees, exiles, emigrants to use their own language in private and common prayer, and generally in their religious life including the religious education of their children. Up to now, although this principle was fully accepted *in praxi*—everywhere priests of their own language and nationality were engaged by bishops for refugees all over the world—opinion was more or less that this solution is a very temporary one. The aid of the refugee priest was needed only until people got sufficient knowledge of the language of the country where they are living. Therefore bishops were not very anxious to organize this work on a more permanent basis. Chaplains for refugees were supported and kindly assisted in their difficult work, but on the whole they were more tolerated than fully accepted as doing the apostolate of the dioceses. By this fact their work was given more a national than a Catholic character, and depended more on the country they came from than the one they worked in. Having no connections with the hierarchy of the home-country, chaplains for refugees from behind the Iron Curtain were far worse off than those for Germans, Italians and so on. They worked as free-lances, and had not the feeling of a proper ecclesiastical authority backing them. The bishops also felt the awkwardness of the situation, and duly and tactfully did not want to press their authority upon them.

Therefore it was absolutely necessary to provide at the highest level—that of the Consistorial Congregation—for pastoral care, some organ for a proper solution and continuous survey of this delicate problem.

The way it has been done in *Exsul Familia* shows again how wisely and considerately the Holy See handles the matter. It does not impose on the bishops the duty of seeking everywhere the erection of national parishes, which would very often be inadvisable.[12] But it emphasizes the duty of Ordinaries to engage for the people concerned priests of their own nationality and to provide those with the necessary faculties as well as to let them have a church wherein to satisfy their obligations.[13]

A surprising feature is that the rights given to refugee priests are equivalent to those of a parish priest. Personal jurisdiction as opposed to territorial is not in great favor in Church Law, but without this absolute jurisdiction over their subjects the whole of the work would simply depend on personal likes or dislikes. The refugees must feel in their priest the authority of the Church reminding them of their duties as Catholics and not merely a voluntary helper to whom they turn only when in need.

Also without doubt *Exsul Familia* was in this point strongly influenced by the present Catholic situation in the U.S.A. where a great number of the so-called national-personal parishes are flourishing. In the age of emigration from Europe towards the New World, which was not a Catholic country, this way seemed to be the only possible one to provide for the masses of Catholic immigrants of all nationalities. So today when again millions are on the move, and in the receiving countries the parishes are not capable of dealing with the newcomers, the most sensible solution seems to be just the same in order to save the faith.

Everybody knows that these personal parishes for aliens were not always associated with the most pleasant experiences for Ordinaries, even in America. Exaggerations, seclusion from the Catholic life of the country (approaching to sectarianism), relations to the home country touching the limits of politics, inside differences between political parties, denunciations against their own priests, are not too rare. But all that is yet a *minus malum* compared with the loss of the faith through emigration.

It would be far worse if priests of their own nationality would not be engaged for the exiles. To have sufficient knowledge for everyday life, even for listening to sermons in the church, or going to confession validly does not mean everything. To join a new community in the new country means a lot more than that. There are different modes of dress, different ways of thinking and feeling, different ways to express oneself, different devotions. Those very slight so-called emotional differences cannot be neglected in Church life. The real differences amongst peoples relate less to language than to mentality. This cannot be learned out of books, cannot be taught in schools. It is bred of history, tradition, blood, geographical and social factors. It is something so complicated, that we find it always extremely difficult if we try to give a precise definition to the word "nationality" I emphasize: nationality does not make an essential difference between man and man. We know well that it is not the great apparent differences that are the solid obstacles to reciprocal understanding, but the very fine and very subtle ones, a special way of thinking and feeling, traditions revealed in music, folklore, customs and sagas of the different nations, and also in the religious life in devotions, hymns, etc. We are fortunately Catholics, having so much in common all over the world, but even this wonderful and real universality of our faith has to take into account these differences. That has always been the Church's policy.

Besides that, there is another point yet to be considered. The emigrants would never give up hope of returning again to their own country. They know perfectly well that humanly speaking there is no hope. But even then they hope, as the man sentenced to death hopes for his life. They are loyal to the new country, but their emotional self—they cannot help it— lives for the past. Even if they would, they could not sacrifice it, and they should not sacrifice it. Because in these patriotic feelings there is the religious duty of piety towards their country, their persecuted Church, their suffering pastors and brethren. They could not charge a new community with the burden of their souls. They would be left alone with it. If they have no religious *milieu* wherein to relieve their souls in satisfying this duty of piety, wherein to foster the hope of lighting again the sanctuary lamps where the faith of their fathers is being extinguished, I wonder how they could lead a religious life at all. Even good, highly educated Catholics find it extremely difficult to bear alone responsibility for their country. How could we expect it from simple ones, whose faith is very emotional and is greatly supported by the community they live in? I do not wonder if they find the religious life they had to join in the new country empty and shallow, not only because they are not used to its forms and ways, but because they do not find there a support in the most excruciating problem of their hearts.

Exsul Familia is not a theoretical study of how Catholics should live amongst Catholics when abroad, but the rules laid down in it urge us to reconsider the views we formerly held upon this problem.

Generally we thought that a Catholic having learnt the language of the foreign country is all right and does not need anything else in order to ensure a full practice of his religion there. Do we realize that by thinking so we were not only omitting to consider the grave reasons which influenced the Holy See in the decisions of *Exsul Familia,* but that also we were implicitly indulging the false theory that religion is a private business between God and man? If only the man is Catholic and his Catholicism has nothing to do with his nationality, I do not see how religion could be more for him than a personal relation with God being practiced according to the prescriptions of the Church, in whatever parish or territory he is living. Catholic internationalism propagated in this way by abstracting from the national community of origin and descent of nation is atomizing the Church just as effectively as socialism atomizes human society.

Exsul Familia leads us out of this insidious error in thought and gives full rights to the national feeling based upon the natural virtue of piety. It is really an extension of the fourth commandment of God. Piety being one of the most important elements of every religious feeling, we may understand how deeply right patriotism is rooted in religion.

Nationalism itself and also patriotism have been so often abused in the recent past that we fear to use them. The new, or more correctly the old, original sense of these words has to be revived through us Catholics in the spirit of *Exsul Familia*. We have to make clear the distinction between the loyalty due to other nations and to the political state, and the piety we feel towards the nation and country of our origin.

In a Catholic state there would be no problem for Polish or Hungarian Catholics about retaining their national feelings towards their country, even fostering them in a religious *milieu*. But in non-Catholic states such a community will be regarded more as Polish or Hungarian than Catholic. Also the hierarchy in such states are looked upon as representatives of a foreign power, and therefore they, having already their own difficulties, do not like to foster the development of a foreign community under their jurisdiction. It's hard enough for them to prove that they are, *e.g.*, as English as the ministers of any other denomination. Also they have, besides loyalty to their own state, piety towards their own country and nation, and it is quite understandable that they are anxious to assure this piety in everybody under their jurisdiction. *Exsul Familia* does not raise the question about civil duties towards the new state; but declaring in such a clear manner the religious needs of aliens, it forces us to think further and to make the above distinction. This solution avoids the overestimating of nationality as well as the ignoring of it.

Through these instructions, the Holy See, without having any intention of influencing politics, leads the way towards rapprochement between nations, teaching them to acknowledge and respect each other's due piety on a purely religious basis.

I would say that through *Exsul Familia* a new—in fact very old and always used in the Church, but alas! today so much forgotten—way is indicated for Catholics on how to face the most excruciating problem of Europe: the national differences.

I feel I am not very wrong in saying that the decline of the West (*Untergang des Abendlandes*) is mainly due to nationalism losing the braking-power of Christian universality. After the great schism in the West the *Respublica Christiana* of the Middle Ages became a faraway dream of a golden age lost for ever. The sovereign nations corrupted by the division of Christianity gave up slowly every religious basis in national life and became more and more neutral, indifferent social formations, states. Where it is indifferent, the state is concerned merely with the temporary welfare and security of its citizens. This diminishing of the social life of a nation and its human needs left an empty space in the soul. This lack of spirituality in national social life gave room on the one hand for the exaggerations of nationalism and on the other for the rather similar exaggerations of socialism. The national state having lost the religious basis of its sovereignty, has as its only target its own welfare; so consequently it must arrive at an idolatry of its own interests, lastly of itself. Socialism on the other hand, confessing a purely materialistic humanism, loses completely the understanding of man, and will sooner or later culminate in Communism. Both have surprisingly the same characteristic: the unconscious replacement of religion. This is clearly revealed by the fact that they presume to make such absolute claims as only religion is justified in making. For the sake of a utopia (national or international), of an earthly paradise, man in his individual existence will be ruthlessly sacrificed.

Naturally, it would be morally unjustifiable to force even the true religion upon a nation or upon the whole of the human race by laws passed by a majority. But certainly freedom of conscience must not mean that national as well as international relations must be handed over completely to the secular power to be dealt with. When *Exsul Familia* declares the rights of aliens to a full practice of their religion in their own language, led by priests of their own nationality, it is defending freedom of conscience for those people to fulfill their duties of piety towards their own country and nation. At the same time, the aliens are educated to another kind of patriotism which is not inspired by the vain ambitions of nationalism, and which is not opposed to the loyalty towards other nations, especially towards the state whose hospitality they are enjoying.

If we Catholics of the receiving countries, as well as aliens, accept and carry out the instructions of the *Exsul Familia,* I think we are preparing the ground for the United Europe we hear so much about. Perverted human justice and good will helped to destroy what the centuries left of the *Respublica Christiana,* but this religious basis for national feelings which *Exsul Familia* is so anxious to assure certainly will do its work if we do not fail to cooperate with the graces offered to us. The aliens, the sufferings, homeless ones are now in the first line: the passions of nationalism in their hearts must be purified through prayer and a closer union with the suffering Lord Jesus;

and hence they are the objects of the paternal love and care of the Vicar of Christ.

1. *Exsul Familia, AAS,* vol. XLIV 30th September, 1952, No. 13, pp. 649-704.
2. *John xi.*
3. Cap. I, pp. 1-4.
4. Cap. I, pp. 7-8.
5. Cap. II, pp. 9-17.
6. Cap. III, pp. 18-31.
7. Cap. IV, pp. 32-34.
8. Cap. IV, 35-39.
9. Cap. IV, p. 40.
10. Cap. V.
11. Cap. VI.
12. *Exsul Familia,* p. 32.
13. *Ibid.,* pp. 33, 34, 37.

BIBLIOGRAPHY

TEXTS

Pope Pius XII. "Exsul Familia", (Latin Text of the Apostolic Constitution) *Acta Apostolicae Sedis*, XLIV, Aug. 1952, 649-704.

──────. Costituzione Apostolica sulla Cura Spirituale degli Emigranti ("Exsul Familia"). Rome: *La Civiltà Cattolica*, 1952

──────. Constitution Apostolique "Exsul Familia" sur l'aumonerie des émigrants. Publication de la Conférence Catholique Canadienne du Bien-Etre. Montréal, Canada.

──────. Constitucao Apostolica sobre os cuidados espirituais emigrantes (Exsul Familia), Sao Paulo, 1955.

──────. "Spiritual Care of Emigrants: Titulus Alter: Normae pro spirituali emigrantium cura gerenda. (Excerpts from the Apostolic Constitution "Exsul Familia"), *The Clergy Review*, XXXVIII, Jan. 1953, 40-48; Feb. 1953, 110-113.

Sacra Congregatio Consistorialis. "Normae et facultates pro Sacerdotibus in spiritualem maritimorum curam incumbentibus nempe pro Cappellanis et Directoribus operis "Apostolatus Maris" iussu Sanctissimi Domini Nostri Pii Divina Providentia Papae

Duodecimi editae", *Acta Apostolicae Sedis*, XLVI, 248.

—————. "Normae et factultates pro Sacerdotibus in spiritualem navigantium curam incumbentibus, nempe pro Cappellanis Navigantium et Cappellanorum Directorum, iussu Sanctissimi Domini Nostri Pii Divina Providentia Papae Duodecimi editae", *Acta Apostolicae Sedis*, XLVI, 415.

—————. "Normae et facultates pro Sacerdotibus in spiritualem emigrantium curam incumbentibus, nempe pro Missionariis emigrantium et Missionariorum Directoribus iussu Sanctissimi Domini Nostri Pii Divina Providentia Papae Duodecimi editae", *Acta Apostolicae Sedis*, XLVII, 91.

Catholic Foreign Secretariate, Beuel-Bonn. "Title two of the Apostolic Constitution "Exsul Familia".

BOOKS

Carretta, Antonio. *I Missionari degli Emigranti nella Costituzione Apostolica "Exsul Familia"*. Rome: Giunta Cattolica Italiana per l'Emigrazione, 1957.

Ferretto, Giuseppe Cardinal. *In Normas et Facultates pro Sacerdotibus in Spiritualem Navigantium, Maritimorum et emigrantium curam incumbentibus*. Rome: Vatican Press, 1956.

—————. *La Costituzione Apostolica "Exsul Familia"*. Pompei, Italy: I.P.S.I., 1958.

Grentrup, Theodor. Die Apostolische Konstitution "Exsul Familia" zur Auswanderer-und Fluchtlingsfrage, Verlag "Christ Unterwegs", Munchen, 1955-6.

International Catholic Migration Congress. (Second) The Hague: Pax International Publishing Company, Ltd., 1954.

International Catholic Migration Congress. (Third) Geneva: International Catholic Migration Commission, 1957.

International Catholic Migration Congress (Fourth) Geneva: International Catholic Migration Commission, 1960.

O'Leary, Humphrey, C.SS.R. *Migrant Chaplain*. Ballarat, Australia: Majellan Press, 1956.

Sokolick, Alexander *The Apostolic Constitution "Exsul Familia"—An Historical Synopsis*, (Pro Manuscripto). Washington, D.C.: Catholic University of America Press, 1955.

ARTICLES

"Constitution Regulating Migration", *The Jurist*, 12, October 1952, 486.

"Die Apostolische Konstitution 'Exsul Familia'", Herder-Korrespondenz, VII, Aug. 1953, 492-494.

Donnelly, F.B. "New Provisions regarding Emigrants and Seamen", *The Homiletic and Pastoral Review*, LIII, Feb. 1953, 418-421.

Fabregas, Michael, S.J. "Adnotationes in Constitutionem Apostolicam 'Exsul Familia'", *Periodica de Re Morali Canonica et Liturgica*, LII, 1952, 318-325.

Ferretto, Joseph Cardinal, "Adnotationes", *Monitor Eccelsiasticus*, LXXVII, 215-219.

————. "The Apostolic Constitution 'Exsul Familia'", *The American Ecclesiastical Review*, CXXX, Feb.-March, 1954, 73-83; 146-162.

————. "In Constitutionem Apostolicam 'Exsul Familia' Animadversiones", *Monitor Ecclesiasticus*, LXXVIII, 7-22.

Fus, E.A. "Priest Emigrants under the Constitution 'Exsul Familia'", *The Jurist*, XVI, October 1956, 359-386.

Henkey-Honig, C. " 'Exsul Familia': The Care of Migrants", *The Irish Ecclesiastical Record*, LXXIX, May, 1953, 329-341.

Kindermann, Dr. Adolf-Koenigstein-Taunus, Articles in "Mitteilungen fuer die heimatvertrebenen Priester aus dem Osten", 1953, Nos. 1, 2, 3. Priesterreferat, Koenigstein.

Ledit, J.H. "La Constitution Apostolique 'Exsul Familia' sur l'Emigration", *Relations*, XII, Oct. 1952, 276-277.

Milini, Francesco, P.S.S.C., "Exsul Familia e l'Assistenza Spirituale agli Emigranti", *Le Missioni Scalabriniane*, XLI, 1952.

"Régles pour l'Immigration", *Relations,* 1952, 294-295.

Sartori, Giacomo, P.S.S.C. Attualita' e dimensioni Pastorali della "Exsul Familia", L'Emigrato Italiano, LI, 1962.

"Spiritual Care of Emigrants", *Tablet,* CC, Aug. 16, 1952, 137-138.

Tellechea, José Ignacio Idigoras— Pastoral Care of Emigrants: Commentary on the Apostolic Constitution "Exsul Familia", Revista Espanola de Derecho Canonico, III, 1953.

Wycislo, A.J. "Apostolic Constitution on Migration", *The Homiletic and Pastoral Review,* LIII, January, 1953, 318-326.

INDEX